From Madness to Mutiny

The Northeastern Series on Gender, Crime, and Law

edited by Claire Renzetti, St. Joseph's University

For a complete list of titles in the series, please see www.upne.com

FROM MADNESS ||||| ||||||||||| TO MUTINY

Why Mothers Are Running from the Family Courts —and What Can Be Done about It

Amy Neustein

Michael Lesher

Foreword by Raoul Felder

||||||||||||||||||||||||||||||||||| **Northeastern University Press**

Boston

Published by University Press of New England

Hanover and London

Northeastern University Press
Published by University Press of New England,
One Court Street, Lebanon, NH 03766
www.upne.com
© 2005 by Amy Neustein and Michael Lesher
Printed in the United States of America
5   4   3   2   1

Library of Congress Cataloging-in-Publication Data

Neustein, Amy.
    From madness to mutiny : why mothers are running from the family courts—and what can be done about it / Amy Neustein, Michael Lesher; foreword by Raoul Felder.
        p.   cm. — (The Northeastern series on gender, crime, and law)
    Includes bibliographical references and index.
    ISBN 1-58465-462-7 (cloth : alk. paper)
        1. Domestic relations courts—United States. 2. Child sexual abuse—United States. 3. Mothers—United States. I. Lesher, Michael. II. Title.
    KF505.5.N48 2005
    346.7301′5′0269—dc22   2005000916

Contents

Foreword

This book paints a very disturbing picture of the family court system. That doesn't surprise me. To tell the truth, I've suspected for a long time that someone who knew the system at first hand would write a book like this one.

It was eighteen years ago that Dr. Amy Neustein first walked into my office to talk to me about New York's family courts. At that time, she was locked in a bizarre battle over what was described to me as an eyewitness report that her six-year-old daughter had been sexually abused by her ex-husband. The facts, from the information I had, all pointed one way, but the system—the judge, the law guardian, the social service agencies, the whole mix—was going the other way.

Instead of going after her ex-husband, as anyone from outside the family courts would have expected, the system was putting *her* on trial.

She asked me what could be done to set things right.

I had been a matrimonial attorney since 1963—so I knew the answer that I had to give her wasn't pretty. I knew that what happens in domestic litigation is not like what happens in our civics textbooks—or, for that matter, what is described in law books.

I told Amy Neustein the truth. I told her that no matter how strong the facts were on her side, her battle would be a tough one, especially since the institutions that are so important in family court—law guardians, social service agencies, visitation supervision agencies—have so much arbitrary power. "It's very hard to fight the system," I told her. Which I knew was putting it mildly.

A few years later I saw Dr. Neustein again. This time, we met at a television studio where we were both taping shows. We spoke again about the problems of family court, and Dr. Neustein clearly wasn't a naive newcomer any more. Now she knew of dozens of cases besides her own. She had learned shocking things about other mothers who had been punished for making good-faith reports of child sexual abuse by their husbands, ex-husbands, boyfriends. She catalogued the injustices of the system with a thoroughness and zeal that made me wonder if she might be planning to put it all into a book, one day.

Lawyers who, like me, have spent decades practicing matrimonial law know that the way our courts deal with sex abuse allegations against parents can be crazy—downright sadistic. Not long ago the *Daily News* asked me about a case in which a mother lost custody of her four-year-old twin daughters to a father who was accused of molesting them. The father had never married the mother—he was married to another woman throughout their relationship, lived across the country, had never spent more than one night with the children, and had urged the mother to abort the children. Not only did the millionaire father win custody; he got an order that limited the mother's contact with her children and even tried to force her to pay child support. I told the reporter, "It's like pulling the wings off a fly."

Another time, Leslie Eaton of the *New York Times* asked me about the power of controversial mental health "experts" who make custody recommendations in horribly biased and unscientific ways. These "experts"— psychologists, psychiatrists, social workers—are rarely seen outside the family court system. But inside it, they can label a mother who reports sex abuse of her child a "fabricator," or a "parental alienator," and strip her of custody of a child she has raised since birth. Not only that—with a judge's help, these "experts" can force the mother to pay their outlandish fees, too. I told Ms. Eaton about how these evaluators have become so powerful that they've undermined the judicial process, and I said, "The whole thing is a train wreck waiting to happen."

Now Amy Neustein, who is a sociologist, has joined forces with a lawyer, Michael Lesher. The two of them have obviously done their homework on the family courts throughout America. They have collected and analyzed information from a large body of cases all across the country. Their conclusions—contained in this book—represent the end of the process Dr. Neustein began eighteen years ago, when she first discovered the harsh realities of our nation's system of family litigation.

The book you have in your hands is about the treatment of children who have been sexually abused (and of mothers who receive reports of sexual abuse), and about the mothers who try to protect their children. That is, it is about a critical task of America's family court system. And it illustrates just how badly that system fails to protect our children when they have been sexually abused by a father. It shows how often mothers who believe that their children have been sexually abused end up receiving punishment from the courts. And how the children have ended up not only not being protected but, in some cases, being cut off from the parent whose crime was caring about their welfare. It gives a mother a Hobson's choice. Keep quiet about a belief of sexual abuse and put her child at risk of it continuing, or speak up and risk losing the child to the abuser.

I think this book is essential reading for every American who cares about the justice system that is supposed to safeguard our welfare. For I do not know of a more comprehensive, or a more damning, presentation.

What I have seen as a practitioner, this book reveals in punishing detail. The book shows how untested theories can be used to discredit women who make reports of sexual abuse, without an examination of the evidence behind the charge. It shows how child protective services agencies—which are supposed to look out for children's welfare—have come to be so powerful they can derail almost any sex abuse case into an attack on a mother they don't like or don't believe. It shows how lawyers specially appointed to protect children's interests in court can abuse their roles—and get away with it. And it shows how judges have allowed all this to happen, presiding over a system that, all too often, has forgotten how to act like a justice system.

Neustein and Lesher argue that the whole system is in need of thorough reform, and they have laid out some proposals for building a better system. They believe that until the system is reformed and rethought at every level, it will continue to be a dangerous one—dangerously malfunctioning, dangerously betraying its critical task. They believe that, as it stands, our nation's family court system isn't a safe place to send children who have been sexually abused—or to send the mothers who care about them.

Are things really as bad as that?

Read this book and see for yourself.

Raoul Felder, Esq.
New York, New York
September 14, 2004

Acknowledgments

We are deeply grateful to the University Press of New England for their un-wavering belief in the academic, social, and political importance of this book. In particular, we express our gratitude to Phyllis Deutsch, Executive Editor (and newly appointed editor of the Gender, Crime, and Law series), for helping to bring this book to fruition. We also wish to acknowledge the entire team of professionals at the University Press of New England, who under the leadership of its director, Richard M. Abel, at each stage of the project showed an uncompromising commitment to perfecting the work.

Throughout our two-decades-long study of the family court system, we drew inspiration and strength from a number of individuals, in several pro-fessional disciplines, who have worked to shed light on the family courts' scandalous treatment of mothers who seek help for children they believe are being sexually abused. These men and women are too numerous to thank individually here, but special acknowledgment must be given to Jere-miah B. McKenna, former chief counsel to the New York State Senate Com-mittee on Crime and Correction, whose tireless efforts (dating back to 1986) to expose the cruelties of the family courts have been a source of hope to many despairing mothers.

More recently, Siena psychology professor Maureen "Mo" Therese Han-nah has emerged as a dedicated proponent of family court reform. She performs the invaluable service of bringing together child advocates and professionals from all over the country for an annual conference at Siena College that addresses the problems of mothers in the family courts. Among the other leading figures in this social movement, we wish to acknowledge Washington lobbyist Mariam Bell, who has been urging legislators on Capi-tol Hill to look into the family court system, and Eileen King, regional di-rector of Justice for Children, who for many years has offered information and encouragement for mothers trapped in a hostile process.

Writing this book would have been even more difficult without the patience and support of a handful of sympathetic supporters and close friends. Dr. Martha Lindemann's prayers and encouragement fortified us throughout the project. Larry Cohler-Esses, a journalist who does not fear the unknown, helped to shape and focus our early investigation into the subject. New York State Senator David A. Paterson held investigative hearings on the mistreatment of mothers by the family courts at a time when few politicians would even mention the issue. Professor Kathleen Faller took the time to answer our many questions. Grace Charnow's broad shoulders and eternal optimism were invaluable during dark times.

A.N. and M.L.

Introduction

This has not been a pleasant book to research or to write. It will not be a pleasant book to read. It deals with a profoundly disturbing topic: a system of justice, designed to protect children from sexual abuse, that has gone so terribly wrong that it often abets the very evils it exists to correct. The failure of any judicial system is bad enough; the failure of the American family court[1] system, resulting in the systematic mishandling of sex abuse charges, exposes children throughout the country to grave dangers. That is something anyone would rather not know, given the choice.

But the truth is simply too serious to ignore. If it is true—as we have found—that the American family court system, built to safeguard the welfare of children and their families, has all too often become a place where civil rights are thrust aside, where the search for truth is subordinated to "junk science," and where children are forced into unwanted relationships with parents they have accused of sexually abusing them—while the parents who try to protect them are punished with the loss of custody—then none of us should be indifferent to family court malfunction. While the family courts treat too many mothers who believe that their children have been sexually abused as guilty until proven innocent (guilty of parental unfitness, of hysteria, of "hostility" toward the accused parent), and take away their children as a result, ignorance of the system is clearly too high a price for any of us to pay.

Indeed, the American public is already aware that something is wrong with the system that is supposed to protect our children. Over the last twenty years, the child welfare system has attracted increasing public attention and controversy. Again and again, the public has learned of astonishing judicial lapses as a result of which children are kept in the custody of physically or sexually abusive parents—until it is too late.

Yet there has always been much more to the story than this. The public is aware that the family court system sometimes fails to protect children from sexual abuse. But it is only just becoming aware that the system may actually *place* children with sexually abusive parents because the other parent (usually the mother) is stigmatized for making the accusation in the first place. That is the phenomenon we examine in this book.

Although ours is the first book to analyze this pattern in objective detail, we are not the first to notice the evils we examine. Well over a decade ago, several researchers, including activist attorney H. Joan Pennington, coined the term "protective parent" to describe those parents, usually mothers, who engage the family court system to protect their children from alleged sexual abuse by the child's father. In many cases, Pennington complained, these parents faced a fierce backlash from judges, law guardians, caseworkers, court-appointed mental health experts, and others.[2]

Pennington (now retired) founded the National Center for Protective Parents, based in Trenton, New Jersey, in 1990. Over the following six years, the center published a number of well-documented studies on the plight of mothers in the family courts. In 1992, Pennington testified before the House Judiciary Committee on how to educate judges about the protective parent problem.[3] Pennington has argued that family courts not only fail, in many cases, to stop the abuse of children but actually go much further, punishing mothers for trying to protect them.

In 1999 Kim Gandy, then vice president of the National Organization for Women (NOW), was moved to write to one of us that this problem cried out for legislative reform: "[T]here is a frightening trend in both the juvenile and family law courts of the United States, which is placing literally thousands of children in danger. In court cases across the county, children who have disclosed abuse by a parent . . . are being placed in the sole custody of the abusive parent. . . . Congress must be made aware of how prevalent this problem is. . . . "

In April 2004, Kathryn Mazierski, president of the NOW chapter in New York State, echoed Gandy's denunciation of the family courts. Mazierski, joined by other NOW state chapters and national child advocacy organizations, demanded a federal investigation of the family courts. Mazierski's press release did not mince words: "in case after case, the mother who makes the report of sex abuse is punished—stripped by the court of her custodial rights . . . this phenomenon can be observed in so many states, and involves such profound violations of the rights of mothers and the children concerned, that a federal investigation into the Constitutional and civil rights violations of mothers caught in the family court system is the best way to seek a remedy."

According to Mazierski, "One out of every two calls I get on a daily basis is from a mother who just lost custody because she tried to get the family court to protect her child from sexual abuse committed by the father." Similarly, Rita Henley Jensen, editor in chief of Women's eNews, an online daily news service reaching twenty thousand members of the press, has told one of us that "the bulk of the daily incoming emails to Women's eNews are desperate pleas from mothers who have lost custody of their children they tried in vain to protect from sexual abuse."[4] This suggests that, if anything, the plight of protective parents is worsening: six years earlier, the director of the Violence Against Women Office of the U.S. Justice Department had written to one of us that at least "two calls a week" received by her office were from protective parents "desperate for assistance."[5]

If this sounds to you like the product of judicial madness, you are not alone. During a 1997 Mother's Day press conference held on the steps of the Capitol in Washington, D.C., a devastated Georgia mother, whose contact with her five-year-old son had been completely suspended by a family court, shouted: "Family court is a bad dream that you can't wake up from!" The other fifty mothers at the rally plainly agreed.

Our own look into the "bad dream" of the family court system began in 1986, when Dr. Amy Neustein, one of the authors of this book, lost custody of her six-year-old daughter to a man an eyewitness had accused of sexually molesting her—despite the confirming account of the girl herself and the corroboration of experts. Appalled by what she had experienced, Dr. Neustein founded the Help Us Regain The Children (HURT) research center in Brooklyn, New York, in 1986, moving the center to New York City in 1999.

HURT advertised itself to protective mothers primarily by word of mouth as well as through local and national television talk show appearances, during which the center's address and phone number would be posted on the screen. Referrals were also made to HURT by women's organizations in New York and nationwide, and battered women's shelters listed the center's phone number as a resource in their printed literature.

The results were astonishing. HURT was contacted in well over four thousand cases. About one thousand met the study requirements set forth by HURT, which required its research subjects to provide as full a court record as possible: motion papers, court transcripts, decisions, and orders. Later, this book's other author, Michael Lesher, Esq., undertook a legal review of HURT's cases and added others from his own experience. The authors found that those cases tragically confirmed the warnings of H. Joan

Pennington, Kim Gandy, and Kathryn Mazierski. Family courts really were ignoring evidence of sexual abuse and awarding custody to fathers against whom credible cases of sexual abuse had been presented.

Of those mothers who lost custody to allegedly abusive ex-husbands or former partners, the majority had been primary caretakers of their children—the main nurturers—and in a number of cases the children had been very young when they were removed from their mothers. Some had not even been weaned. Others had disabilities that made them particularly dependent on their mothers. None of these facts made any consistent difference in the results of the cases. Healthy children and sick ones, teenagers and toddlers, were just as likely to be removed from their mothers when allegations emerged of sexual abuse by the father.

We found that such results cut straight across the American demographic pie. Both rich and poor women lost custody of their children to alleged sex offenders, as did women at different educational levels. The judicial outcomes were largely the same in large metropolises and in rural areas.

The evidence we have collected has enabled us to demonstrate in detail—and to analyze—the backlash against protective parents that activists have complained about for decades. We offer this book as a detailed analysis of a system that has turned far too much of its energy toward the punishment, not of parents who abuse their children, but of those parents (almost always women) who reasonably suspect their spouse or partner of child sexual abuse.

Just as the evidence we have amassed enables us to remove any doubt as to the reality of this problem, it has enabled us to address two important reservations sometimes voiced by skeptics. These should be dealt with at once.

First, we do not claim—nor do we believe—that the miscarriages of justice we dissect in this book characterize all family court cases across the country. But it remains true, unfortunately, that severely mishandled cases are not uncommon. As we will show, other investigations, formal and informal, have found—as we did—that far too many cases of alleged sexual abuse have ended with inexplicable punishments meted out to a mother whose "crime" was to try to protect her child from sexual abuse. And the consistency of this finding is all the more striking because court records of sex abuse cases are nearly always barred from public review, making large-scale surveys unusually difficult. The same may be said of the sheer volume of desperate calls and e-mails from bewildered protective mothers to women's organizations and other groups.

Take the case of Childhelp USA. Founded in 1959 as a groundbreaking purveyor of child abuse prevention information, Childhelp later established a telephone hotline for child abuse "crisis counseling," the number of which (1-800-4-A-CHILD) slowly began to make appearances on daytime television in the 1980s. By 1992, after several years of running the hotline, Childhelp officials had received so many calls from mothers claiming that they had tried to protect their children from abuse, only to have the children taken from their custody, that they decided to investigate the phenomenon more fully. Dubbed the "System Failure Project," Childhelp's investigation was straightforward: a detailed questionnaire was mailed to a several thousand callers who had complained of losing custody of a child after reporting sexual abuse by the other parent. The questionnaire addressed the specific actions of the salient figures in each case: judges, law guardians, social service caseworkers, court-appointed mental health experts, and others. Fully 10 percent of the questionnaires were completed and returned (a large figure for any survey, particularly one involving several pages of questions). The results showed such consistent accusations of misconduct, from hundreds of independent respondents, that Childhelp decided it was necessary to address legislators about the seriousness of the problem. Mariam Bell, Childhelp's director of governmental affairs at the time, approached one congressional committee after another, telling lawmakers what her organization had found and urging them to convene a federal hearing into the issue.[6]

Thus, whatever the exact proportion of family court cases involving a "backlash" against protective mothers, it is impossible to doubt that the problem is serious, widespread, and intractable. Indeed, in this book, we have attempted to go beyond numbers to identify the sociological and legal patterns that result in such outcomes—thus revealing an entrenched system that will continue to wrong allegedly abused children, and their mothers, until it is checked. It is difficult to say exactly how large, numerically, this problem is. But no one can question its gravity.

Second, we are well aware that not every father accused of sexual abuse is actually guilty. What is more, we know that as the courts operate—and must operate—even parents who are guilty of sexual abuse must sometimes remain uncorrected, because of the absence of acceptable proof. We do not seek a system in which the accused is denied the presumption of innocence. Nevertheless, the all too common voices that complain of an assault against innocent men in the courts, that worry loudly that sex abuse charges pose a lopsided threat to the accused—with the inevitable corollary that such charges must be received with skepticism—are seriously wrong. Public fears of a "witch hunt" against fathers are not borne out by the facts. The existing literature clearly establishes that false or malicious accusations of sexual abuse, even in custody litigation, are not at all common. Dziech and Schudson (1989) point to several sources—Thoennes, Pearson, and Tjaden (1988), Quinn (1988), Berliner (1988), and Corwin, Berliner, Goodman, Goodwin, and White (1987)—as examples of well-respected studies showing that "even in family courts, false allegations [of sexual abuse] remain rare. . . . [M]ost . . . are substantiated" (p. 204). More recent empirical studies, as well as critical analyses of the published research, confirm these findings (Thoennes and Tjaden 1990; Faller, Corwin, and Olafson 1993; Faller and DeVoe 1995; McDonald 1998; Denike, Huang, and Kachuk 1998).

Nor is it true that sex abuse charges must be met with judicial resistance because such accusations are all too easily made and all too readily endorsed by credulous psychologists. Again, the professional literature belies this claim. The exact opposite seems more likely to be the case: experts often fail to diagnose abuse when it has actually occurred. In a 1992 article in the *Journal of Interpersonal Violence,* psychologists Lawson and Chaffin stressed the difficulty of obtaining a disclosure from an abused child. Lawson and Chaffin interviewed twenty-eight children, ranging from three-year-olds to adolescents, and found that more than half (57 percent) of those with sexually transmitted diseases did not report having been sexually abused during the initial interview.[7] What is more, even when credible evidence supports a sex abuse charge, there is no reason to believe it will help the legal position of the mother who makes it. For example, an ominous 1995 study by K. C. Faller and E. DeVoe at the University of Michigan found that forty mothers concerned about possible sexual abuse of their children had incurred "negative sanctions" from a court of law, which included being jailed, losing custody (to the alleged offender, to a relative, or to foster parents), losing some or all visitation rights, being ordered not to report alleged abuse again to the court (or to child protective services or the police), and being barred from taking the child to a doctor or a therapist because of sex abuse concerns. Disturbingly, the researchers found that the parents who had received such punitive measures had actually scored higher on a composite scale of likelihood of sexual abuse—a calculation of the likelihood that their child had been abused, taking into account such factors as the existence of medical evidence—than those parents who had not received such "sanctions."[8]

It follows that the sufferings of protective parents in family courts cannot be explained away with pat answers. To understand what is happening, one must delve into the culture of the family courts, carefully documenting what occurs, and then explaining how such acts fit within a framework that makes sense to the system's practitioners—though to anyone else they look like sheer madness.

That is the purpose of this book.

As the reader will find, there is no shortage of madness to discuss. Family courts can punish protective mothers in a bewildering variety of ways. They can, and often do, transfer custody of the allegedly abused child to the parent accused of abusing him or her. In fact, some judges go further, forbidding mothers to see their children more than a few hours a month, and even then only under strict supervision. In some cases, a mother's visits have been suspended indefinitely because she suspected sexual abuse. Judges have been known to ban telephone calls, letters, and e-mails between mother and child. In one California case, a mother was criticized by a family court judge for waving to her children when she saw them in another car on the highway.

Hand in hand with family court madness is a growing pattern of parental mutiny—a refusal by protective parents to accept the procedures or orders of courts whose logic they can no longer comprehend. Faced with judicial rulings that seem to them contrary to the most basic parental instincts and values, they have begun to rebel. In defiance of family court orders they believe put their children at risk, they litigate furiously, take their stories to the press, go on hunger strikes, or turn fugitive with their children with the help of a modern-day "Underground Railroad."

Like judicial madness, parental rebellion against the family courts has taken many forms. Protective mothers have organized grassroots groups throughout the country—in New York, Ohio, Michigan, Georgia, North Carolina, Washington, and California. The groups monitor court cases, hold candlelight vigils, and in some cases actively support the Underground Railroad that hides mothers who have gone on the run with their children.

Some mothers have pursued legislative reform, becoming unpaid activists. They offer lawmakers and administrators a grim look into the family courts. In response, a few legislators have become champions of protective mother causes. Some have actually drafted legislation on the subject, though little of it has reached the statute books. In his book *In Defense of Public Order* (1961), political theorist Harold Lasswell has argued that "the history of legislation often shows that pressure groups . . . are developed long before an issue becomes a burning question on the calendar of the Congress or state legislatures."[9] This is clearly true for the fighting protective parents.

Our goal in this book is to provide a thorough picture of the infestation of the family courts by a special form of judicial madness, and to illustrate its causes and its consequences. We will show how family court judges and law guardians, child welfare workers, court-appointed mental health experts, visitation supervisors, and others have created a system that all too often betrays its own principles. We will also discuss some practical reforms that can help to redirect the system toward healthier goals.

It should be stressed that our study of the backlash against mothers by the family courts is an empirical analysis, concentrating on how more than why. That is, we have avoided speculation as to the underlying psychological or historical forces that may cause family court personnel to react so violently when mothers accuse fathers of child sexual abuse. This is not to say that some writers, aware of the same phenomenon, have not attempted this. One attempt in particular, the theory put forth by the feminist writer Louise Armstrong, deserves mention here as probably the best known.

Armstrong argues that charges of sexual abuse provoke such a hostile response from family courts because they pose a threat to the inherent patriarchal structure of the family. In *Rocking the Cradle of Sexual Politics: What Happened When Women Said Incest* (1994), Armstrong writes that fathers accused of sexual abuse have answered such charges with "a political war, a war to safeguard their rights." And she adds that men are winning the war: charges of sexual abuse have left women "vulnerable to charges of hysteria or vindictiveness," whereas "in men sheer rage can be taken as reasonable outrage, for righteous indignation: for a sign that their circumstance is indeed demanding of remedy" (p. 138).

Such a theory is, of course, extremely difficult to prove. It is clear that women's greater aggressiveness in domestic litigation has inspired the creation of "fathers' rights" groups (the activities of which are noted below, in chapter 1) and that some of these organizations have agitated for a return to "biblical" patriarchal rights. But this extreme is a fringe phenomenon. Our research has shown that male judges and social workers have no monopoly on hostility to sex abuse charges that women level at men. The same backlash can be observed whether the family court personnel are predominantly male or female, liberal or conservative, religious or agnostic. We have chosen, therefore, to concentrate on methods that dissect family court madness as an institutional phenomenon, describing what the system clearly *is*—we are less concerned with inevitably more debatable attempts to reveal the madness's ultimate source.

A word about our research methods is certainly in order here. As noted above, it is impossible to undertake a large-scale, random review of family court case files, since these are not available to the public. However, we have been as thorough as circumstances permit. The research for this book spans twenty years and states all across the United States. Cases were analyzed longitudinally over all or most of their litigation history, including appellate review when applicable. Other accessible and relevant sources were also examined: reports of statewide judicial conduct commissions and gender-bias task forces; published case digests of decisions; and testimonial records of state and federal public hearings. We interviewed judges, private attorneys, law guardians, social workers, and mental health experts. Litigants were interviewed on multiple occasions over extended periods of time. On a few occasions, we were able to observe videotapes of trials.

To enhance this book's analysis of family courts, we have employed a form of sociological inquiry known as ethnomethodology. Using this approach, we sought to discover, describe, and analyze the collaborative ways in which "social interactants" in the family courts accomplish the situated production of social order in their day-to-day activities. For example, this book attempts to explain how judges, as members of a family court "culture," *methodically*[10] re-create, on each occasion that they rule on the issues before them, the family court entity itself as a socially organized system. In developing this analysis, we reviewed the existing ethnomethodological studies of courts and court processes (Atkinson 1979; Atkinson and Drew 1979; Drew 1992; Holstein 1983, 1988; Holstein and Gubrium 1995; Komter 1995, 1998; Lynch 1997; Matoesian 1993; Maynard 1984; Meehan 1997; Pollner 1979; Travers and Manzo 1997; Watson 1990, 1997), although none of these was directed at the study of the family court institution per se.

One particularly important feature of our case research is our emphasis on studying the progress of a single case over time. Judicial madness often follows an evolutionary process. As a bitterly contested case progresses, rulings may become increasingly bizarre. As that happens, madness may sometimes be glimpsed merely by reading the court record as it unfolds over time. For example, a Georgia family court judge, whose ruling on a child neglect question that had caused two young children to be placed in foster care was reversed on appeal as "not supported by the appropriate considerations and findings of fact,"[11] reportedly insisted to the litigants that the appellate judges' order would not affect him, saying, "There's nothing they can do to me; I'm bullet proof!"

Parental "mutiny," likewise, is an evolutionary process. Some parents who have never before participated in a political protest begin to challenge the system after being caught up in it and then develop, step by step, into ardent activists. Some parents choose a more radical path. After protracted court proceedings, in which (they believe) issues of child safety are being dangerously mishandled, these parents defy court orders outright. They become either fugitives or prisoners.

One other comment seems appropriate here. As we have written, this book is an objective study, presenting objective data. But objectivity is not the same as indifference. Throughout this book, we have been at pains to be accurate, but when the facts we reveal are outrageous, we have not minced words about them. Nor do we expect our readers to be dispassionate about what we describe, for the truth about the family courts gives the lie to some cherished American assumptions. Americans believe they are safe from arbitrary abuse of governmental power—yet child protective services, "law guardians," and family court judges can cast aside the norms of due process when suppressing an allegation of sexual abuse. Americans believe that constitutional protections follow them everywhere—but family courts are an exception, at least for protective parents; as one family court judge put it, "There is no First Amendment in my court." Americans believe that sexist stereotypes have been soundly expelled from American political life—yet family courts still stigmatize mothers who make abuse allegations as "hysterical," "vindictive," and "hostile," as if, in family courts, the appearance of an angry woman still scandalizes. We see no point in trying to minimize the injustice of such phenomena.

On the other hand, simply to identify the abuses perpetrated by the family court system is not enough. One must also try to understand how they arise, how they become part of an institutional phenomenon—and we have devoted considerable effort to this question. Finally, one must consider how the system can be reformed. And we address that issue as well.

This book is divided into three parts. The first gives an overview of family court malfunction and the parental mutiny that results from it. We outline the madness that has infected the family courts and describe the new legal landscape that has helped make the madness possible. We show how the system has reacted—or rather, failed to react—to severe criticism from commentators, newspapers, and even legislators. We also explain the roles that judges, lawyers, and other official "auxiliaries" play in the family court process.

For example, one important modern development is the increased role of child protective services (CPS) agencies, whose workers have formulated their own criteria for determining who is a fit parent. In many cases, CPS workers have charged mothers with child neglect solely on the strength of a claim that these mothers "brainwashed" their children into believing they had been sexually abused.

Corresponding to this new legal landscape is a new sort of parental rebellion, and we describe this, too, including the formation of a new "Underground Railroad" for mothers of allegedly abused children and the women who have risked their freedom to lead it.

The book's second part presents our observations in greater depth. First, we discuss in some detail the history and applications of ethnomethodologists' approach to sociological inquiry, and demonstrate how this approach can be applied to the study of the family courts. Next, we present detailed observations of the abuse of judicial powers in family courts—both the kinds of abuse and reasons they seem to occur. We discuss the function of "law guardians," lawyers intended to advocate solely for the welfare of children in abuse cases who all too often have other agendas. We discuss in depth the behavior of child protective services agencies and how they, too, often fail to protect the children they exist to protect. We also chart the evolution of controversial mental health theories that have been given great evidentiary weight in the family courts. These theories—with names such as "Malicious Mother Syndrome" and "Parental Alienation Syndrome" (PAS)—are unique to family litigation and seem to have been created specifically for use in counterattacking abuse allegations in court. Finally, we treat in detail the behavior of mothers who rebel in various ways against the system and the effects on them of the courts' violent disruption of their family life.

The third, and last, part of this book discusses possible ways of revamping the system. In so doing, we examine what is required to "rebirth" the system, starting with a radical change in the beliefs that drive it. In addition, we examine a number of legislative proposals that have been introduced in New York, California, and Texas with the aim of improving the family courts. We add to these existing proposals a number of suggested reforms to redress particular shortcomings of the system that we describe in this book. Our suggestions are aimed not only at judges but also at law guardians and social workers, who are an integral part of the system.

The full significance and impact of the failures and abuses this book describes will only be clearly seen many years from now. But even now it is possible to document how a court system designed to protect families has been tearing too many children and innocent mothers apart.

Part I

FAMILY COURTS

The Problem

Chapter 1

An Overview of Family Court Madness
—and Mothers' Mutiny

Media Highlights

Today's popular media have already begun to report on the gravity of the family court problem. In January 2003, the *Boston Phoenix* ran a ten thousand-word, front-page feature story profiling the severe malfunctioning of the family court system.[1] The article's subtitle alone was alarming: "Across the nation, family court is the last place a mother concerned about child sexual abuse by the child's father wants to find herself."

Shortly after the *Phoenix* article appeared, Garland Waller, a Boston University communications professor, appeared on *Katherine Crier Live* (Court T.V., January 24, 2003) to discuss the same issue. Professor Waller had produced a film documentary in 2001 (*Small Justice: Little Justice in America's Family Courts*)[2] that profiled several protective mothers and the children who had been taken from them after they reported their suspicions about the children's fathers. On Crier's show, Waller was blunt and passionate: "Our family courts have become a national scandal . . . a system unto itself" in which mothers "pleading for protection" [for their sexually abused children] are "often punished by the judge" with loss of custody and even deprivation of their right to visit their children.[3] She called for "immediate action" to redress this "national crisis."

Such tocsins could actually be heard a decade earlier when, in 1992, the Oscar-winning actress and film director Lee Grant produced and narrated an HBO documentary called *Women on Trial.* That film presented the stories of four Texas mothers whose children were placed by court order with their fathers, despite strong evidence that the fathers had abused them.

Stories of mothers losing custody of their children to sexually abusive ex-husbands or former partners have appeared in women's magazines, and the issue has received attention in both the national and local newsletters of the National Organization for Women. In 1988, *Good Housekeeping* published an article about seven mothers from several different states—New Hampshire, Massachusetts, Ohio, Mississippi, Nebraska, and

Georgia—who were thrown into jail for contempt of court for refusing to turn their children over to allegedly abusive fathers for unsupervised weekend visitation.[4]

That same year, *U.S. News and World Report* printed a feature story on April Curtis, a twenty-seven-year old San Bernardino, California, schoolteacher who, after making an appearance on the *Sally Jessy Raphael Show* to tell her story, fled with her four-year-old daughter into the "Underground Railroad."[5] Her charges that her daughter had been sexually abused were substantiated by the fact that the girl had contracted condyloma, a sexually transmitted disease. Nevertheless, the evidence was ignored by a family court judge.

In 1989, *Newsweek* published a My Turn column written by D.C. cosmetic surgeon Elizabeth Morgan, who spent twenty-five months in jail rather than turn her daughter over to the man she had accused of sexual abuse, as ordered by a family court. That same year, one of the November feature articles in *New York Woman,* titled "Women and Children Last," carried a provocative tag on the magazine cover that summed up the issue in a phrase: "The Horror of Family Court."

Stories of courageous mothers who have fought the system to protect their sexually abused children have appeared in newspapers as well. *USA Today* columnist and editor Barbara Reynolds wrote two columns: "Children's Cries for Help Deserve More Attention" (1993) and "Judges Sentence Kids to Life of Pain" (1995). Former *New York Times* columnist Anna Quindlen, in one of her last columns for the paper, wrote: "While we are quick to believe in the stranger pedophile . . . conventional wisdom has it that sexual abuse is the cry-wolf of the vindictive, a common ploy in custody battles. That's simply wrong. . . . Yet some judges, out of denial or ignorance, continue to label women who insist their children are being molested as crazy, bitter, unfit."[6]

Michael Lesher, one of the authors of this book, co-wrote a major article for the *Village Voice* in the fall of 1996 on a mother's futile struggle to get a New York family court to investigate the charges that her ex-husband had abused their six-year-old daughter—futile despite the fact that an eyewitness had confirmed an act of abuse and that the charge had been corroborated by one of New York's leading authorities on sexual abuse. Not only was the father never investigated; the mother lost custody and, later, her visitation rights as well.[7] Daily newspapers in such states as California, Texas, Indiana, Arkansas, and Iowa have described similar cases.

In 2004, the New York case of Bridget Marks, who lost custody of four-year-old twin daughters because she accused the father of sexually inappropriate behavior with them, attracted national attention. The case presented some unusual features. The children's father, a millionaire casino executive named John Aylsworth, had fathered the girls during an extramarital affair with Marks, a model who had once been featured in *Playboy.* Aylsworth had urged Marks to abort the twins during her pregnancy. He had refused to divorce his wife and marry her even when Marks insisted on bearing the children, prompting the end of the couple's relationship. As a result, the girls hardly knew Aylsworth when he filed his request for full custody in New York's family court system.

Meanwhile, Marks had begun to worry about Aylsworth's conduct around the girls. A babysitter reported that the children told her their father had "touched their pee-pee." A police investigator thought enough of the issue to recommend that a prominent forensic psychologist interview the children—an interview that never took place. Another psychologist recommended strict supervision for the father's visits with the girls. Marks produced expert witnesses at trial who confirmed that her suspicions of sexual abuse under the circumstances were not unreasonable.

Nevertheless, the Manhattan Family Court judge—true to the patterns established in the cases described above—granted full custody to Aylsworth, although this meant removing both four-year-olds from the only parent who had ever cared for them. The judge even denied Marks any visitation with her daughters except under conditions of strict supervision—which Marks had to pay for. The judge claimed that Marks's belief that her daughters had been molested revealed such "unbridled anger" that she could not be trusted to foster a "loving" relationship between the man she had accused of abuse and the children she was trying to protect. Responses to the case in the popular press and on the Internet were prompt and, for the most part, outraged. Family court madness had once again found a place in public view.[8]

Published Studies on the Plight of the Protective Mother

The plight of protective parents has also begun to draw the attention of lawyers and social scientists. A growing body of professional literature is reporting that the family courts are failing to protect sexually abused children, while punishing mothers who report abuse. Sharon S. Keating, a Louisiana lawyer, wrote in 1988 for the *Loyola Law Review:*

[I]t is feared that if a parent makes . . . an allegation [of abuse against the other parent], that parent will be automatically branded as a paranoid, vindictive person. . . . These attitudes can easily lead to a prejudice so strong that the likelihood that a court will choose an accusing parent as future caretaker for the child is greatly diminished. Thus the parent is in a no-win situation. If the . . . parent remains silent about the abuse, it will surely continue. But if accusations are made, the [nonoffending] parent could lose custody completely, placing the child in constant danger."[9]

In the *Journal of Child Sexual Abuse,* Neustein and Goetting (1999) illustrated specific patterns of judicial responses to a "non-offending" parent's complaints of sexual abuse, showing the "interplay of judges, guardians ad litem, caseworkers and forensic experts in cases where sexual abuse claims were raised [prior to] or during child custody proceedings." Analyzing three hundred cases over a ten-year period, from 1988 to 1998, the authors found that in 70 percent of the cases the mothers were forced by court order to send their children on unsupervised visits and to share custody with the alleged abusers. In 20 percent of the cases the outcome was far worse: mothers lost custody completely to the allegedly abusive parent. Among this group of mothers who lost custody to the former spouse or partner, a large number also lost all visitation rights.

Family courts' treatment of sex abuse allegations is demonstrably out of step with contemporary literature: by the mid-1980s, Russell (1983, 1986) had demonstrated with her random sample of San Francisco women that serious and damaging incest was more prevalent than had been thought and appeared to be increasing over time. Yet protective mothers are still overwhelmingly disbelieved in the family court system, according to Myers (1997). Finkelhor (1986) pointed out that judges would rather believe that a mother would "brainwash" a child to make up stories than face the fact that incest not only exists but is found in every culture, in every socioeconomic group, and in every class of society, including the educated and articulate.

Faller (2000), in a *University of Arkansas Little Rock Law Review* article,[10] concluded that notwithstanding the literature on child abuse and clinical experience showing that allegations of sexual abuse during divorce and custody are deemed likely in two-thirds to three-quarters of all cases,[11] family court judges usually respond to such allegations with much skepticism (pp. 429–430). Penfold (1997), in a law journal article exploring "questionable beliefs about child sexual abuse allegations," added that judges often react harshly to mothers who allege sexual abuse, even to the point of transferring custody to the father.[12]

In *The Hostage Child: Sex Abuse Allegations in Custody Disputes* (1996), Rosen and Etlin similarly describe what happens when the battered wife seeks to protect herself from abuse and "is viewed [by the court] as unwilling to share access to her children with her abusive husband": her punishment "is to lose custody to the abusive father who in the court's eyes is a better parent than one who cannot protect her children" (pp. 142–143). Clearly, sexual abuse of one's child does not appear to preclude an award of custody to the abuser: "[T]he current trend which effectively refuses protection to children whose mothers allege sexual abuse and punishes their mothers, may be seen as part of the backlash against feminism . . . [wherein] mother's rights had been deteriorating for some time before the main backlash received the [feminist] movement's attention" (p. 144).

In 1998, Massat and Lundy, two professors of social work at the Jane Addams College of Social Work of the University of Illinois, reported in *Child Welfare* on their three-year study of the hidden costs to mothers who attempt to protect children allegedly abused by their fathers. They used four criteria (relational, financial, vocational, and residential), which they applied to a sample of 104 nonoffending parents whose cases were before family courts, and drew the following conclusion: "Learning that one's child has been sexually abused is to learn not only that one's child has been harmed but harmed in a way that does not bring about public support in the same way that a physical accident or illness may."[13]

Besides the growing corpus of studies of family court malfunction, there have been several published reports by prominent women's organizations and gender-bias task forces commissioned by state courts that have expressed similar concerns.

In 2002, the California chapter of the National Organization for Women (NOW) issued the results of a three-year investigation into "the ways women are abused by the family court system in California."[14] NOW conducted extensive interviews with mothers and reviewed their court documents. Some of the issues covered in the NOW report were gender biases, denial of due process, conflict of interest and corruption, and the use of false "syndromes" to discriminate against mothers in family courts.[15] After the report was completed, NOW's California chapter urged its subsidiaries throughout the state to press for serious changes to the family court system.

In November 2002, the Wellesley Centers for Women published the findings of a study that analyzed the cases of thirty-nine Massachusetts mothers who reported both "intimate partner violence" (abuse by a partner or spouse) against themselves and sexual abuse of their child or children by the allegedly violent partner. The 106–page report, titled *Battered Mothers Speak Out: A Human Rights Report on Domestic Violence and Child Custody in the Massachusetts Family Courts,* documented instances "in which the Massachusetts family courts are violating internationally accepted human rights laws and standards . . . [and] are violating Massachusetts law and policy" (p. iv).[16] In the June 2004 issue of the *American Journal of Public Health,* the authors summarized their findings, which revealed "a consistent pattern of potential human rights violations by state actors [judges, law guardians, social service agency workers, and others] of the Massachusetts family courts against women participating in the project and their children." These human rights violations included "failing to investigate allegations or consider documentation of child abuse as relevant evidence in cases of disputed child custody"(pp. 952–953).[17]

The Massachusetts Battered Mothers' Testimony Project was copied in other states, with similar results. In June 2003, the Arizona Coalition against Domestic Violence released a report titled *Battered Mothers' Testimony Project: A Human Rights Approach to Child Custody and Domestic Violence.* Fifty-seven women were interviewed for this study. Its conclusions amounted to an indictment of the family court system. The authors stated: "state law was violated virtually at every turn," and "Constitutional issues such as due process, equal protection and the fundamental right of parenting were violated by arbitrary rules and actual practice." The report concluded with a "call for action to policy makers, the legal community, state government and, most importantly, the public" (p. 7).[18]

The findings of such reports documenting serious abuses by the family court system in its treatment of protective mothers, startling as they are, were not unprecedented. The state-funded Judicial Council of California Administrative Office of the Courts produced a lengthy report in 1990 (*Achieving Equal Justice for Women and Men in the Courts*)[19] that found evidence of gender bias in the courts, including "serious problems . . . in decision making, court practices and procedures, the fair allocation of judicial resources, and in the courtroom environment" (p. 1):

> Similarly, the Judicial Council Advisory Committee showed that while the conduct of judges constituting gender bias has resulted in judicial discipline by the Commission on Judicial performance . . . many more examples of conduct exhibiting gender bias or the appearance of gender bias have oc-

curred that have not resulted in judicial discipline and include . . . openly
hostile behavior; the utterance of sexual innuendos or dirty jokes; the occasional and offensive use of terms of endearment to refer to women participants in the courtroom; hostility and impatience toward causes of action
uniquely involving women. (pp. 5–6)

Writing in *Judicare* in 1987, New York attorney Lynn Hecht Schafran
summarized some of the critical findings of the New York State Task Force
on Gender Bias in the Courts:

The Task Force has concluded that gender bias against women litigants, attorneys and court personnel is a pervasive problem with grave consequences.
Women are often denied equal justice, equal treatment and equal opportunity. Cultural stereotypes of women's role in marriage and in society daily
distort courts' application of substantive law. Women, uniquely, dispropor-
tionately, and with unacceptable frequency must endure a climate of con-
descension, indifference and hostility. (p. 283)

Karen Winner, a veteran investigative journalist, wrote in *Divorced from
Justice: The Abuse of Women and Children by Divorce Lawyers and Judges*
(1996) about "the gaping black hole of justice" in domestic litigation, describing a lawless system in which judges and lawyers "are governed by
their own system of self-rule" (p. 93). Winner, a former policy analyst for
the City of New York Department of Consumer Affairs, also studied various counties in California, paying specific attention to protective mother
issues, and concluded that the family courts sorely mishandle charges of
sexual abuse. Under the auspices of Justice Seekers, Inc., a privately funded,
nonprofit, New York–based court watch and citizen's action organization
founded by Winner in 1997, Winner authored several reports on the family courts across several northern California counties.

Here are some of Winner's conclusions regarding cases she investigated:
"the judge and commissioner put power . . . and self-interest over the welfare and safety of children and litigants";[20] "pedophile-friendly views . . .
are deeply entrenched in the Sacramento court system and surrounding
areas. . . . This report [shows] that the psychological evaluations produced
for the courts were so flawed and skewed in many cases, that they
amounted to hoaxes perpetrated on the litigants and on the judges deciding the outcomes."[21]

In fact, Ms. Winner expressed to us the urgent need for civil disobedi-
ence to combat the disastrous treatment of protective mothers and their

children in America's family courts. And her report has received important confirmation: a prominent matrimonial attorney in Marin County, California, has told a journalist, "Although I disagreed with some of the factual details of the Winner report, I thought that overall, in general, it described the situation."[22]

Clearly, the reality of family court malfunction is well documented. But nearly all reports and studies of family court malfunction attempt to abstract a "root cause" for the system's failure. Most studies have relied on traditional gender-based explanations built on a sociohistorical view of child sexual abuse awareness and society's readiness to acknowledge abuse.

For example, Olafson, Corwin, and Summit (1993) performed a thorough historical analysis of the "cycles" of discovery and suppression in the complex history of sexual abuse awareness. Myers (1997) calls 1975 "the great divide in the professional literature" (p. 132), when the predominant skepticism about abuse charges eroded in the face of the strong feminist movement of the 1960s and 1970s.

Although such sociohistorical analyses are indeed of importance in their own right, the focus of our book—as we have remarked in the introduction—is somewhat different. We examine the inner dynamics of the ways the family courts have evolved into oppressive, biased dispensers of justice, whose decisions so often run counter to the best interests of children.

Where the Madness Comes From

Family courts can work only as well as the lawyers and judges who inhabit them. Yet we have found serious deficiencies in both the bench and bar of the family court system.

LAWYERS

Though this may surprise the uninitiated, most lawyers who handle divorce and custody litigation in family courts are poorly equipped to deal with charges of sexual abuse that arise in child custody litigation. In *The Hostage Child,* Rosen and Etlin (1996) give many examples of woefully inadequate legal representation in child abuse cases, citing among other instances a Texas mother who "pressed for a speedy trial on her daughter's best interests" only to have her attorney "threaten to quit rather than try the case" (p. 79). Her experience was not exceptional: in 1989, Colorado activist attorney Alan Rosenfeld testified at a New York State legislative hearing on family court malfunction that *most* attorneys are reluctant to pursue claims of child sexual abuse.[23]

This attitude on the part of much of the matrimonial bar has the effect of making child sex abuse allegations much more difficult to pursue in the courts—and this is ironic in view of statistical evidence that such charges are seldom fabricated. In 1988, the American Bar Association, in cooperation with the Association of Family and Conciliation Courts, issued a report on an in-depth study of allegations of child sexual abuse made in the context of custody and visitation proceedings. Nicholson and Bulkley, who edited the report,[24] found that "[d]eliberately false allegations made to influence the custody decision or to hurt an ex-spouse do happen, but they are viewed by knowledgeable professionals as rarities" (p. 17). Along similar lines, the relevant section in a highly respected treatise for lawyers, *American Jurisprudence Proof of Facts* (3rd ed., 1995), after thoroughly analyzing all sides of the custody/abuse debate, concludes: "[C]oaching is not a common occurrence in custody cases involving child sexual allegations."[25]

Yet the bulk of family law attorneys, hardened to the realities of family courts, are reluctant to risk making, or supporting, a sex abuse allegation. The *Proof of Facts* article quoted above notes that "alleging child sexual abuse rarely gives the mother an advantage" (contrary to popular belief) because "[w]omen who claim such abuse in a custody proceeding are often met with immediate suspicion. Even if true, the abuse allegation is difficult to prove . . . [and if] the allegations are not substantiated, the complaining parent risks losing custody, even if he or she would have won on the merits without such a claim."[26] So most protective mothers are likely to find themselves without eager representation. A prominent Brooklyn matrimonial attorney (and former president of the Brooklyn Bar Association matrimonial committee) told one of us that the bulk of sex abuse allegations in divorce litigation were acts of "revenge" and that even validation by a professional was meaningless in such cases because "those validators were feminists who had their own issues with men."

Family court lawyers who bring to these courts the expectations learned in other tribunals may find themselves swimming against the tide. A Massachusetts divorce attorney told one of us recently: "The reason I do a diligent representation of my clients is because my practice entails other specialties of the law; I bring to family court [litigation] what I bring to my cases in other areas."

Julia Heit, a New York City divorce attorney whose practice also includes criminal and civil appeals, reported to us that she was once driven to ask an old colleague from the Legal Aid Society: "Can it be true that in the Family Court the Constitution is thrown to the winds?" Against this background, it is not surprising that most lawyers who work in the family court system have come to accept as standard practices what might be regarded as highly questionable in other arenas.

Heit also told us that "family court isn't a court, it's a club." This means that protective mothers often find local practitioners and experts unwilling to jeopardize their relationships with family court judges by presenting an unpopular sex abuse allegation. In a Green Bay, Wisconsin, case, for example, two school-age boys were held in the custody of a father whose behavior included showering with the children and other "inappropriate conduct of the nature that can be considered sexual." Only when the mother, with the help of an out-of-state activist, changed attorneys (selecting a new one from the other end of the state) and brought in new experts (including one from out of state) did she persuade a judge to alter a previous ruling and transfer custody to the mother (and order supervised visitation for the father). Evidently the conventional local network of lawyers and experts was not prepared to advocate for these steps.

Something similar occurred in a New York City case in 1991. A popular court-appointed expert testified that the mother had "a personality disorder" with "borderline and schizotypal features," because she complained that her eight-year-old daughter was forced to sleep on Saturday nights in her father's bed (an arrangement against which the child also protested). The mother's lawyer (according to the mother's report to us) would not take any action to challenge the expert's testimony. The mother hired new counsel who did challenge the expert, and in the end the judge put an end to the sleeping arrangement, writing in his decision that the mother's concerns were absolutely justified: "the recognized phenomena such as nocturnal erections could, under such sleeping arrangements, have the effect of frightening the child." It would seem likely that the mother's first lawyer was reportedly unwilling to fight an expert he would probably see again in future cases.

The difficulty for advocates who oppose the tide is compounded by the glacial pace of many family courts. In the mid-1980s, popular TV talk show personality "Judge Judy" (Judith Scheindlin) was a sitting judge in the Manhattan Family Court. Sheindlin ruled in favor of a Russian immigrant mother whose nine-year-old daughter had been removed from her by child protective services without sufficient legal grounds. But the mother had to wait six long months before Judge Scheindlin could even hear her case.

MEN'S RIGHTS/FATHERS' RIGHTS GROUPS

The feminist writer Louise Armstrong, in *Rocking the Cradle of Sexual Politics: What Happened When Women Said Incest* (1994), described the emergence of the fathers' rights movement in the early 1980s as a "corrective" to "increased pressure to enforce child support" (p. 68). Armstrong points to the Men's Equality Now International Coalition as one of the first men's rights/fathers' rights organizations to circulate an official bimonthly newsletter offering advice on winning child custody cases as well as reducing or eliminating child support burdens by claiming alienation of affection and/or denial of visitation, among other litigation goals.[27]

The effect of the fathers' rights movement should not be taken lightly. The American Coalition for Fathers and Children (ACFC), founded in 1986, is one of the largest fathers' rights groups in the country. Sporting a distinctive logo, the ACFC has sprouted chapters all over the United States. On its website (www.acfc.org), the ACFC states its primary goal: "disseminating the truth about fathers and families" and exposing "the hypocrisy that exists in the news media." And the organization can boast of some success: several legislators we interviewed have told us—using language that closely parallels ACFC's literature—that women frequently fabricate sex abuse charges to gain an advantage in custody litigation.

Matrimonial attorneys often play leading roles in fathers' rights groups, and this means that these lawyers may have close relationships with family court judges—relationships that can easily be misused. This was evident when Jay Shoulson, an attorney who was then chief counsel to the Fathers' Rights Association of Metro New York and Long Island, appeared at a legislative hearing specifically to defend Leon Deutsch, a Brooklyn Family Court judge notorious for his punishment of mothers who alleged child sexual abuse.[28]

Shoulson testified to state legislators, who had assembled to hear complaints about Brooklyn Family Court, that Judge Deutsch was "a really caring individual" and that the mothers who had testified against him were "vindictive."[29] The outraged mothers and their supporters confronted Shoulson in a corridor outside the hearing room, where he heatedly insisted that the women who had testified about Deutsch's judicial abuses "had an axe to grind."

One of those mothers later became acquainted with Humberto Middleton, a legal client of Shoulson and an active member of his Fathers' Rights Association. In a remarkable letter written in December 1991, Middleton disclosed to her that Shoulson's advocacy for Judge Deutsch, and his implicit attack on one of the judge's victims, was prearranged with Deutsch himself. Shoulson, he wrote, had boasted of his relationship with Brooklyn Family Court judges including Deutsch:

> He [Shoulson] went on to say that he was connected with Judge Deutsch and that as a favor to the Judge he had promised to discredit [you] whenever possible. . . . One of the things that Rabbi Shoulson requested of me was to inform him of everything and every time you had some involvement with the Fathers Rights Association of which I am a member. When I refused and told him that I did not have the time or desire to monitor your activities . . . that triggered another response from him.[30]

According to Middleton, Shoulson in effect had volunteered to be both advocate and spy for a family court judge. What is more, he saw no reason not to boast of it to a client. This anecdote has much to say about the role fathers' rights groups may play in the family court system, at least in some cases.

JUDGES

Matrimonial lawyers take their cue from the judges who rule the family courts. The published findings about the scarcity of deliberately fabricated allegations, cited above, have had little discernible impact on judges, who continue to believe that women charge sex abuse out of "vindictiveness" during an acrimonious custody proceeding. For example, Judge William Thompson—New York State's chief appellate justice for the state's Second Judicial Department—told investigative journalist Karen Winner, "You know what happens in every matrimonial case now? They go to the lawyer and the lawyer says, 'You know we're going to holler sexual abuse.' Everything stops. . . . That's become the password now. . . . Holler sexual abuse and every goddamn thing slows down. It's getting to be a disaster now because that's the password now."[31]

Beliefs like these have much to do with the family court system's persistent mishandling of sex abuse allegations and its tendency to make the accuser, rather than the accused, pay the price of such charges. In 1992, New York state senator David A. Paterson declared at a press conference, the purpose of which was to bring public attention to the family court system's mishandling of sex abuse cases: "This is about as serious an indictment of government as I can think of in all the time I've been in office."[32] Paterson was not a lone voice; more than a half dozen legislators and members of the New York City Council echoed his indictment at the same press conference.

During a two-day legislative hearing into family court malfunction held in 1989, New York State assemblyman (now congressman) Jerrold Nadler exclaimed: "I've been shocked to discover in case after case the consistent denial of due process rights to women attempting to protect their children from sexual abuse . . . [and] the public is not aware of the terrible miscarriages of justice."[33]

Midway through the hearing, after listening to "so many cases where the child is handed over to the abuser and the mother is punished," Nadler referred to what was happening in the family courts as "'the judicial rape of children.'"[34] After that comment appeared in the *New York Post,* a high-ranking official of the New York State Bar Association publicly challenged Nadler to retract it. He refused.

How the System Responds to Criticism

Jerrold Nadler may have been surprised that his well-deserved criticism of family courts drew a denial, rather than sympathy, from a prominent Bar Association official. But his experience is typical. The family court system is largely impervious to the sort of criticism presented above. In 1988, the *Journal of the American Academy of Child and Adolescent Psychiatry* published an extraordinary public rebuke of a popular expert witness in child sexual abuse cases, Dr. Arthur Green, signed by psychiatrist Graeme Hanson and eighteen cosignatories, all of them specialists in child sexual abuse, which stated: "Our major concern is that Green's assertions may be taken as a standard of practice by those clinicians relatively inexperienced in the area of child sexual abuse . . . [and] it is our fear that Green's [assertions are] likely to be used in judicial settings to the detriment of a large number of children caught in custody battles who have actually been sexually abused."[35]

That sharp criticism, however, had no apparent impact on Green's reputation in family courts. Roughly a year after this warning about Green's work appeared, the *New York Law Journal* undertook an informal survey of New York City judges to determine their attitudes toward Dr. Green's controversial theories—theories that claimed, in essence, that divorcing women frequently lie about sex abuse to get back at their husbands. Out of forty-five family court judges, only two expressed any definite concern about having an expert such as Green testify in their courtrooms. According to the *Law Journal,* one of those two judges, Abraham Jurow, "suggested the court should ferret out experts who have published articles stating strong opinions about the truth or falsity of allegations of child sexual abuse and accord their predispositions proper weight in evaluating their testimony."[36] But that comment stood alone. Evidently, the great majority of New York City's family court judges were unperturbed by Dr. Green's ominous reputation among his peers.

In fact, when a family court judge departs from the "mad" logic typical of the system, she may actually be subject to reversal by a higher court (on those rare occasions when an appellate court even reviews the facts underlying a family court decision). That happened in a 1999 New York case in which the judge awarded custody to a protective mother even though the judge was not persuaded that the father had sexually abused the child. The judge found that the mother had not been malicious in making her allegations; rather, she was "hypersensitive" to issues of abuse (perhaps because she was allegedly abused herself as a child). The judge found her a fit parent, "more in tune" with the child than the father, and awarded her custody based on her history of being primary caretaker. However, the appellate court discarded the judge's findings, stating that the mother's motivation was irrelevant—all that mattered was that her allegations of sexual abuse were not ultimately substantiated.[37] The court then reversed the trial judge and awarded custody outright to the father despite the trial court's findings about both parents. The appellate court went so far as to criticize the mother for taking the child to a therapist and for causing the father's visits to be temporarily supervised—even though these are fairly routine steps when abuse is suspected. Family court orthodoxy was thus ensured by the reversal of an unusually sensitive ruling by a family court trial judge.[38]

Family Court System under Attack:
Federal Judge Champions Mothers' Cause

In 2002, Chief Judge Jack Weinstein of the U.S. Court for the Eastern District of New York, in a landmark decision, gave voice to the plight of at least some of the mothers victimized in family courts. Although Judge Weinstein did not address the problems of child sex abuse allegations, his long decision in a high-profile case sheds important light on family court malfunction.

In *Nicholson v. ACS*,[39] Judge Weinstein considered the claims of mothers who had been needlessly separated from their minor children solely because the mothers had been battered by a husband or lover. Judge Weinstein concluded that New York City's child protective services agency (CPS) had indeed taken this astonishing approach to domestic abuse: "the abuser [is] left unaccountable because it is administratively easier [for child protective services] to punish the mother by separating her from her children."

Judge Weinstein found that the CPS agency had penalized mothers for enduring abuse on the theory that they had "failed to protect" their children from abuse, or potential abuse, by a father—even where their circumstances made it difficult for the mothers to leave the marital home. (One of those circumstances, ironically, was the fear of losing custody if they did leave. Louise Armstrong noted in *The Home Front: Notes from the Family War Zone* [1983] that when a woman is battered and threatens to leave, the batterer may counter with a threat that he will sue for custody.) Judge Weinstein found that "statistics, individual cases, expert testimony, and admissions of ACS (Administration for Children's Services) employees demonstrate that many more separations of abused mothers and their children are made by ACS than are necessary for protection of the children" (p. 50).

In summarizing the facts concerning removals of children from battered mothers, Judge Weinstein declared: "the Thirteenth Amendment should protect exploited workers, *abused mothers,* neglected children, and all other victims of relationships reminiscent of *slavery*" (p. 76, emphasis supplied). The bitterness of the judge's analogy—as well as the fact that in the case of abused mothers it is the machinery of the family court system that adds to the mothers' oppression—is a measure of family court madness.

How Mothers React to the Madness

In light of all this, it is not surprising that more and more mothers who have cases in family courts are rebelling. H. Joan Pennington and Laurie Woods of the National Center on Women and Family Law began their 1990 report, *Legal Issues and Legal Options in Civil Child Sexual Abuse Cases,* with this announcement:

> Recently there has been an increase in the number of cases in which mothers who are convinced that their children have been sexually abused by their fathers have taken away or hidden their children, sometimes in violation of court orders . . . because they have concluded that the legal system will not protect the children. These mothers believe that they have only one way left to them in order to protect their child. In many situations, friends, family, or a network of supporters have helped the mothers and children leave the area and go into hiding. This has become popularly known as The Underground Movement (p. 1).

The "Underground Movement" has grown up recently and rapidly. Phyllis Chesler's *Mothers on Trial* (1986) surveyed the literature on child custody from the 1970s and early 1980s and found that "studies of 'child snatching' or parental kidnapping confirm that most parental child kidnappers are fathers [and not mothers]" (p. 446). Yet by 1990, parental abductions by mothers who suspected abuse were sufficiently organized to be called a "movement."

The "mutiny" of protective mothers against the family court system today has many of the earmarks of a movement. For example, many of the rebellious mothers have come to see the unaccountable judicial actions in their cases as part of a larger social and legal malady, rather than as aberrations or anomalies.

Activist mothers have aggressively sought the attention of lawmakers. Though new legislation seldom results from this activism, the protective mothers can be profoundly affected even by sympathetic words. In March 1989, at a legislative press conference on the eve of the first of a series of hearings held by then New York State assemblyman Jerrold Nadler on the family courts, Faye Yager—founder of an Atlanta-based organization she later called "Children of the Underground"—exclaimed to Amy Neustein: "I can't believe what I'm hearing. Why didn't I have a legislator speaking out in my day when I all alone was up against a court system that refused to protect my daughter, who contracted gonorrhea from her father?"

In January 2004, the activist movement reached another milestone. Nationally recognized attorneys, advocates, and protective mothers from all over the country convened at Siena College, just outside Albany, New York, for a two-day summit on the abuse of mothers in the family courts. The conference, organized by Siena psychology professor Maureen Therese Hannah and an activist North Carolina mother, Liliane Heller Miller, was intended by the organizers to "kick off a campaign of activism" that would take the family court scandal to "the highest levels" of government and to the public at large. New York State assemblyman Felix Ortiz was among the featured invitees. The conference began with a special invocation by journalist and author Barbara Reynolds, former columnist and editor of *USA Today,* who called it a "historic moment" in the movement for equality for mothers in the family courts throughout the nation.[40]

PRO SE PEBELS

Protective mother "mutiny" may take many forms. Taking on her own representation in court is often the decisive step that turns a protective mother into a rebel. Such mothers become increasingly strident in their court behavior: they lash out at the judge and the auxiliary players, demanding their rights, accusing the officials of misconduct, sometimes accusing them of "conspiracies." Some mothers have shocked themselves with their conduct. One New York State protective mother told the Director of the Women's Office at the Archdiocese of New York, "I didn't know I had it in me to be so bold." Sometimes such mothers are punished by angry judges for their tirades; on other occasions, family court personnel simply seem to ignore them.

As a strategy, however, pro se rebellion is not particularly beneficial to protective mothers. Court personnel tend to regard pro se litigants as eccentrics. Thus they may give them unusual leeway when it comes to "acting out," but this tolerance rarely implies sympathy with their position in the litigation. In some cases we have reviewed, it was precisely a protective mother's behavior as her own attorney—defending herself at great length, accusing the social workers of misconduct, "rambling" as she tried to explain her view of the entire case—that supported the judge's ultimately hostile rulings concerning her. That is, mothers who had been good, nurturing parents (providing for their children's basic needs and more) were evaluated in family court not for their parenting but for their awkward conduct in the courtroom.

FLEEING

Another way women may rebel against the family courts is by literally running away from them.

An organized "underground" movement for protective mothers began in 1987 when two Mississippi mothers, Karen Newsom and Dorrie Lyn

Singley, made headlines for defying the orders of family court judge Sebe Dale, who had ordered them to surrender their children into their fathers' custody.[41] Judge Dale had refused to hear compelling medical evidence that supported the allegations of abuse in each case.[42] While Karen Newsom went to jail—after placing her two preschool daughters in hiding—Dorrie Lyn Singley took flight with her child and disappeared into an impromptu underground network of sympathizers.

Neither story ended happily. After forty-three days in jail, Newsom "broke," according to her supporters, and disclosed her children's hiding place in order to win her release from prison. Singley, twenty-seven, died of a brain aneurysm while on the run.

At almost the same time, Virginia LaLonde of Massachusetts spent six months in jail for refusing to reveal the whereabouts of her daughter, whom she had hidden in a "safe house" run by a friend, in order to prevent her ex-husband from gaining access to the child.[43]

These three highly publicized cases caught the attention of many other mothers. Among them was Faye Yager, who transformed an embryonic underground into an organized, transcontinental network of safe houses.

Yager, a successful entrepreneur and the wife of an Atlanta family doctor, had suffered her own family court tragedy years earlier when a family court judge had awarded sole custody of her four-year-old daughter to Yager's former husband, in spite of medical evidence that he had sexually abused the girl. Spurred by what she read, Yager joined the mothers' movement in 1988 and turned her energy and organizational talents to the formation of a nationally known movement of fugitive mothers.[44] Through the late 1980s, and for most of the 1990s, Yager frequently made front-page news and was a regular guest on popular national talk shows. In 1988, she was profiled by CBS News's *60 Minutes,* along with another high-profile activist and safe house operator, Lydia Rayner, the wife of a popular Mississippi obstetrician.

Yager's expansion of the new Underground Railroad (she would later call her organization Children of the Underground) encouraged other activists to form undergrounds of their own. Attorney H. Joan Pennington testified in 1992 to the House Judiciary Committee that "there is a vast underground network, where hundreds, perhaps thousands of parents and children live as fugitives."[45] By 1997 McKenzie Carpenter, a reporter from the *Pittsburgh Post-Gazette,* had identified four major underground railroads in the United States for mothers of abused children in a five-part series she did for the paper.[46]

Yager's high profile has had disadvantages. She was sued several times by fathers whose children she had placed in hiding. In the late 1990s, Yager—having spent all her money on her own legal defense—finally quit the Underground Railroad. Nevertheless, she continued in her harsh criticism of the family court system. In 2001, she told a Pennsylvania newspaper: "It's a crisis. . . . We're not free from anything if we can't free our own children."[47]

POLITICKING

Many protective parents who do not seek refuge in the Underground Railroad do, however, seek the attention of legislators and the media. This is not an easy task. It generally requires a mother to assemble copious documentation on her own case and (if possible) other similar cases. And few legislators and newspaper editors are prepared to challenge the popular assumption that women frequently invent sex abuse charges to gain leverage in custody disputes.

Organizations such as Justice for Children (based in Houston, Texas) have tried to stimulate greater interest in the protective mother problem among legislators and other officials. Regional Director Eileen King, who has been taking calls at Justice for Children's Washington, D.C., office since 1995, reports receiving hundreds of calls each month, from states all over the country, from protective mothers seeking help. She says her organization is steadily seeking the ear of public officials who can do something to improve the situation. But Justice for Children's lobbying efforts have so far borne little fruit, though King says she will persevere.

In some instances protective mothers' assiduous preparation and "politicking" have paid off to some extent. New York State senator David A. Paterson, in a 1995 letter to the deputy acting chief of the Child Exploitation and Obscenity Section of the U.S. Department of Justice, was sufficiently convinced by one Brooklyn, New York, mother's case to write: "there is such an intensely ferocious effort made by judges, social services and law guardian agencies . . . to protect the father from an [abuse] investigation." Still, the Justice Department took no action. The details of mothers' rebellion against the family courts will be described in part II, chapter 8.

Chapter 2

The New Legal Landscape

F amily courts have reached the state they are in, at least partly, through the development of new and unusual features in the family court system. These developments were intended to improve the family courts, but their actual effect has often been remote from the intended one.

Court Auxiliaries

One special feature of family courts, particularly when sex abuse allegations are involved, is the special roster of auxiliary actors: law guardians, child protective service (CPS) caseworkers, visitation supervisors, court-appointed mental health experts and evaluators, and sometimes others.

These auxiliaries enter family court litigation in many ways. In most states, child abuse allegations are now referred to child welfare agencies, known in some states as "presentment agencies," which function much as prosecutors do in criminal cases. The child welfare agencies (or presentment agencies) in turn rely on social workers, evaluators, and psychologists. In addition, many states now require a family court to appoint a special representative for a child in a private custody suit, on the theory that since the parents are in conflict the child needs an advocate of his own to ensure that his rights are protected.

This process was clearly intended to aid the investigation and presentation of sex abuse charges, which by their nature tend to require the intervention of experts. But we have found that many (though not all) of the auxiliary family court personnel are actually among the leading contributors to the insanity of the courts.

For instance, one common way for auxiliary players to enter custody litigation is through a judge's order for a "home study" by the state's CPS agency. This sometimes occurs in conventional custody disputes but is much more common when charges of sexual abuse are raised. In such cases, all parties are likely to be evaluated, including the parent who made the allegation.

But protective mothers often present a special problem to the social workers who must evaluate them. Unlike indigent parents, who are accustomed to being at the mercy of state agencies for subsistence, many protective mothers are appreciably better educated and earn a better income than the caseworkers do. They are not prepared to be dictated to, and they do not meekly accept the state employees' assessment of them. This can often lead to antagonism between mothers and child protection caseworkers. In several cases we have studied, the formal charges pressed against mothers in family courts by child welfare agencies were essentially based on allegedly "difficult" or "insulting" behavior of the mothers toward the caseworkers—not their capacity as parents. What is more, some CPS workers simply resist accusations of child sexual abuse. Researchers M. D. Everson and B. W. Boat (1989) have found that a certain proportion of CPS workers are more skeptical of children's claims of sexual abuse than is warranted by the actual rates of false reporting (which are low). Such skepticism adds a crucial irritant to the relationship between protective mothers and child welfare workers. The role of social service agencies will be discussed in more depth in part II of this book, chapter 6.

"Law guardians" or "guardians ad litem" are not new to the courts, but they, like the social workers, have attained special prominence and significance in abuse litigation. And since they function in family courts as the voice of the child, their acts of commission and omission have a profound effect on the progress of any abuse allegation. In one case, after a child disclosed to his mother that his father had molested him—and confirmed this to a pediatrician—the boy's law guardian, without even meeting with the boy (supposedly his client), recommended in court that the boy and his younger brother be removed from their mother's home, because otherwise "we're going to be in and out of this courtroom the rest of our lives." This was certainly not what his client wanted—but his position as law guardian apparently convinced the judge to remove two small children from the mother's home without even considering the boy's charges against his father. The role of "lawless" law guardians in the family courts will be examined in detail in part II of this book, chapter 5.

The involvement of auxiliaries dramatically changes the landscape of custody/abuse litigation. When a mother makes an abuse allegation that is not supported by social workers, for instance, she finds herself fighting not only against one adversary (her ex-husband) but against an array of other actors who may then lend considerable official support (free of charge) to the mother's adversary.

The influence of CPS social workers and lawyers on a family court goes far beyond mere advocacy. Family court judges, who work with these officials day in and day out, ordinarily defer to their recommendations. Indeed, they are under heavy pressure to do so. When New York City's mayor made the unusual decision "not to reappoint a particular family court judge for a new term, some defense lawyers bitterly complained" to the *New York Law Journal* that the only reason was the judge's "reputation for aggressively pushing [CPS] . . . to provide services to families and to conduct its work expeditiously"—rare among family court judges—and that denying him reappointment "only reinforced an already widespread tendency on the part of most Family Court judges to defer to the recommendations of ACS [New York City's CPS agency]." As one lawyer put it, "if you criticize ACS and don't do what ACS wants, you are not going to get reappointed." Another lawyer, who specialized in representing battered women, complained that the mayor's decision made other family court judges "even more afraid to stand up to ACS." (Unwittingly dotting the i's of this attorney's point, CPS lawyers told the *Law Journal* the judge deserved to lose his job because he had been "disrespectful" to them.) By contrast, a family court judge criticized by many defense lawyers for "being too inclined to accept the government's position" was readily reappointed.[1]

The support of the auxiliary actors in a family court case can mean more to an accused father than legal leverage. The father can derive financial benefit as well. For example, in a New York case litigated in the early 1990s, a law guardian was appointed by the court because of sex abuse allegations against the father. The legal role of a law guardian in such a case is to protect the child's best interest. Yet after the family court judge awarded custody to the mother, limiting the father's visits with the child because of sexually inappropriate behavior, it was the law guardian who appealed the decision to a higher court—thus effectively litigating for the father at the appellate level, although the father was found to have behaved inappropriately toward the law guardian's own client! The added injury to the mother was that the law guardian's appeal relieved the father of the heavy burden of appellate expenses—while the mother had to pay over $25,000 in legal fees out of her own pocket. (Fortunately for the mother, the appellate court affirmed the family court's ruling. However, the mother cannot recoup the enormous financial loss she suffered because of the law guardian's action, while the father enjoyed a free appeal.)

In fact, in some cases we have studied, law guardians who were employed by state agencies and were sympathetic to one parent have used their own agencies' money to purchase trial transcripts for use in an appeal (which can cost thousands of dollars) and then have provided a free copy to that parent—but not the other. Thus, the disfavored parent—the mother in all the cases we know of—was put to a significant financial disadvantage.

"Visitation supervisors" represent another class of interlopers in modern-day custody proceedings in which an abuse issue has been raised. Their purpose is to monitor visits between a child and a parent, ostensibly for the protection of the child. But they are often called on in cases in which a family court judge suspects a mother of having "brainwashed" her children into believing they have been sexually abused. In such cases, visitation supervisors play their role in the family court structure by searching for any sort of evidence of "coaching," improper "involvement" of the child in the lawsuit, or even "overidentification" of the mother with the child. Accordingly, they may permit only the strictest, most limited contact between the child and the mother, where every word the mother says is closely monitored to see if she is "planting ideas" in the child's mind. In some cases, mothers are forbidden to hold their small children on their laps for fear they will whisper in the children's ears.

This is clearly not what such supervisors were originally meant to do. Stern and Oehme opine in *Temple Law Review* (2002) that although "supervised visitation was originally established to provide a crucial service, parent-child access, and was never intended to be used as a backdoor parenting evaluation . . . using supervised visitation to 'document behavior by each parent that either supports or discourages [access to the child]' does just that" (p. 281). And, in fact, the authors point out that "courts . . . may be far too willing to allow unqualified visitation staff to make assessments [about visitation and custody]" (p. 285).

The evidentiary weight that family courts give to visitation reports, according to Stern and Oehme, notwithstanding the "lack of judicial and legislative standards governing their admissibility," leads to a misguided reliance on visitation records in child custody proceedings that "can cause unintended consequences directly adverse to the best interests of the children . . ." (p. 278). And indeed, in some cases, visitation supervisors have presented evidence to family courts that the judges relied on in terminating the visitation rights of the protective mother altogether.

Among the most important figures in the new legal landscape of child abuse/custody litigation are mental health experts (and evaluators) who are hired by litigants or (more often) appointed by the court to evaluate the parenting skills of both parents. They are also called on to present psychological profiles of parents and children, and to analyze any claims of abuse that have been made. Since the mid-1970s, parents have been encouraged by family court judges to agree to the court's appointment of an impartial expert to make findings and recommendations in nearly all custody and visitation cases.[2] These experts wield extraordinary influence over judicial decision making. Unfortunately, the influence they can wield is often out of all proportion to the weight their methods and theories hold among their professional peers.

By 1985, some experts had found themselves under attack from angry family court litigants. Some of the litigants filed federal lawsuits against certain of the more controversial experts, alleging malpractice, negligence, invasion of privacy, and violation of constitutional rights. The suits were dismissed, and most health care professionals agreed with the dismissals. As William Curran, a regular legal editorialist for the *New England Journal of Medicine* at that time, wrote in 1985 about such lawsuits: "Ensuring complete immunity from suit is the only sensible method of discouraging such *angry retaliation*" (emphasis supplied).[3]

The need for such protection in acrimonious custody disputes is clear enough, but protecting the experts does nothing to protect litigants from the spurious or tendentious theories these experts sometimes bring to family courts.

One such theory is "Parental Alienation Syndrome" (PAS). New Jersey psychiatrist Richard A. Gardner coined this term in 1985[4] to describe a special disorder that he claimed was unique to custody proceedings in which child sexual abuse allegations were raised. In *True and False Accusations of Child Sex Abuse* (1992), Gardner defines PAS as "a disorder in which children, programmed by the allegedly 'loved' parent, embark on a campaign of denigration of the allegedly 'hated' parent." Gardner also claims that it is "most often the mothers who are involved in such programming, and the fathers are the victims of the campaigns of deprecation" (p. 193).

Gardner's theories have received extensive criticism in published articles by other mental health professionals. They were officially rejected by the American Psychological Association's Presidential Task Force on Violence and the Family in a 1996 report titled "Violence and the Family." But PAS remains very popular with family courts.

Like Gardner, Dr. Arthur Green (mentioned in chapter 1) claimed that in order to determine whether a child has been abused, the primary focus should be on scrutinizing the mother's behavior.

Green advocated closely watching the mother-child interaction when a child reports abuse to a professional, seeing if the child "checks" with the mother before proceeding. He regarded this as an indication of a "brain-washed" child. But many of Green's colleagues adamantly disagree: "In our experience, children who are anxious . . . 'check' with their mothers for reassurance before proceeding. This does not invariably indicate brain-washing."[5] Nevertheless, Dr. Green remained a highly influential expert in custody and abuse litigation until his death in 1998.

In fact, the influence of the theories of Gardner and Green is so perva-sive that it is reflected, unconsciously, even by legal writers who are very skeptical of the claims on which those theories are based. As noted above, *American Jurisprudence Proof of Facts* states—contradicting Gardner and Green—that coaching of sex abuse charges is rare in custody cases. But the same widely used treatise lists as "guidelines" for determining a sex abuse allegation's reliability some controversial factors lifted right out of Gard-ner's books. For instance, the treatise indicates that a mother's strong reac-tion to the child's disclosure of sex abuse may be indicative of a false alle-gation. It also mentions the importance of determining from the outset if the allegations arose during a custody battle. These are, in fact, among the criteria recommended by Gardner. But such an approach, according to Corwin et al. (1987), can be grossly misleading for the simple reason that sex abuse is more likely to be disclosed by the child when the abuser is al-ready out of the house (leaving the child feeling safe enough to talk) than when a family is intact. And, of course, a protective parent's strong reac-tion may be perfectly appropriate if the charge is genuine.

The antimother bias that thrives in the family courts has accommodated even more extreme psychological theories. For instance, psychologist Ira Turkat (1997) has named "Malicious Mother Syndrome" (MMS) to iden-tify "mothers [who] not only try to alienate their children from their fa-thers, but are committed to a broadly based campaign to hurt the father di-rectly" (pp. 17–18). Like PAS, this theory has the particularly insidious feature of apparently substituting for a factual inquiry into an abuse alle-gation, since it classifies such accusations as "true" or "false" based on the behavior and attitudes of the mother who believes them. Responding to Turkat in *Judges' Journal*, Smith and Coukos (1997) stated: "Courts should be vigilant in evaluating any psychological expert testimony that claims to be able to discern false from true allegations, or that can be used to explain away or cover up abuse," concluding that the "most well-intentioned judges may be completely unaware of how they view protective parents until they are presented with empirical information about . . . child abuse" (pp. 41, 45). This advice is frequently unheeded by family court judges who find it simpler to describe an angry mother than to assess a factually complicated or murky charge of sex abuse. The causes and effects of tendentious mental health theories in family courts will be examined in Part II of this book, chapter 7.

Procedural Peculiarities

Family courts are characterized by procedural peculiarities that often work to the detriment of protective mothers.

First, the proceedings are confidential. This protects family court judges from the restraining influence of the public eye. In some states family courts are closed by statute; in other states, at least in theory, an evidentiary hearing must take place to determine if the case should be closed. But in practice judges can easily seal court records and close hearings to the public. This gives family courts unusual leeway in threatening or punishing litigants without anyone outside the court being the wiser.

"Confidentiality" may be extended even further. Mothers may be ordered not to talk to the public, or to friends, family, or support groups, about what goes on inside the court. If they violate such orders, they may lose custody or visitation rights. Pennington testified before the House Judiciary Committee (1992) that such "gag orders" have become "commonplace" in family court cases. Like the sealing of court records, she said, these orders "are used to keep the public from being informed about the inequities rampant in the system."[6]

Second, family courts are not quite taken seriously by practicing attorneys. A disturbing number of family law practitioners refer to them as "kangaroo courts." They deal with "family problems" (often the problems of poor families) and lack the prestige of other civil or criminal tribunals. The physical appearance of family courts, especially in major cities, is telling. These courts are often set in small, poorly lit, windowless rooms. A New York nonprofit organization called the Fund for Modern Courts measures "improvements" in family courts by such barometers as rodent control and the availability of bathroom toilet paper. (When the Fund for Modern Courts did comment about the behavior of one of the judges—who would resign a few years later in the face of a state senator's complaint about his conduct—its published report praised the judge as one who could be "positive, strong and strict in decisions when the case requires it.")[7] To date, no governmental body with oversight capacity has performed a serious investigation into the operations of family courts, notwithstanding the rising number of complaints over the past two decades.

Unequal Protection

One especially unnerving aspect of today's divorce and abuse litigation is that, in some cases, a family court judge "consolidates" a private custody action with a petition from a state CPS agency charging one of the parents with abuse or neglect. When the charge is against a protective parent—who is often accused of "psychological neglect" for making an abuse report—this has the effect of forcing the mother to fight not only her ex-husband but the state itself in her effort to retain custody of her children.

Since most judges tend to follow the recommendations of state CPS agencies, who form close relationships with judges in their day-to-day handling of neglect and abuse cases (and have political influence over judicial appointments and reappointments as well—see examples discussed above, in this chapter), a parent whose position is opposed by a CPS agency faces extraordinary obstacles. Even worse, this procedure can result in the state literally underwriting one party's legal fees, expert witness bills, and court transcript costs in a private custody action against the other parent. It is difficult to imagine such an arrangement in any other sort of litigation between two parties.

For example, during one New York case, after a change of custody action was combined with an "emotional neglect" proceeding against the protective mother, the father's attorney admitted in court that he could "sit back and do nothing" while the state agency attorneys vigorously represented his client's position, even providing all the witnesses to testify for him at state expense. When the mother appealed the family court's custody ruling, she was forced to pay thousands of dollars for court transcripts—but the state agency provided copies to the father. This father, incidentally, was not poor; he was a practicing physician. Yet he was spared most of the costs of a long custody trial, which awarded him sole custody of his daughter in spite of the child's charges that he had molested her (which were supported by an eyewitness and by a leading New York expert on child sex abuse, Dr. Anne Meltzer).

Failure of the Appeals Process

In theory, appellate courts exist to correct errors made at the trial level, in family courts as in other courts. However, the cases we have reviewed show that appellate review is rarely of much help to protective parents. Appeals from family court rulings, particularly when an abuse or neglect finding is at issue, rarely result in reversal of the lower court's rulings; in fact, the decisions usually uphold the family courts without even giving detailed reasons.

The lack of serious appellate interest in family court rulings is one reason many of these rulings are not appealed to begin with. But there are other reasons as well. First, due process violations may result from an interim order rather than a final one. For example, when a child is temporarily removed from a protective parent's home on an "emergency" basis, or is temporarily transferred into the custody of the allegedly abusive parent pending the outcome of a custody proceeding, the order involved generally cannot be appealed (in most jurisdictions) until after the case is resolved. But by this time, long after the change in the child's residence, an appeal is often useless.

Second, protective parents are often pressured to make deals with CPS attorneys that preempt appellate review. In one typical case, the CPS attorney, having helped the father win custody of his daughter from the mother, pressed the mother to accept a "global settlement" with the agency that was prosecuting her for "brainwashing" her child to believe she had been sexually abused. Settlements of this kind require a mother to agree to accept certain penalties, such as a limitation on visitation—and what is more, they are not appealable. In addition, CPS may still renew its case against such a mother if it is not satisfied with the mother's compliance with the imposed conditions. The mother in this case refused to give in, but not all mothers in her position can resist the pressure. According to a 1989 report by Senator Mary B. Goodhue, chairperson of the New York State Senate Committee on Child Care, at least one-third of mothers offered "deals" by state agencies under which they would accept some penalties, implicitly admitting some degree of guilt, and would waive their right to appeal (arrangements formally known as "adjournments in con-templation of dismissal") have accepted the offers.[8]

That so many cases never receive appellate review means, in practice, that family courts remain impervious to scrutiny by higher courts, which could be making good case law to keep family courts in check.

Part II ||||||||||||||||||||||||||||||||||||||||||||||||||||||||||||||||
OBSERVATIONS IN DEPTH

Chapter 3

Research Methods

The Ethnomethodological Approach

A study that analyzes how our nation's family courts can so seriously malfunction requires a good research method. When we undertook this study, we chose a method that did not begin with a hypothesis of our own that we could attempt to prove or disprove, because we felt such a method would be vulnerable to confusion. Specifically, we realized that if we tried to predict ahead of time which variables to study, and if those variables turned out to be the wrong ones, or if we overlooked the confounding variables that would skew our findings, we would be no closer to understanding the courts than before we began our study.

For this reason, we chose at the outset to suspend our own preconceived hypotheses as to *why* the system was punishing mothers of abused children and examine, instead, the methods of the court participants themselves—to learn how they produce social order and meaning within the day-to-day context of their work. To do this we used a special form of sociological inquiry, known as *ethnomethodology,* to illuminate how the system produces madness and how mothers become mutineers.

The word "ethnomethodology" means the study of "members' methods"—the "members" of a given culture. For the purposes of our study, the "members" consist of the social participants who constitute the interactional setting of the family court, both as dispensers of justice (and their auxiliary agents) and as parents in search of legal redress. Because we examine the methods of the members themselves, we prefer to call this kind of sociological study a *sociological inquiry* rather than a methodology, as the *only* methods to be studied here are those of the social actors themselves, who engage in the situated (that is, produced within the context of the interactional setting) achievement of social order.

But one does not examine members' methods by asking them to explain their social activities—which is why we did not use questionnaires and other forms of survey instruments. Lynch (1997), in fact, describes in *Law and Action: Ethnomethodological and Conversation Analytic Approaches to Law*[1] what happened on one "rare occasion" when he was allowed to meet with the (criminal court) judge in his chambers and ask him to explain his rulings: "The judge laid down a ground rule, saying that he had already given his reasons in court, and therefore it was pointless . . . to ask him for the real reasons for his judgment . . . [which] points to a rich topic of inquiry: the public accountability of judicial actions and reasons as constituents of courtroom hearings" (p. 125). Thus, one can gain a much clearer insight into judicial madness from the "public" accounts of judicial reasoning, by which judges and others make their decisions accountable to coparticipants in the social setting (for example, attorneys, respondents, and prosecutors), than by asking the interactants to simply explain their conduct.

Harold Garfinkel, who founded ethnomethodology some thirty-five years ago, defined this discipline as "the organizational study of a member's knowledge of his ordinary affairs, of his own organized enterprises, where that knowledge is treated by us as part of the same setting that it also makes orderable."[2]

When we apply ethnomethodology to the study of the family court system, we concern ourselves with the practical reasoning of judges (and others) that at each and every instant serves to re-create a system that reflexively gives meaning to their situated actions. Because of the inherently "reflexive" nature of social activity—a setting is re-created each time social action is produced within the setting, which at the same time gives meaning to the situatedly produced social activity—we treat madness and mutiny as informed by a (judicial) setting, which is simultaneously reconstituted during each occurrence of a mad or mutinous act. We draw from the rich corpora of ethnomethodological studies that detail and describe how social interactants in many different settings (courtrooms, jury rooms, police stations, child welfare agencies, etc.) through their situated actions continually re-create the setting that gives contextually relevant meaning to their interactive work.

For example, Lynch (1997) studied "the judge (in criminal court) as a figure within the collaborative production of a courtroom hearing . . ." (p. 99). Lynch followed Garfinkel, who "transforms Durkheim's (1938) classic aphorism, 'the objective reality of social facts is sociology's fundamental phenomenon,' by setting out an ethnomethodological alternative to Durkheim's analytic sociology . . . [which is] to examine the regularities . . . [of social life] . . . and to explicate how social order is achieved reflexively in and through the unrelenting practices of local parties who dwell in a society" (p. 100).

In keeping with the ethnomethodological tradition, Lynch did not "objectify" judges' work by imposing social-psychological interpretations on their social actions—examining gender or race, or trying to go "behind the scenes [to uncover what was] 'in the judge's head,' behind the closed doors of the judge's chambers, or in the judge's social background" (p. 99). Instead, he studied how judges were "publicly available in the embodied production of the hearing" (p. 99) and examined closely how they displayed an orderly, publicly observable (by interactants in the courtroom setting)[3] accounting of "their judicial actions and reasons as constituents of the courtroom hearings" (p. 125).

Like Lynch, we, in our study of the family courts, do not treat judicial decision making as "a composite of variables in a regression analysis [that is] specified by measures of socio-economic status, gender, educational attainment, ethnicity, regional background, or any other social factor or combination of factors" (p. 100). If we were to do so, we might learn nothing more about judicial decision making than our own predetermined variables would allow. We would also be in a quandary when forced to produce some rational explanation (assuming we could) for the fact that female judges in the family courts have handed down the same punitive decisions against mothers as their male counterparts. This fact would seem unintelligible in the light of a simple theory of gender bias.

Lynch's 1997 study of the criminal court also showed that the "role" of judge is itself a situated achievement as opposed to an artifact that is "somehow attached to . . . the individual actor." This is so because such roles are instead as Lynch states "a configuration *in action*" (p. 100)—something that is *reconstituted* on each occasion that situated order is achieved.

By understanding the production of social action, and in particular the fulfillment of the "role" of judge (or law guardian, social worker, etc.) as an inherently reflexive process, we were able to isolate and define those critical moments in which judges and their auxiliaries performed acts of institutional violence as an integral part of judicial madness.

The Documentary Method of Interpretation

The ethnomethodological form of sociological inquiry can help us to better understand how mothers, confronted with bizarre events in their own court proceedings, tend to interpret these events not as anomalies but as part of a bigger picture, and such interpretations often lead to acts of parental mutiny, as the parent fights not just her own case but an entire system at work. Garfinkel (1967) describes how social actors continually make practical sense and order out of what may appear a senseless and chaotic situation as the "documentary method of interpretation":

> The method consists of treating an actual appearance as "the document of," as "pointing to," as "standing on behalf of" a presupposed underlying pattern. Not only is the underlying pattern derived from its individual documentary evidences, but the individual documentary evidences, in their turn, are interpreted on the basis of "what is known" about the underlying pattern. Each is used to elaborate the other.[4] (p. 78)

Here are three brief illustrations of how mothers engage in practical sociological reasoning (the production of rational explanations to suffice "for all practical purposes") to achieve socially ordered meaning for their unique set of family court experiences and in so doing, evince what Garfinkel has described as the "documentary method of interpretation":

1. A woman in the process of divorcing her husband, who has abused their daughter, participates in a study of support services given to mothers of abused children by the Jane Addams College of Social Work (University of Illinois) in the late 1990s. In the course of the interview, the mother "asks hesitantly if there are very many other mothers in her situation . . . [stating] she doesn't know anyone." While Massat and Lundy (1999, p. 42), who conducted this study, had been primarily querying the interviewee about her access to affordable housing, public assistance, and other practical service and support needs, the mother used this occasion to socially constitute her own particular circumstances as part of a "system" by asking the researcher whether there were "very many other mothers in her situation." Thus, in asking for other mothers in her circumstances, she chose to perceive her individual circumstances as presupposing a larger system at work rather than an instance of an anomalous set of events, even though at that time she had no evidence of any other mothers in her circumstances.

2. A New York protective mother, not yet knowing of another single mother who was likewise stripped of custody upon trying to protect her child from abuse, exclaimed to the court-appointed ex-

pert: "You make *me* take psychological tests, when it was he [the ex-husband] who molested my child. . . . *I ought to give a course in this!*" This comment, too, implies that this mother saw her experience as only one example of a pattern large enough to justify the teaching of a "course."

3. Dziech and Schudson (1989) point out that in the celebrated case of Washington, D.C., plastic surgeon Elizabeth Morgan, "even after years in jail . . . Dr. Morgan wrote her supporters not about her anger or pain, but about a legal *system* that had failed to learn and understand" (p. 206, emphasis added).

As protective mothers become increasingly entrenched in their family court cases and they come to see what is happening to them as wholly inexplicable—losing custody and visitation, sometimes going to jail for reasons that are never properly indicated on the court record—they engage in methods of practical reasoning that enable them to convert these unique and bizarre events into a socially meaningful typification or mold, which can be recognized as a "type" or an "instance of" rather than the only one of its kind. These acts of practical reasoning can take various forms, often influenced by the mother's social characteristics such as education, class, and race.

For example, some protective mothers who are black and poor, and generally accustomed to a state of powerlessness, have reasoned that the family court's consistently harsh rulings against them are part of a systematic effort to punish them for being black and female. On occasion, African-American or Latino mothers, particularly those who are well educated, have even posed Marxist arguments, claiming that the system is intent on demoralizing working-class children, perhaps because those who are weakened by troubled childhoods make better candidates for subjugation.

Mothers with a more affluent lifestyle often attribute their court sufferings to the financial power their ex-husbands may have over a politically controlled court system.

Finally, mothers who are believers in "end world" theories have reasoned that their legal nightmares are just a small part of an eschatological drama in which good is rivaled by evil; they see their individual situations as portents of the last days. For example, an upstate New York mother, herself a registered nurse, would often recite (to the members of her support group) critical passages from the New Testament, which gave her solace after losing custody and all visitation contact with her seven-year-old daughter when she sought medical care to treat the young girl's pelvic infection, which she thought was a consequence of sexual abuse by the father.

What we see here is that whatever explanation protective mothers give, they tend to treat the peculiarities of their cases as emblematic of a larger pattern, one that has social meaning far beyond their own situations. Consequently, since the problem is perceived by the individual mother as part of a whole "system" that "sells out" many mothers for various reasons, the solution to the problem, which is an expression of mutiny or rebellion, is naturally seen as serving a constituency much greater than the mother herself. That is, if the problem is collective, the solution is naturally seen as collective too.

When we interviewed mothers it became clear they were constantly "realizing" the presence of other mothers even when they were acting at that particular moment solely in their own case, as if each mother were speaking to a gallery of other mothers not yet visible to her at that particular moment. Thus, it was not at all unusual to hear the mothers we interviewed proclaim they were working hard to change the system for "others," even if at that particular moment they did not actually, directly know of any "others."

Explicative Transactions

One of the ways social order is achieved reflexively (that is, with the production of each social action the system is re-created, which in turn governs or informs the production of situated actions) is through "explicative transactions." Pollner (1979), in his study of the California traffic courts, shows how judges "transform encapsulated episodes into explicative transactions and endow them with their exemplary and definitional power" (p. 229). Pollner defines "explicative transactions" as those moments in proceedings when judges attempt to control the outcome of their decisions so as to give them the intended exemplary effect both on subsequent decisions and (retrospectively) on prior ones. He refers to such moments as special "liminal" moments (Turner 1974), in which "the veil of the illusion is briefly lifted and the enactive (not merely the reactive) capacity (Weick 1969, pp. 63–71) of actions is momentarily visible" (p. 229).

In trying to illustrate explicative transactions, Pollner demonstrates how in case after case the judges' work "occurred in real time, in public, with the consequences of any decision [for example, lenient rulings for traffic violations] unavoidably feeding back into the session and furnishing the conditions and context of subsequent decisions" (p. 242).

Among the examples Pollner gives of "explicative transactions" is that of a judge who, having heard from Caucasian defendants all morning and then confronting a black defendant, made a deliberate point of continuing his stern rulings so that he would not be accused of showing leniency toward minority defendants (pp. 243–244).

In another instance, Pollner explains that a judge's refusal to grant a female defendant in traffic court an extension of time to pay the fine was guided by the explicative force of the case:

> The judge felt that this woman's request had some merit [but] a concession in public would have meant that he might be besieged by similar requests in the future. After stating that he did not give time [for an extension], he had the woman sit until the end of the session, at which time she was granted an extension. (p. 243)

In the family courts, too, judges engage in explicative transactions. For example, an Illinois family court judge, after incarcerating a mother for refusing to send her child on a visit to a family member she believed had sexually abused the girl, justified his actions by asserting, "[M]y orders mean something and I don't take it lightly somebody saying they're going to defy them!" By making this declaration about his orders—"my orders mean something"—the judge was in so many words explicating (showing the exemplary and definitional power of) his rulings as unequivocally inviolable.

In another example, a Brooklyn, New York, judge, when challenged by the mother's attorney to modify an unusually restrictive visitation order, explicated his rulings—showing their exemplary and definitional power—by emphasizing his autocratic control over dispensing visitation privileges: "Supervised visitation is something that I give, and take."

We do not look at the work of judges alone for demonstrations of explicative transactions. Auxiliary actors, too, have been found to engage in similar kinds of explicative transactions in family court cases. For example, in the early 1990s, an Idaho protective mother had her two young boys removed from her and placed in state-run foster care (although at least one of the children's reports of sexual abuse was corroborated by the children's pediatrician) on the recommendation of the law guardian, who unreservedly told the court that such rash action was being taken in order to "teach" the mother a "lesson" about making any subsequent complaints of sex abuse against the children's father, a well-known medical doctor in the local hospital.

Formulating

Garfinkel and Sacks (1970) describe a process by which social interactants use some part of their interactive discourse "as an occasion to describe . . . to explain it, or characterize it, or explicate it . . . or summarize or furnish the gist of it . . . . saying-in-so-many-words-what-we-are-doing or 'formulating'"(p. 350–351).

Here is an example of "formulating": a Massachusetts family court judge, upon ignoring the request of a judge from a different state (who had ruled that all contact between the child and the sexually abusive father be supervised), furnished the gist of his decision to override the out-of-state court with these words: "I don't honor courts outside my jurisdiction, as I won't allow venue shopping!"

But one does not study the formulating practices of family court judges by simply asking judges for the gist or summary of what they are doing in each case. Applying an ethnomethodological form of inquiry, we do not ask social interactants to indicate to us as researchers when they are engaged in the work of formulating, for the simple reason that social actors unproblematically perceive their actions as "taken for granted" rather than open to analytic reflection. Thus, if we were to question social actors, they would not lead us to the gist of what they are doing any better than we would have been led by a complete nonparticipant. Instead, we uncover members' methods of formulating, or summing up, by studying how social participants in the family court setting situatedly achieve social organization, of which the work of formulating is an integral part.

"Maternal Fitness" as a Situated Accomplishment

Holstein and Gubrium (1995) demonstrated, in their study of hospital discharge hearings, how the definition of "family" is neither an a priori concept nor a fixed one but is instead the situated achievement of the participants in the court setting. They looked at court hearings for determining whether a psychiatric patient could be discharged to a suitable setting to see how "domestic meaning and order are produced and situated interactionally," as opposed to representing the "substantive contours of a specific ideal" (pp. 896, 900). In so doing, Holstein and Gubrium showed how the definition of "family" is itself a situated achievement in which crucial judicial decisions about discharging psychiatric patients to "families" are made according to the *negotiated* meaning among professionals (sometimes presenting countervailing opinions) as to what constitutes in each instance a viable "family" unit.

In our study, we similarly show how the definition of a suitable family unit, or specifically a "fit" mother, is the situated accomplishment of the coparticipants in the family court hearing. But when the system becomes infected with *madness,* the "domestic meaning and order" of "maternal fitness" that is produced and managed interactionally as the collaborative achievements of its coparticipants—judges, law guardians, court-appointed mental health experts, et al.—is changed into something that could never be justified outside the family court setting.

What happens in family court is that "maternal fitness," as the defining basis of custody/visitation decisions, moves progressively further from the concept of a mother as the "nurturer" and closer to the notion of mother as *litigant.* As a result of family court's situated definition of maternal fitness—one that is totally dependent on the mother's deportment as a litigator rather than a caregiver—important decisions about custody and visitation may be determined solely by the mother's actions as a litigant. In fact, in their written decisions, family court judges sometimes explain why a mother is "unfit" to be a custodial parent (or even to have visitation) solely in terms of her courtroom behavior and her out-of-court interactions with social workers, law guardians, mental health evaluators, and other members of the special roster of auxiliary actors found in the family courts.

For example, in a California case, a mother lost all visitation contact with her nine-year-old daughter after she was labeled a "vexatious" litigant. This label evidently justified her exclusion from the child's life in the eyes of the judge. Similarly, in a New Jersey case, the family court judge rested much of his finding that a mother had "abused" her two sons on the fact that the mother had quarreled with CPS caseworkers in the boys' presence.

As family court litigation progresses, the locally managed (contextually relevant) definition of what constitutes a "fit" mother becomes increasingly at variance with how maternal fitness is practically reasoned by members of society (that is, society outside the parameters of the family court setting), until a family court judge's definition of what constitutes a "good" mother may become almost unrecognizable when compared with the standards of society at large. This is why protective mothers, having lost custody and visitation in the family courts, often encounter incredulity from peers, neighbors or colleagues who cannot understand why these "good" mothers lost their custody and/or visitation.

Judges themselves, as members of society at large, appear to be very much aware that their indigenous definitions of maternal fitness (based on the mother's behavior as a litigant) are at odds with society's views of maternal competence. When family court judges see their own (situatedly formed) definitions of maternal fitness collide with society's views, they are at pains to reconcile these dichotomous views of what constitutes parental competence.

For instance, in one case, a family court judge justified severe restrictions on a mother's interactions with her children, in part, with the rationale that the mother's "shameful displays" of anger toward social workers and her "emotional outbursts before the Court" (as she pleaded to be allowed to make telephone calls to her children) were "certainly causing harm to these boys." In so saying, the judge endorsed the argument of the CPS attorney that these actions by the mother would teach her children disrespect for "authority." And in another case, a judge justified terminating contact between a mother and her daughter by claiming that if the mother were to have continuing contact with her child, she would put the girl in "danger" of growing up not to trust men and develop good relationships.

In some of the more extreme cases, judges have punished protective mothers by terminating their parental rights, allowing the child to be adopted by total strangers—even though the mother was never found to be unfit in conventional terms.

Excising a mother from the life of her child, as draconian as such a measure naturally appears to the outside world, is quite easily understood when examining the situated production of "domestic meaning" in the context of a family court proceeding. In such proceedings, the "mother-as-nurturer" is completely eclipsed by "mother-as-litigant" as a situated achievement of what constitutes maternal fitness. When the family court judge, acting in accordance with his/her own locally constituted meaning of "good" parenting, does exclude a mother from the life of her child, all the judge has really done is to remove a "vexatious" litigant from the life of her child because the "nurturing" mother has been forgotten in the family court setting.

The reader can begin to see that by employing an ethnomethodological form of inquiry, in which we examine the practical reasoning and practical accomplishments of judges in their day-to-day rendering of decisions such as these, we can illuminate how social organization actually occurs in this setting. Then we can begin to understand how the family court system has evolved into such an inverted form of justice whereby, for instance, judges situatedly define parental fitness by a mother's litigation activities.

Because "maternal fitness" assumes a negotiated meaning as the collaborative achievement of both mothers and court personnel, we not only examine how judges achieve situated meaning for motherhood; we employ the same ethnomethodological approach to describe how the mother herself comes to define her own parental competence as a practical accomplishment.

For example, we have observed that it is common, at the beginning of a litigation, for mothers to focus their attention on stressing their mothering skills (for example, taking their children for timely checkups, attending parent-teacher conferences). However, their defenses change dramatically as the court system shifts its focus from mother-as-nurturer to mother-as-litigant. For example, when mothers see that the system attacks their litigation posture (by accusing them of "abusing" the court process by bringing "too many" motions or of being "harmful" to social workers by making demands for information) rather than questioning their nurturing skills, they respond by defending their litigation as opposed to their caregiving.

By following the hearing record, one can see how the meaning of "maternal fitness" for the mother herself is thus produced and situated interactionally. While the mother engaged in the litigation process may begin by attacking the father's caregiving (and defending her own), she later directs her attack on the litigation process itself, making accusations of denial of due process and gender-based discrimination. In more extreme cases, mothers have accused the courts of engaging in cover-ups and conspiracies that include law guardians, visitation supervisors, child welfare workers, and mental health evaluators. And in out-of-court statements (for example, legislative hearings and press conferences), mothers likewise continue to defend their parental fitness by attacking the unfairness of the system.

Making and Managing the Meaning of "Maternal Fitness"
for a Projected Courtroom

As part of our study of the madness and mutiny found in the family court system, we also examined the interactional work that is "practically accomplished" by mothers and auxiliary agents, such as child protective service caseworkers, before the case ever gets to court.

Lynch (1997) demonstrated how social interactants accomplish the making and managing of the meaning of a defendant's guilt or innocence for a "projected courtroom," by showing that even before a case gets to court, "attorneys invoke the judge as an organizational principle that locally governs the presentation of the case at hand" by projecting what a judge "would treat as a serious charge or accept as a reasonable basis for reducing the charges . . . " (pp. 102–103). Similarly, in our study we have paid careful attention to the intricate ways in which mothers and social workers incorporate the judge into their locally managed meaning of maternal competence.

In a discipline closely related to ethnomethodology known as conversation analysis—the study of the interactional organization of talk—Heritage and Sefi (1992) have shown the interactive work of mothers of newborn infants with government agency social workers in Great Britain. British social workers (referred to as "health visitors") are required by federal law to perform home visits on a weekly basis, usually unannounced, for the first couple of months of a child's life. Mothers in those settings must attend to the fact that their rights to care for their newborn babies can be open to serious legal challenge. Heritage and Sefi carefully studied the interactive dialogue that takes place between the mothers and the "health visitors" during such "visits."

They noted that these visits have "an unavoidable dimension of surveillance and social control . . . [as] may be inferred from the fact that health visitors are the largest single source of information and referral in cases of child abuse and neglect in the United Kingdom" (p. 362). They found that, as a result, the mothers they studied engaged in routinely patterned ways of interacting with social workers so that they would not risk being socially constituted as "neglectful" mothers.[5]

In our family court study, we found that when a mother is first interviewed by caseworkers, before her case has even reached court, both mother and caseworker "project" the judge in their collaborative production of the situated meaning of maternal fitness. However, mothers and social workers often invoke the judge as an organizational principal from opposing viewpoints.

Such opposing projections of how a judge would assess maternal fitness are most sharply apparent in those early interviews between mothers and CPS workers in cases in which the mother believes a child has been sexually abused and before litigation has commenced. What commonly occurs is that a mother, in her effort to prove to the caseworker that the child is in danger of continuing abuse by the father, gives graphic details of the abuse, speaking with urgency and alarm, hoping the caseworker's report will persuade a judge to protect her child from the abuse. The caseworker, however, may be likely to project the judge as one who will seriously question the mother's parental fitness for not "preventing" such abuse from occurring in the first place or for displaying an "obsessive" concern with her suspicions. Here is where the contrasting projections of court participants can play easily into the madness of the courts—for the mother's presentation of the urgency of her situation can result in her being made the target of a CPS "neglect" charge for "failure to protect her child from abuse" or for "obsessive" or "alienating" behavior.

Child Protective Service Agency Records as Practical Accomplishments

As part of our study of judicial madness, we closely examined the participation of child protective service agencies and, in particular, their production of case notes and neglect petitions for court purposes. For this book, we draw on ethnomethodological studies that look at how the construction of agency records, as an ongoing practical accomplishment, anticipates what Garfinkel and Bittner (1967) call "contractual" rather than "actuarial" uses. What this means is that the primary goal of such records is not to produce a purely statistical profile (a statement of facts) concerning the individual but rather to produce a record that serves the purpose of entering into a "contract" (for example, a social service plan on a neglectful parent) between the organization and the person served.

Albert J. Meehan (1997), in studying the record-keeping practices of police, explained this contractual use as an "assembling process [that] may involve the selection, recasting, and, on occasion, even fabrication of 'the facts' and the sequence in which they occurred" (p. 187). Meehan called attention to "processes by which . . . [an] arrest report framed . . . [the] incident in anticipation of its likely contractual uses in the court setting" (p. 187).

In much the same way, in our study of the family courts and their related agencies, we have found that the construction of social work records (for example, case notes, neglect/abuse petitions, removal orders, case plan summaries) is informed by the madness of the family court and child welfare system, which is re-created each time such records are situatedly produced. Since protective mothers lose custody of their children to sexually abusive fathers, the "contractual," rather than actuarial, purpose of CPS agency records causes the records to anticipate such custodial transfers of sexually abused children to abusive parents.

This fact helps to explain the otherwise baffling tendency of CPS agencies to make contradictory charges against protective mothers in the "neglect" petitions they file with family courts. Such petitions commonly state that the mother has "failed to protect" her children from sexual abuse—or, in the alternative, that she has "brainwashed" or "coached" her children to believe, falsely, they have been sexually abused. The mothers who are the targets of such petitions understandably begin to doubt the sanity of the court system at the very outset of the process, for they see that the two charges against them are plainly inconsistent. However, the use of *both* charges—even though the two are patently contradictory—actually works to facilitate the real, "contractual" purpose of the CPS petition, namely, to support a transfer of custody to the father. The first charge—"failure to protect"—indicates an immediate danger, thus creating legal grounds for CPS officials to remove the child from the mother. The second charge—"brainwashing"—can be used against the mother as evidence of "alienation" in the ensuing custody dispute and thus allows the state to recommend a transfer of the child out of temporary foster care and into the custody of the father. Neither charge, standing alone, would have the same legal effect.

If CPS records were truly intended to serve an actuarial purpose—that is, to create a true presentation of the mother—CPS neglect petitions would seldom contain such contradictory claims, since caseworkers could hardly believe simultaneously that a child is in continuing danger of abuse and that the same child is not being abused at all.[6] These documents are clearly intended for "contractual" use within the family court setting in which judges, law guardians, and social workers reenact the madness of the family court system in each of their actions—actions that, in turn, are informed by the demands of the topsy-turvy system. This also explains why many caseworkers, matrimonial attorneys, and family court judges are not disturbed or perplexed by such petitions—though a layman would be (and the mothers on the receiving end certainly are)—since the petitions have come to serve common, everyday contractual purposes in the family court system.

Meehan's research on record-keeping practices is helpful in our study of

CPS agency files and court records in another way as well. In studying law enforcement agencies, Meehan (1997) identified a practice by which the police "create a stock of knowledge about local individuals and situations" that he calls the "running record": "an oral history of persons, places and incidents constructed by virtue of the police officer's access to the everyday activities of individuals . . . [that] is a collaboratively produced and shared reporting of persons and events . . . " (p. 199).

We likewise have found that CPS agencies, law guardians, judges, and others describe protective mothers more by the "running record"—a selective dossier[7]—than by the full and accurate history of their cases. This is how mothers whose court-ordered psychological profiles are essentially normal come to be called "crazy," sometimes even "psychotic," by the judge and the auxiliary players. (For instance, although one mother's psychiatric evaluation showed no mental illness, the judge, referring to her allegedly excessive litigation, called this a product of her "sickness.")

Meehan (1997) showed that the "running record" in the police department is an oral instrument clearly distinguished from the written record, which "attains its legitimacy because it is impersonally produced and read" (p. 199). The protective mother's "running record," in which she is labeled, for instance, a "vindictive" ex-wife, is likewise an oral production rather than a written one. It is part of the very nature of running records as oral instruments that their "information sharing," according to Meehan, "is shaped by the political alliances and personal agreements" among members of an organization. This type of information sharing prevents anyone from the outside from learning about (let alone affecting) what goes on inside.

This is one reason why, when state and federal investigators have tried over the years to uncover the causes of abuses of the family courts, they have not been particularly successful. A great deal of the systemic madness has all too often been contained in "running records" of protective mothers who seek relief from the courts; and these "running records," communicated orally, are selectively shared with an inner circle that fits the political purpose for the construction of the running record in the first place.

We have found that "running records" have become so prevalent in protective mother cases that it is a widespread practice for family court judges to engage in ex parte communications (that is, communications between a judge and some individuals concerned in a case without the knowledge or participation of the other parties) with CPS workers, law guardians, mental health experts, sometimes even the father's own attorney.[8] In these communications, criticism of the (absent) mother is commonplace.

Meehan observed that these running records are "evoked at key points in decision-making," such as when the police determine whether to make an arrest of a juvenile based on information about the parents and the likelihood that they will "challenge the officer and side with their child" (pp. 200–201). We found that in the family courts the dependence on the running record, rather than on the substantive facts of the case, carries over into a judge's decision making. We have found that some crucial family court orders are based on "facts" that were never properly in the record—and may not even have been facts.[9] Sometimes, critical rulings pertaining to custody and visitation are handed down at hearings at which the mother and her counsel are absent.

We can thus begin to see how the application of the ethnomethodological form of sociological inquiry to the family court system provides special insight into how judges and their auxiliaries produce and manage social organization as a situated achievement. By applying ethnomethodology, we learn how both judges and protective mothers organize their situated practices and, in so doing, re-create the judicial madness and parental mutiny that have come to characterize the American family court system today.

Chapter 4

Robed Rage

F amily court judges have many ways of attacking protective mothers who appear before them as litigants. Since many of these attacks make little sense either logically or legally, one tends to look elsewhere for an explanation. A likely underlying reason is that the protective mother (or her attorney, sympathetic caseworkers or therapists, or others who support her position) presents a perceived threat to the judge's authority. That is, a judge afraid of losing control of his or her courtroom to a protective mother treats the legal system as a way of beating down the threat—and the proper inquiry in a case of alleged child abuse is obscured behind a screen of "robed rage."

Examination of court documents reveals this phenomenon in several different guises. Generally, robed rage means that an abuse case is transformed, unofficially, into an inquisition into the complaining mother's character, with a judge apparently finding so many reasons to criticize the mother that he has no time to investigate whether her charges are justified. In more extreme cases, judges who feel their authority threatened actually take the law into their own hands, ignoring rules and violating judicial ethics in order to ensure that any challenge to the judge's finding is reliably punished. "Robed rage" can also express itself in an abuse of a judge's power to hold litigants or witnesses in contempt of court; in unnecessary and traumatic private interviews by the judge of a child claiming abuse; or in the use of name-calling from the bench. In nearly all cases, however, "robed rage" is not spontaneous or arbitrary. In protective parent cases it is part of a vicious cycle, a symptom of a system gone awry. The judges' actions in these cases are *reflexive*—each instance of robed rage acts to "recreate" the system of madness that paved the way for this latest action; the new act then helps to govern each of the judge's subsequent actions as well.

Family court judges' intemperate behavior when faced with sex abuse charges is no secret to the matrimonial bar. Several attorneys we interviewed have admitted that when representing a mother in a custody/visitation action, they generally decline to present evidence of sex abuse even if the charges are corroborated. Likewise, many of the mothers we interviewed have reported being turned down by one attorney after another, the lawyers saying they could not fight a judge known for his angry reaction to sex abuse claims.[1]

What sometimes happens to attorneys who *do* choose to risk such anger shows that the danger is not imaginary. Julia Heit, a New York matrimonial attorney with many years of experience, complained in an appellate brief about the rage of a Brooklyn Family Court judge who had repeatedly threatened her for trying to present evidence that her client's daughter had been sexually abused. In the brief, Heit described how the judge "persistently berated [her] for attempting to make offers of proof and on a number of occasions threatened to hold counsel in contempt if she persisted."[2] Heit told us: "You can't see from the transcript what it was like. He shouted. He threw down his pencil. He pointed his finger at me and warned me he'd hold me in contempt. He shouted at me that he was 'appalled' when I tried to put evidence in the record. And it was over and over again." Heit reported that before each appearance during the trial, she would make arrangements with neighbors to take care of her dogs in case the judge threw her in jail that day.

Taken together, the different aspects of robed rage constitute a central vein in the madness of the family courts.

Accusing the Accuser

A judge who is strongly disposed to disbelieve a charge of child sex abuse by one parent against another can often manage to avoid an inquiry into the troubling issue simply by shifting the blame to the accuser.[3]

For example, in a case that arose in Brooklyn, New York, CPS officials accused the father of sexually abusing his six-year-old daughter based on an eyewitness account. However, the family court judge was less interested in investigating the abuse report than in evaluating the mental state of the mother. He ordered her to submit to a psychological evaluation, warning bluntly that if she did not appear within fourteen days for the examination, he would immediately order her daughter removed from her home. In fact, the judge did not even wait fourteen days; just four days later, he ordered the child placed in foster care, though there was no evidence of any abuse or neglect committed by the mother, nor any evidence that she was mentally ill. The judge did this because the mother had missed an appointment with an evaluating psychologist—ignoring the fact that she had gone, instead, to a hospital complaining of chest pains. He also ignored the fact that she was ready and willing to reschedule the psychologist's appointment within the court-ordered fourteen days.[4]

Ultimately, the mother was convicted of "neglect" on the sole ground that she believed that her child had been abused—though the charge was supported by the child, several psychologists, and an eyewitness. In other words, the danger the mother posed to her child was that she believed the child was endangered by someone else. Clearly, the family court could not tolerate the mother's belief. The only alternative to accepting it, however, was to punish the accuser—which is what, strange as it sounds, the court chose to do.

An equally startling example of this tendency can be seen in a child sex abuse case litigated in Connecticut in the 1990s. In that case, two boys reported being sexually abused by their divorced father, and extensive corroboration of their reports was developed in Vermont, where the boys lived with their mother.[5] However, the father (who lived in Connecticut) found a local family court judge more sympathetic to his position. The Connecticut courts ultimately assumed jurisdiction over the case. When a Connecticut judge ordered the children "temporarily" transferred to the custody of the accused's sister (who denied the abuse charges against her brother and who had herself been charged with participating in the abuse), the mother hesitated to bring the children into that state while she fought the change of custody, clearly fearing that the children would not be safe if the court's order was carried out. At that moment the entire case was turned on its head.

The Connecticut judge, apparently indifferent to the evidence of sex abuse, expressed indignation at the mother's attempts to evade his jurisdiction, shifting the focus of the court's interest from the charge of abuse to whether the mother was shamming a back injury to stay out of Connecticut: "[She] made misrepresentations to the Court that she was so sick she could not travel to the state of Connecticut and yet was sighted in the state of Connecticut. . . . " Then, as if it were a logical continuation, the judge snapped to the attorneys present:

> I think the children are at risk, that the behavior has been so odd and so outrageous and I would also request of the Department [of Children and Youth Services] . . . to contact the Federal Bureau of Investigation.

The judge was still not finished; he also fulminated against Vermont case-workers and prosecutors who did not appear to support his point of view:

> I don't know what the behavior of the prosecutor in Vermont is, but I think at this point in time that leaves a lot to be desired. . . . Somebody ought to get a handle on it and not just let another child drift down the wood via some person who travels around the country and plays the role of goddess. [There was no proof that the mother had traveled anywhere with the children outside Vermont.]

When one of the attorneys present gave the judge the name of a Vermont caseworker involved in the father's investigation, the judge erupted again:

> I'd like to thank you for giving me the name of that party because I will ask that that be noted for the record, that that is among one of the people that I will be looking to as being responsible in the event that anything happens to those children. . . . This game that's being played, that seems to be, may have even be [sic] fostered by the State's Attorney of Vermont, I don't know, but that's why I'm asking you to contact the Federal Bureau of Investigation, I think that there's something amiss. . . . I think there's been essentially a violation of the anti-kidnapping statute and I think, you know . . . I want the name you gave me, you gave me the name, Mr. Adams. . . . I gather his namesake may have acted more responsibly.

In a few short minutes, the judge had wiped the slate clean of the extensive evidence of abuse by the father and had labeled the mother an "outrageous" woman who played "goddess"; he had then taken the illogical leap of declaring the children "at risk" (though there was no evidence of any neglect or abuse by the mother) and of accusing the mother of "kidnapping" (a crime she had not even been charged with) and had even gone on to attack Vermont prosecutors and caseworkers for not attacking the mother (which, of course, would have been directly contrary to the conclusions they had reached in the case)! What began as irritation with a party who resisted the jurisdiction of his court ended as an inversion of the inquiry the judge was supposed to pursue, from an investigation of alleged sex abuse to the denunciation of a recalcitrant litigant.[6]

A similar result occurred in a case in Idaho in 1993, in which a nine-year-old boy reported that his father had fondled his genitals on at least two occasions. A pediatrician testified that the boy's disclosure was credible, and the boy repeated his account to the judge in a special session in the judge's chambers.[7] The judge, however, concluded that although the boy sincerely believed he had been abused, the charge must have resulted from an "abuse atmosphere" that supposedly infected the boy's home, which in turn must have been caused by the mother. Though no one had charged the mother with any sort of neglect or abuse, and no evidence against the mother had been presented to the court, the judge immediately ordered that *both* boys living with the mother be removed from her home and placed in foster care.[8] Throughout the long and agonizing litigation that followed, the judge repeatedly justified his rulings against the mother by ridiculing her legal efforts to clear her name and to retain custody of the children, efforts the judge termed "obsessive and compulsive."

Ten years earlier, a mother in Buffalo, New York, bore the brunt of another family court judge's unwillingness to believe an allegation of child abuse. Her husband had been charged by CPS with touching the eleven-month-old child's vagina and with placing her hand on his penis. [9]After the judge refused to consider the mother's request that the father's visits be supervised, she pleaded to have visits limited to "four hours at a time so as to not interfere with breastfeeding the [infant] child."[10] According to the mother's sworn affidavit, the judge then "screamed across the courtroom" that if the mother "did not want to go along with his [the judge's] liberal visitation order, [the mother's] maintenance and child support would be reduced from $150 per week to $25 per week."[11]

During a court appearance almost a year later, the mother again urged the court to curtail the father's visitation due to allegations of continuing abuse. The judge did limit visitation but warned the mother that if she "wasn't careful," he would remove the infant from her custody altogether.[12] During that hearing, the judge repeatedly and sarcastically referred to the mother as "the Virgin Mary" because she testified to overlapping sexual relationships at the time the child was conceived.[13]

The judge continued to stigmatize the mother throughout the proceeding. On one occasion, when the father sought a change of custody in the form of an emergency motion, the judge arranged for the sheriffs to pick up the mother and bring her to court, where, she says, she was "placed in the criminal's chamber in the courtroom [and] threatened with handcuffs" while the judge "acted in a jovial manner" as the father sat in court laughing with his attorney.[14]

Along similar lines, in a New Jersey case, a mother discovered that the mere fact of her suspicions concerning her ex-husband's conduct toward her daughter could provoke a harsher reaction from a family court judge—against *her*—than the possibility of sexual abuse could trigger against *him*.

A family court judge had appointed a psychologist to make a recommendation as to custody and visitation of the parties' young daughter. Two days
before Christmas 1997, just before that report was received, the father filed
an "emergency" motion seeking more holiday visitation time. Since the
original judge was on vacation, a new judge presided over the "emergency"
hearing that afternoon. Earlier, the mother had conveyed her suspicions of
possible sex abuse by the father to CPS, but the issue was not supposed to
be before the new judge that afternoon. However, stating that the mother's
suspicions about the father were "escalating," the new judge decided, without having taken any evidence or hearing from any witnesses, to transfer
the girl's custody to the father. She claimed that the mother's concern that
the father might have abused the child (a suspicion that the judge believed,
after a quick review of the case file and without taking any evidence, to be
groundless) was "worse" for the child than the possibility of abuse itself.
The judge went so far as to claim that the mother's mere suspicions of
abuse could "place [the child] in danger."[15] We are not aware of any sound
psychological doctrine to support such a view—and certainly no evidence
was before the court to support it in this case. (In fact, when the custody
evaluator's report was received shortly thereafter, it did *not* recommend
transfer of custody to the father, even though the evaluator was well aware
of the history of abuse allegations.)

Since the judge's stated reasons for her transfer of custody were clearly
insufficient, it is hard to resist the conclusion that her real motives were un-
stated ones. Like the other judges described in this section, she was probably driven by an overwhelming desire to stop allegations that threatened
her control over the litigants in a divorce case. The judge could not stop
the accusations without punishing the accuser. So that is what she did.

Naturally, certain judges are more prone to this behavior than others.
Two of the cases we examined—cases, incidentally, in which the protective
mothers eventually went "underground" with their children—involved the
same New York family court judge. These two mothers never met, and they
did not even know of each other's existence, but they both told their stories (at different times) to New York State legislators examining a disturbing pattern of child abuse accusations being turned against the accusers.

In the first case, an abuse allegation against the children's father was but-
tressed by substantial medical evidence. Medical experts testified to telltale
"anal scarring" and chlamydia (a sexually transmitted disease) in the three-
year-old girl, and a "vaginal canal [that] was found to be rounded instead
of oval, [and] roughened instead of smooth . . . and a stretching of the

hymen" in her seven-year-old sister.[16] Nevertheless, the mother was subjected to a grueling cross-examination that lasted a total of twenty-one
days[17] in which at least one of the major topics of questioning was her
"born-again" Christianity.

Again and again, she was asked about her religious beliefs, the clear im-
plication being that her fundamentalist views were abnormal. In fact, according to the mother's report, the judge himself interrupted the attorneys
(none of whom was Christian) to ask her if she "actually believes that
'Christian' means 'Christ is in her'"? The mother answered, "Yes." We have
learned that the judge later referred to this mother, among his associates,
as "the nut." Even a popular family law attorney who had barely met this
woman freely called her "crazy" in speaking to one of us.

In the second case, the mother was forced to submit to an evaluation by
a court-appointed psychiatrist known for controversial views about women
who make sexual abuse charges. The psychiatrist, Dr. Arthur Green (described in more detail in chapter 7), diagnosed the mother as emotionally
"labile," suffering from a "histrionic personality disorder" with some "paranoid features." Despite some corroboration of her abuse charge against the
father,[18] Dr. Green's diagnosis settled the case in the eyes of the judge, who
began to refer to the mother as "the paranoid." So another mother had been
accused in family court—because she had accused a father of sexual abuse.

Though some judges are more prone than others to accuse the accuser,
a pattern of turning a sex abuse allegation against the accusing mother can
be seen in a wide range of family court cases. Indeed, a remarkable number of court decisions have awarded custody to a father precisely because
the mother accused him of sex abuse. Though there is no written law in
any state that making a charge of sex abuse (even if it is ultimately unproved) renders a mother unfit for custody, many family courts function
as though there were, applying what is in a sense the ultimate penalty
against protective parents.[19] H. Joan Pennington, former president of the
National Center for Protective Parents, has reported to us that in more
than half of the 3,145 cases her center reviewed in which a mother accused
the father of child abuse, the father was ultimately awarded custody.

Vigilante Judges

When a family court judge has singled out the accusing mother as the root
of all evil in his courtroom, accusing the accuser is not always enough.

Sometimes robed rage goes further. In some cases, judges have taken the law into their own hands in order to ensure that abuse accusations are not investigated and that mothers who insist on pressing them are punished—legally or not.

In one case that arose in Brooklyn, New York, the Family Court judge, according to a formal complaint lodged by the mother's lawyer, "deliberately and knowingly suppressed highly incriminating evidence of sexual abuse [by the father]."[20] The judge had already ignored the claims of the children themselves—the daughter said her father had held her little brother in an oven while sexually abusing her—and the pleas of the children's therapist, who said, "I don't think these kids will make it if the father gets custody."

Instead, through private communication with child welfare officials, the judge encouraged CPS officials involved in the case to charge the *mother* with "child neglect" because she had moved her children from one mental health facility to another.[21] Significantly, such communication of a judge with officials connected with a case, without the knowledge of the litigants—termed ex parte communication by lawyers—is a breach of judicial ethics.[22] Here, then, was a judge—a guardian of the law—apparently ignoring his legal and ethical obligations in order to punish a mother whose resistance to his view of the case the judge clearly found intolerable.

A family court proceeding in Buffalo, New York, was equally marred by judicial overreaching to punish the protective mother. The mother, in the end, lost custodial rights to her three-year-old daughter and was given instead severely restricted, supervised visitation. This was not the outcome of dispassionate deliberation by the judge. In fact, it allegedly occurred in violation of the rules of law. In a formal statement, the mother's attorney has written:

> the proceedings . . . in which I have participated in the past year have been characterized by rudeness and anger of the Court directed at my client, myself . . . [and by] ex parte communications and meetings between the Court and counsel for the defendant [ex-husband], law guardian and witnesses; substantial disregard of ordinary procedural law; [and] substantial disregard of the substantive law with respect to transfer of custody. . . . [23]

The judge's alleged violation of his legal and ethical obligations was, again, clearly connected with his rage at the mother's conviction that sex abuse had actually occurred. In a sworn statement, the mother has described a conversation she had with her former attorney, who told her "that during a phone call Justice Doyle screamed at him [and] asked him 'did it ever occur to you that *she* [the mother] is teaching the baby to say these things?' "24

When judicial rudeness and ex parte communications did not suffice to silence the mother, the judge apparently resorted to civil rights violations. In legal papers filed with an appellate court, the mother's attorney has stated the following (under penalty of perjury)[25] about the judge's order switching custody of the three-year-old to her father:

> Said Order, dated June 30, 1986, by Justice Doyle was made and entered ex parte without any written application and without any notice to [the mother's counsel] nor opportunity to be heard by telephone or other-wise . . . where the Court's ex parte custody transfer was by its terms based solely on the Letter/Report dated June 17, 1986 of Dr. Bruce Bleichfeld, a psychologist appointed as the Court's witness . . . and where no evidentiary heaing has been held as to its contents, nor opportunity permitted to cross-examine the Court's psychologist-witness as to his credentials and expertise. . . . (pp. 1–3).

According to these statements, the mother had become a "bad" parent to the family court judge because of the way she pursued her claims in court. And the judge had bent the law out of shape to put her in her place. Robed rage had become vigilante justice.

Lest the unwary reader conclude that this sort of justice is dispensed only in the state of New York, a case in Idaho deserves mention here as well. In the early 1990s, during divorce litigation between a couple with four children, one of the daughters alleged that the father had sexually abused her. In response, the father—rather than fighting the charge—agreed to waive all claims to custody, and even to visitation, with that child. Later, in the spring of 1993, one of the boys made a similar accusation. The case was then transferred to a different judge, who interviewed the nine-year-old boy in his chambers, barring the mother's counsel from the room during the questioning. Transcripts of the interview show that the boy described to the judge two incidents in which the father had fondled his genitals. A pediatrician testified that the boy's report was credible. Nevertheless, the judge, without holding a full hearing into the issue (though he had earlier promised the mother's attorney he would do so) and without even sharing the boy's testimony with the mother or her lawyer, promptly ruled that no abuse had occurred; he blamed the boy's belief he had been abused on an "abuse atmosphere" that allegedly pervaded the mother's home, presumably because of the previous accusation against the father by one of his daughters. (As noted above, that accusation was never examined in court by agreement of the parents, since the father waived all custody and visitation claims concerning that girl.) The judge abruptly ordered the boy and his younger brother into foster care.[26]

The children's mother, not surprisingly, fought vigorously for her children's return. For weeks she was scarcely allowed to speak to them. When, after several months, she was told that the foster parents intended to place the children "temporarily" with the very father accused of child abuse, she signed an agreement with her ex-husband that allowed the children to return to her home provided (among other things) that she would not accuse the father of abuse and that she would not seek a new counselor for the older of the two boys unless his current counselors agreed to the change.

The mother later arranged for a meeting between the boys and Dr. Lenore Walker, a prominent expert in child sexual abuse, with the consent of one of the boys' counselors. (The other counselor appears not to have known of the meeting.) She later testified that Dr. Walker did not actually provide counseling; she said she only intended to let Dr. Walker get to know the boys in case something happened in the future. No one else testified about what had happened at the meeting.

The judge responded with outrage. First he rewrote the terms of the agreement the mother had signed: the agreement spoke only of "counseling" and affected only one of the two boys, but the judge claimed from the bench that that her agreement meant "that there will be no contact, counseling, interviews, assessments or visits with psychologists, psychiatrists or other mental health professionals without both [counselors] having approved in advance such contact or counseling."[27] Then the judge ruled that the mother was in contempt of court—even though no one who was present at the meeting with the psychologist had testified to anything that violated the mother's agreement—and sentenced her to five days in jail. In his decision, he again called the mother's behavior "obsessive," questioned her "reason and common sense," accused her of excessive challenges to his orders, and stated that her jail sentence was intended as a "clear message" that such conduct "must come to an end."[28] This was too much for the appellate judge who supervised the court in question; he overturned the contempt finding and the jail sentence, finding the contempt conviction "procedurally flawed and substantively deficient."[29] In a word, the wheel of justice had come full circle: the family court judge, who accused the protective mother of misusing the courts, had in fact been the one guilty of abusing his judicial power, ignoring procedural law, and glossing over facts in his desire to punish the mother. And although the jail sentence he ordered was never served, he continued to malign the mother throughout the case. Eventually the mother lost custody of both her boys to the alleged abuser.

In a 2002 New Jersey divorce case, a three-year-old girl, one of four children, made statements suggesting that her father had sexually abused her. The father had a history of serious drug and alcohol abuse. The psychologist to whom CPS referred the child concluded: "My meetings with [the child] confirm the Division's assessment that [she] has experienced inappropriate sexual contact with her father while at visitation."[30] However, CPS ultimately dropped the charge against the father and then charged the mother with physically abusing two of the children. (That case is still being litigated; the mother continues to deny the charge against her.)

The effect of CPS's charge against the mother was rapid and severe. The family court judge, without taking evidence or hearing from witnesses, promptly removed all four children from the mother's home and even denied her visits with the elder children and telephone contact with all of them—even though the mother had yet to have her day in court on the charges against her.[31] Remarkably, all this was done in direct violation of a higher court's ruling (in an earlier case) forbidding family court judges from making temporary transfers of custody without actually taking evidence.[32] Yet this is exactly what the judge did. Why did a judge ignore the law? Could it be because not to do so would have allowed a protective mother to go on complaining of sexually inappropriate behavior by her ex-husband?

Star Chamber Sessions

In family courts, there are forms of vigilante justice to which even children may be subjected. Perhaps the most startling, to an uninitiated observer, is the use by family court judges of private interrogations of a child who has reported abuse. In theory, such interviews are designed to give a child a forum for telling his or her story that is less intimidating than a formal courtroom. But unscrupulous judges can turn this benign theory on its head. For instance, in one New York case, the family court judge[33] insisted on four separate, lengthy *in camera* (that is, "in chambers," or private) interviews between himself and a four-year-old boy who had accused his father of sexually abusing him. These interviews occurred without counsel for either parent being present. Ostensibly, the interviews were for the purpose of determining "whether the father should be given visitation rights in light of the claim of sexual abuse of the child and whether the child's statement of sexual abuse should be credited." However, during the four interviews—each of which lasted over an hour, and which produced 221 transcript pages—the judge asked relatively few questions about the alleged sex abuse, or even about the boy's visits with his father.

Instead, the judge concentrated on a charge (previously made in court) that the father had claimed that he had "the power to 'fix' the judge." When the child repeated this to the judge in chambers, the enraged judge (in the words of New York's Commission on Judicial Conduct) "lost the sense of detachment required of him, vented his displeasure on the child and engaged in what the referee correctly termed a 'relentless and tenacious interrogation of the child.' "[34] The transcripts of the interviews reveal that the judge "turned the sessions with the [four-year-old] child into a series of grueling cross-examinations in which he became preoccupied and obsessed in pursuing the source of the 'fixing' remark and all but abandoned the serious allegations of child abuse that bore directly on the issues he was to determine."[35]

Specifically, the judge (a) called the child a liar or stated that he was not telling the truth more than 200 times; (b) told the child approximately 40 times that he had given contradictory testimony; (c) admonished the child to tell the truth more than 200 times; (d) asked the child approximately 150 times who had told the child to testify as he had (it was clear that the judge suspected the child's mother, but no evidence ever proved the mother was the source of the child's remark); (e) told the child more than 10 times that he had "better remember" or "must remember" after the child had indicated that he did not know the answer to a question; (f) inaccurately indicated to the child on 4 occasions that he might go to jail if he did not tell the truth; (g) inaccurately pointed out to the child that handcuffs carried by the court officer were used for people who did not tell the truth; and, (h) told the child more than 50 times that there would be "serious" trouble or "serious consequences" if he did not tell the truth, including that the child would be punished by God, that he could not leave the court, that he would have to repeatedly return to court, that lies would "hurt" the child's mother, that the child might be handcuffed by a court officer, that the child would have to live with his father against his expressed wishes.[36]

Under these attacks and threats, delivered by the judge "roughly and in a rapid-fire fashion," the child "cried" and "protested that he was tired or needed to rest," but the judge "did not suspend or terminate his questioning of the child on any of those occasions."

This case had a happy ending. The mother retained custody of her son, and the father was given monitored, supervised visitation. The judge was officially censured by New York's Commission on Judicial Conduct—a rare and relatively serious penalty. But had not the mother's lawyer (a prominent attorney) obtained transcripts of the private interviews, the judge's shocking tactics would never have come to light. Indeed, the judge had already selected the notorious Dr. Arthur Green to make the custodial recommendation, and Green had—predictably—labeled the mother "delusional" and recommended giving custody of the boy to his alleged abuser.[37] As for the judge, he remained on the bench for years, even after the facts of this case brought about an official censure.

Other mothers and children have not been as lucky as those in the previous case. In a Brooklyn, New York, case, a six-year-old girl who had accused her father of sexually abusing her—whose report was corroborated by an eyewitness and supported by Dr. Anne Meltzer, one of the state's most respected evaluators of child sex abuse accusations—was repeatedly interrogated by the family court judge in private sessions from which the mother's counsel was barred. The judge then sealed the transcripts of all these interviews and refused to give them to the mother's lawyer even after she appealed his ruling, which awarded custody to the father. The judge claimed, on the record, that the child had admitted during these closed sessions (after how much time, or what sort of questioning, we can only guess) that the abuse incident never occurred. Yet sworn affidavits filed in that case reveal that even the mother's adversaries, including the law guardian (who recommended giving the girl into her father's custody), knew that the incident did indeed occur. (The only doubt was whether the father had ejaculated or the six-year-old girl had urinated in her clothes to account for the wetness observed by the eyewitness.) To this day the mother has never had access to the transcripts of these secret interrogations.[38]

In another New York family court case, the judge rejected strong medical evidence of sexual abuse: a pediatrician, who believed abuse had occurred, reported "an enlarged clitoral hood" in the then eight-year-old girl, as well as a "clearly visible" introitus with margins that "were rather easily stretched." The judge nevertheless insisted that the father was innocent of sex abuse. As the case dragged on, the judge repeatedly interviewed the girl in chambers, supposedly to find out about her living conditions in the father's home. But the mother's lawyer was not allowed inside; nor were the mother or her lawyer allowed to see the transcripts of those interrogations. Instead, as the mother later testified at a legislative hearing, she would wait anxiously outside the judge's chambers while her daughter told the judge (and afterward repeated to her mother) that her father had allowed her to smoke cigarettes and marijuana, had allowed boys at his house to "feel over her," and had left her unsupervised with family members who were using and selling crack cocaine. She was also allowed to watch X-rated movies and drink alcohol. (She was eleven at the time.)

These revelations infuriated the judge—but not with the girl's father. Instead, he turned his anger on the girl.

"My daughter has come out of these interviews crying and yelling," the mother testified at a hearing held by New York State senator David A. Paterson. "She reported to me that he [the judge] yelled at her, called her a liar." Noting that she had never been allowed to see the transcripts, the mother added, "I believe if these interviews were made available to the public it would clearly prove this judge has not [acted] in the best interest of my child, but has clearly put my child's welfare at risk."[39] In fact, the mother has reported that after one of the judge's interviews, the child (who suffered from severe depression) told her she wanted to find a way to the roof of the courthouse so that she could throw herself off and die.[40]

The special dangers of *in camera* hearings have long been acknowledged by the courts. New York's highest court has stated that "grave risks" are always associated with a process that allows questioning children out of the hearing of the parents and lawyers.[41] Yet family courts regularly ignore these "grave risks"—with often ghastly results.

Judicial Jailings

One of the ways in which robed rage is "practically accomplished" is through the use of judicial jailings—that is, by heavy-handed use of a judge's power to punish a litigant or another party for "contempt of court." The power to hold a party or witness in contempt is intended to give courts the power to compel compliance with court orders or to enforce proper behavior during the legal process. And, in theory, jail sentences are very rarely imposed except as a last resort. (Significantly, jail is rarely used as a sanction against fathers who violate child support orders.) But in the mad, mad world of family courts, mothers (and sometimes their attorneys and expert witnesses) find themselves facing jail sentences with startling frequency—and for reasons they cannot seem to comprehend.

The case of the Idaho mother whose children were removed from her home without the mother's even knowing the evidence used against her has been discussed above. That mother was held in contempt—and sentenced to five days in jail—because the judge disapproved of her way of fighting his personal attacks.

The mother had learned that two of her children, after three months in foster care (during which she was rarely permitted to see or talk to them), were to be transferred suddenly, and without a court hearing, to the very father one of them had accused of sexually abusing him. (The younger child would later make similar disclosures to a therapist.) Faced with this threat, the mother signed an agreement with the father that allowed the boys to return to their mother's home under certain conditions. One was that the father would no longer accuse the mother of having a mental disorder—a condition the father and his attorney would later violate with impunity. Another was that the mother would not take the boy who had reported abuse to any counselor except one approved by two health care professionals who had, in turn, been approved by the father.

When the mother took the two boys to meet with a psychologist—even though her undisputed testimony later confirmed that the new psychologist did not perform the "counseling" forbidden by her agreement—the judge erupted. In two written decisions, he claimed that the mother suffered from a mental disorder and called the mother "obsessive and compulsive," suggesting she was vindictive, mentally unbalanced, and dishonest. Then he ruled that she was in contempt of court and sentenced her to five days in jail.

That ruling was eventually reversed by another judge. But the threat of incarceration had a long-lasting effect on this mother. In conversations with us, she often displayed the scars of the psychological violence to which she had been subjected: she worried constantly about being jailed for contempt in the future. She was not consoled by the fact that she had not violated any orders; as she said, "I didn't do anything wrong the first time." As financial support for her case wore thin and as she saw herself losing more and more of her custodial rights and visitation privileges, she oscillated between agitation and depression, between the inspiration to fight and a sense of hopelessness. The more hopeless she felt, the more she would talk about her fear of being jailed in the future for no good reason.

Her fears were not unfounded. In 1997, her ex-husband demanded the disclosure of all the records of a Texas psychologist to whom she had taken her sons for an evaluation two years earlier. The elder child had consistently alleged that the father had fondled his genitals; he had also shown great anxiety over the possibility that his father could learn what he told therapists. (He had refused to talk to one evaluator because his father worked in the same office building; on another occasion, he allegedly told his mother he was afraid of talking to anyone who was "an undercover Dad agent.") Accordingly, the mother opposed the disclosure of the therapist's records to her ex-husband.

The psychologist shared her concerns. He wrote to the court that the forced disclosure of his private records "could be clinically detrimental to the children," adding that the two-year-old records "would not be relevant to their current functioning" in any case.[42] Idaho law supported the mother; the Idaho Supreme Court had already ruled that experts' information that is ordinarily subject to professional privilege (and psychologists' records are ordinarily subject to such a privilege) is not subject to disclosure in litigation.[43] Courts of other states have likewise recognized that "the threat of court-ordered disclosure [in a custody case] can too easily become a strategic weapon for the other parent. Compelled disclosure of treatment information will impair the potential benefits of treatment. . . ."[44]

The Idaho family court disagreed, however, and ordered the disclosure of the psychologist's entire file to the father. When the mother appealed, her legal arguments went largely unanswered by the father's attorney—but even this did not help her.

The appellate judge affirmed the lower court's ruling compelling disclosure. What is more, he did this without even attempting to maintain the appearance of judicial objectivity. He began with the claim that the mother was barred by court order from taking the children to a psychologist for an evaluation in the first place. (This was not true: there was no such order.) Then he unleashed an attack on the mother and her lawyer for trying to protect the boy's privacy, ending with the literal threat of another contempt conviction for the "crime" of trying to keep a child's confidential statements confidential:

> The father is clearly entitled to the records. . . . The contentions of the mother in this area, that the records are privileged or should be withheld from the father because of implications of abuse fly in the face of repeated findings and orders of this court and the court below. *The allegations con-*

tained in the brief of counsel border on contempt, in light of specific findings and orders of the court in previous proceedings.[45] [Emphasis added.]

The appellate judge did not say what those "specific findings and orders" were; presumably he meant the trial judge's insistence that no abuse had taken place, despite the boy's sworn testimony (backed by a pediatrician) that it had. The judge was clear on one point, however: anyone who so much as mentioned the abuse allegation the boy had made against his father—though the boy had certainly made it, and though it was certainly relevant to the proposed disclosure of the psychologist's records to the father (because, if nothing else, it underscored the boy's fear that what he said about the father might find its way back to him)—risked being held in contempt of court.

And when the trial resumed in the lower court, the family court judge told the psychologist, by telephone, that if all the records were not produced to the father that same afternoon in court, the mother "would be held in contempt and put in jail until she complied."[46] The mother's fears of being jailed for no valid reason had been proved reasonable after all.

Something similar happened to a Long Island, New York, mother during family court litigation. She spent twenty days in jail on a contempt charge for allegedly violating a visitation order she says she never had a chance to oppose. And, while she went to prison in handcuffs (for a crime she says she did not commit), she lost custody of her children. In fact, she has not even seen her children since 1994.

In 1992, this mother and her ex-husband had agreed in writing, during their divorce, that she would have full custody of the couple's two boys (ages four and seven). Their agreement included a temporary visitation schedule. But after a visit with his father, one of the boys allegedly complained that "he puts his finger inside my tushie."[47] The mother then sought an order requiring supervision of the father's visits, using the family court in Suffolk County, where she lived at that time. The court appointed a law guardian to evaluate the situation.

On one occasion, the mother blocked the father's visits because of her fear the child was being abused; CPS ruled her complaint "unfounded," and she was found to be in contempt of court. After that experience, the mother sent her children on visits to the father according to the terms of the stipulation, but she says the children periodically reported continuing abuse. The mother has told us she spent months trying to get the ear of the law guardian, but without success. (She says her children had no more success; she later complained to a grievance committee that "my sons had no contact with their law guardian since the initial interview and after many phone calls to him requesting a meeting with my children.")[48]

Finally, after the children returned from a weekend visit with their father complaining of severe pain and soreness, the mother felt she could not wait any longer for the law guardian to take action. She took the children to Nassau County Medical Center, where doctors found "possible sexual abuse by Hx [history]" in the older child and an "enlarged (purple) blood vessel" and a "large rectum for age" in the younger one.[49]

CPS then began its own investigation, during which the mother says she was warned she could be charged with "neglect" if she allowed any more unsupervised visits with the father. According to the mother, the father did not seem to object at first. Besides, his temporary visitation order had expired, and the mother's lawyer advised her not to do anything until CPS decided whether to proceed in court against the father.

One day, to her surprise, the father appeared at the mother's door demanding to see both boys. He had obtained a court order—as the result of an ex parte motion—but the mother says she had never seen the order, much less had the opportunity to argue against it, before the father came to her door. She told him he would have to wait for the results of the CPS investigation.

Almost immediately, the mother received an order to show cause, signed by the family court judge, accusing her of criminal contempt for violating the new visitation order (obtained without any prior notice to her). Once before, the mother had been found in contempt of a visitation order. This time the father wanted more than a warning or a fine: he was also seeking an immediate change of custody because of the mother's "contempt."

When the mother and her lawyer came to court to defend against the contempt charge, they met an unpleasant surprise. The judge would not consider any of the evidence of sexual abuse, despite its obvious bearing on the reasonableness of the mother's conduct, to say nothing of its relevance to the father's demand for custody. Instead, the judge sentenced the mother to a jail term. And that was not all: granting the father's request for a punitive change of custody, the judge turned the two young boys over to the father on the spot. The mother was punished still further by being allowed only one hour a week of visitation with her children—under strict supervision.

In jail, she says, she was strip-searched, attacked by another inmate, and "violated in every which way."

These events form one more concrete manifestation of family court madness. Like the mother accused of playing the "role of goddess," this Long Island mother had run afoul of a family court culture in which to complain of suspected abuse, and to challenge the behavior of court auxiliaries (in this case a judge's ex parte order and the inaction of a law guardian), is to invite the label "rebel." Thus it hardly mattered, in the end, that the mother's violation of a visitation order may not have been willful or even unreasonable. It hardly mattered that jail is a harsh and unusual penalty for contempt in any case, and that a change of custody is a bizarre penalty for unwittingly blocking a single visit.

This mother never regained custody of her boys; her visitation eventually dwindled to nothing, partly because the father failed to deliver the boys for visits. The father was never held in contempt for those failures. The mother has not seen or heard from her boys since 1994, and says she has suffered from stress-related illnesses. She says she is trying to insulate herself somewhat from the "indescribable pain" of a system that "has no form of escape."

An even more extreme example of outsized contempt rulings was described in testimony during the July 1989 legislative hearing into family court abuses sponsored by New York State senator David A. Paterson. A Brooklyn mother, an African-American schoolteacher, began her testimony by stating that she had been repeatedly jailed by Family Court Judge Leon Deutsch[50] for reasons she could not comprehend: "This case has been in the Family Court for six years since my child was five years old . . . [and] during these six years I have spent one night in jail, one afternoon in jail without a hearing or a trial, and I have been sentenced to fifteen days in jail."

After describing repeated acts of alleged sexual abuse, corroborated by several doctors and psychologists, the mother resumed her talk about jail, saying that the judge "can sentence me and put me in jail as he already has," and concluding, "Are his powers limitless?"[51]

Indeed, the judge had not only jailed the mother—he had even threatened to hold a treating psychiatrist in contempt for believing the child who said she had been abused. The psychiatrist, who headed a clinic where the child underwent treatment for "suicidal depression," testified at Senator Paterson's hearing that the mother had taken the then eight-year-old girl to a pediatrician, "who determined sexual abuse, and reported the findings in detail."[52] (The pediatrician had found "an enlarged clitoral hood" and a "clearly visible" introitus with margins that "were rather easily stretched.") Judge Deutsch, however, stating that he doubted the child's story and wanted a "neutral" evaluation, referred the girl to the psychiatrist's clinic, which made a positive finding of sexual abuse and presented it to the court.

When the judge learned that this psychiatrist's clinic was treating the child for sexual abuse trauma (in group and individual therapy), "there was an angry response from the judge, insisting that when he had determined that the girl was lying, the clinic had no right bringing up the issue of sexual abuse or treatment for her [the child]."[53] The psychiatrist told the legislature that, in response, "an explanation was presented to the court, stating that during the evaluation, findings of sexual abuse were made, and the child was indeed suffering from suicidal depression due to the specific trauma . . . [and that] the clinic's responsibility was to treat her [the child] for it." The judge reacted by choosing another validator, who "decided" the girl was lying.[54] Then, having obtained the assent of the law guardian, the judge transferred the girl's custody to the father.

The psychiatrist exclaimed to the legislators present at the hearing: "Now in addition [to transferring custody to the father] he [the judge] also ordered the therapist from my clinic to stop contact immediately with the child. He made sure that no time was given for properly terminating any therapeutic contact. . . . " When the girl's therapist pleaded with the court, "asking at least to have some time to terminate with the child—as it is she's losing her mother, she's losing a therapist, and she's losing all the support systems—the therapist was warned in an open court that if she ever tries to contact the child, or makes any contact with the child, she'll be held in contempt of court!"[55]

Why do family court judges so often resort to the heavy-handed application of contempt powers? As we have argued throughout this book, family court "madness" is closely related to parental "mutiny." Judges who see their authority questioned in a case involving the highly emotional accusation of child sex abuse seem to use contempt rulings, or threats of contempt rulings, to rein in the litigants (or their advocates) making such accusations. And when the litigants resist the contempt rulings, this only reinforces the judges' original concern. Thus, a judge's misuse of contempt powers (that is, using them not to enforce legitimate orders but to bully protective mothers or others who support them) reflexively re-creates the mad family court system, a system that in turn governs or informs each of the judge's actions.

A close look at still another case helps to make this even clearer. In 1990, a Staten Island, New York, judge threw a mother in jail for contempt of court for filing a petition that asked the judge to vacate a temporary custody award he had just made to the father. The judge stated that the petition "on its face is a contemptuous statement,"[56] because the mother had charged in the petition (which she wrote herself) that the judge and the father's attorney and the law guardian were acting "in collusion" with one another to strip her of custody of her seven-year-old daughter, who, she believed, was subjected to sexually inappropriate behavior during weekend visitation with the father.

To assess the judge's ruling, it is important to understand the proceedings the mother's petition complained of.

A court in another jurisdiction, where both parents had lived at the time, had awarded the mother custody of her daughter a year earlier, granting weekend visitation to the father. But, according to the mother, the girl came home from her visits complaining of having to sleep in the same room with her father and his new girlfriend.

After failing to obtain her ex-husband's agreement to change the sleeping arrangements, the mother made an abuse report against him to CPS. The father responded by seeking a change of custody. The judge ordered forensic mental health evaluations for the whole family.

The examining psychiatrist, experienced in the ways of family courts, considered it important to sound out the mother on her willingness to obey court orders, even if they required her to send the child to visits with the father that she might consider harmful. When the psychiatrist pressed her about what she would do if the judge forced her to send her daughter to her ex-husband for such visits—pointing out that if she refused to obey she could be held in contempt of court—the mother said, "If I have to be in contempt, then I will be in contempt."

The mother had said nothing—and had been asked nothing—about taking her child out of the court's jurisdiction. But within this interactional setting—within a court system continually threatened by mothers' mutiny—the psychiatrist "situatedly" defined the mother's defiant statement as a declaration of her intent to go "on the run." His report stated that the mother did "not appear concerned with contempt of court" and *therefore* "could abscond with her child."[57] Indeed, the psychiatrist claimed she was the "type" to abscond with her child, and concluded—in another discursive leap—by recommending a change of custody: "It is this examiner's opinion that the child's interests would be best served if she were in the care of her father."

Of course, the psychiatrist had not really been retained to evaluate the likelihood that the mother would kidnap her child. If he had been, perhaps he would have paid more attention to the mother's family situation and physical condition, both of which militated against her becoming a kidnapper. She was a middle-aged mother who lived with two children, not one; the elder child, a fifteen-year-old girl, could not be abandoned and would be very difficult to bring with the mother if she fled; and the mother had a serious heart condition. What is more, there is no evidence that the mother had ever actually violated any court order; the psychiatrist simply determined (by means best known to himself) that she was the "type" to do so.

What had really happened was that the mother's behavior had been situatedly defined by the terms of the family court culture. Determination equaled defiance; defiance equaled mutiny; and mutiny, as usual, brought about judicial madness.

After the psychiatrist's report was given to the judge and to the law guardian (not to the parents), the father suddenly "learned" of the report and made an emergency application for a change of custody.

According to the mother (in statements made afterward on the court record), when she arrived at the family court to oppose her ex-husband's custody petition, she found her ex-husband's attorney already in the courtroom speaking to the judge. She then immediately asked for court-appointed counsel or, in the alternative, for an adjournment so that she could obtain her own counsel.[58] Both requests were denied; she was ordered to sit outside while her ex-husband's lawyer and the law guardian met with the judge in his private chambers for hours.

While she waited nervously outside, she saw her ex-husband's attorney give two boxes of tapes to the law guardian, which were then taken into the judge's chambers. (The mother was never told what was on the tapes; the judge later confirmed having listened to them but did not say what they were.) The mother also saw her ex-husband try to telephone the child's teachers, apparently making arrangements of some sort, as if (she later thought) he knew already what was about to happen.

At almost 4:55 that afternoon, the judge finally entered the courtroom proper and, reading from "two yellow pieces of paper," told the mother he "already had given him [the father] temporary custody" of the child.[59] The mother protested vehemently, asking, "How could you issue it [temporary custody] when I don't have an attorney and I'm asking for an attorney?"[60] (She might have added, "And when I never even heard the evidence that was used against me?") That evening, the law guardian came to the house with the child's father and the police and took the child away from the mother. A court date was set for several months later for a trial to determine permanent custody.

The mother, not wanting to wait several months to seek the return of her child, promptly wrote a petition asking the judge to vacate his award of temporary custody to the father. The petition, for the most part, described the events recounted above, but the mother also claimed there had been a "conspiracy" between the judge, the father's attorney, and the law guardian to strip her of custody without due process of law, essentially because of the long, private conference they had held in her absence and during which they had apparently listened to tape recordings.

The judge scheduled a hearing on the mother's petition. She appeared at the hearing to represent herself—as she told the judge, "They [attorneys] want ten thousand dollars and I can't give them that."[61] It was at this point that the illogic of her case reached a Kafkaesque pitch. Rather than addressing the merits of her petition (which, in our opinion, deserved attention), the judge insisted on focusing on the mother's use of the word "conspiracy" in her petition. Over her repeated denials, the judge angrily claimed that this was a personal attack on him, the judge, which he characterized as "contemptuous on its face."[62] He insisted that the mother's petition (filed, remember, in an effort to win back custody of her child) was an outrage; no reasonable challenge, he said, could be made to his order transferring temporary custody because of the psychiatrist's "prediction" that she would "abscond with the child"—in other words, no objection from the mother to this bit of psychiatric fortune-telling, nor any evidence presented in her favor, could have mattered in any event in his courtroom. Thus, in effect, the judge reasoned completely around the mother's right to confront the evidence against her—a legal maneuver that turned the U.S. Constitution on its head.

And yet the infuriated judge was so sure of his position that he told the mother to her face that he could not understand why she had petitioned for a change of his procedurally bizarre order in the first place: "For you to come in here and expect me to unilaterally reverse myself is absurd!"[63]

Needless to say, the judge did not vacate his temporary custody order. Instead, he forced the mother to spend several days in jail for contempt of court, based solely on the language of her petition—specifically, her use of the word "conspiracy." And this despite the fact that the mother repeatedly denied she meant any personal insult to the judge. In the end, she also lost permanent custody too—all because she objected to her ex-husband's practice of having the seven-year-old girl sleep in the same room with her father and the father's girlfriend.

Judicial Name-Calling

After everything described above, it will come as no surprise that family court judges sometimes use name-calling as another way of attacking protective mothers. "Vindictive," "malicious," "neurotic," "paranoid," and "mentally ill" are all labels we have found in the mouths of family court judges as they describe protective mothers.

Judicial name-calling may seem a minor matter next to the abuses already described in this chapter. However, name-calling deserves serious attention because it helps to shape the progress of a case. It is a way of using part of the court proceeding to accomplish what is commonly done in a variety of interactional settings, in which participants use some part of their interactive discourse as an occasion to describe it, or explain it, or furnish the gist or upshot, or in other words to engage in the practice of "formulating" (Garfinkel and Sacks 1970). In short, when judges apply labels to protective mothers who are litigants in their courts, they are providing a steadily unfolding explanation (or "summing up") of their actions through the use of pejorative names.

Heritage and Watson (1979), in their description and analysis of the conversational work of "formulating," found that formulations may have a "special role to play" when the topic has been "the object of contest or negotiation" (pp. 149–150). In keeping with this finding, our analysis of court records reveals that judicial name-calling, as a "type" of formulation, arises when the case takes on problematic meaning—as judges and mothers come to see the facts of the case from diametrically opposed points of view.

For instance, in the Idaho case described earlier in this chapter, the protective mother was not diagnosed with a mental illness by the court-appointed psychiatrist. It was only when she began to protest the court's actions that the labels "obsessive and compulsive" and "borderline personality disorder" began to stick to her.

The mother's troubles began when the court-appointed psychiatrist (a professional colleague of her ex-husband, a physician) commented favorably on the ex-husband in a "home study" report he offered to the family court. The mother contends that the psychiatrist did not disclose his professional relationship with the father and misrepresented the comments of the children in his report. Accordingly, she filed an ethics grievance against the psychiatrist. (No official action was ever taken against him.)

Thereafter, when the psychiatrist testified during trial, he abruptly changed his diagnosis of the mother who had accused him. Now he claimed she suffered from "borderline personality disorder." He based this claim partly on the fact that the mother had filed a grievance against him and partly on the fact that, according to him, another psychiatrist involved in the case had made that diagnosis. This was, however, denied under oath by the other psychiatrist.

Despite the flimsy basis for this "diagnosis"—a self-serving response to an ethics complaint and a bit of testimony that was possibly perjured and almost certainly inaccurate—the judge accepted it. Now the mother had been tarred with the label "borderline personality disorder."

The abuse allegation had been settled between the parties with the agreement that (1) the father would have no visitation or custodial rights to the girl who had accused him, and (2) the mother would not seek to prove abuse had occurred so long as the father did not claim it had not. But when the family court judge issued his decision in the divorce case, he devoted much attention to the mother's request that her ex-husband cover most of her legal fees (his annual income was over $163,000, while hers was negligible), and while ostensibly discussing this financial issue he implied that the father had been unfairly accused of abuse.[64]

Now labels that announced "mentally ill" and "false abuse accusation" had been firmly planted on the mother—though without any real justification in the factual record. Family court's process of "formulating" the issues by means of its own labels was off to a running start.

The effects were visible almost at once. While the decision quoted above was still being written, another of the children disclosed that he had been sexually abused by the father—and a pediatrician confirmed that the boy's report was credible and did not appear to be the product of coaching. The judge's reaction was not to require an investigation of this new charge. Instead, he announced that he was removing himself from the case, claiming that the new accusation prejudiced him too much against the *mother* to enable him to continue to preside. (This did not, however, prevent him from issuing the harsh criticism of the mother already quoted.) Evidently, he simply assumed, before seeing any evidence, that the charge could not possibly be true.

A new judge took over in June 1993. But so decisive was the unwritten record summarized in the first judge's name-calling that even the new judge's first determination in the case—that the boy who said he was abused believed what he said—only convinced the judge that the boy was suffering from a delusion and had to be removed from the "abuse atmosphere" of the mother's home. He ordered both him and his younger brother immediately placed in foster care, where for weeks the nine- and five-year-old children were virtually unable to see or hear from their mother. This judge also stated for the record, without even giving the mother an opportunity to present her case at a full hearing, that no abuse of any kind had taken place![65]

The mother fought for the return of her children. She and the father did, in fact, agree that the boys could return to her home, though on rather onerous conditions. But as the father fought for a reduction of his child support payments and the mother continued to defend herself, the new judge began to characterize her as "obsessive and compulsive" for what he called her excessive litigation (ignoring the legal battles launched by the father). He used the same label in more than one decision, including one that granted the father the child support reduction he wanted. The judge cited the "extraordinary legal expense" the father had supposedly incurred due to the mother's "obsessive and compulsive" litigation.[66]

Significantly, the factual record (as opposed to the unofficial record created by judicial labeling) did not tally with the judge's findings. As justification for reducing the father's child support obligation, the judge had stated, "The [father] has had to defend multiple appeals and new litigation since 1993 with no end in sight." Yet in fact the mother, who had appealed exactly twice, had been successful in one appeal and had already paid the father's attorney's fees in connection with the other. Analysis of the father's other claimed legal expenses—which were accepted without a single amendment by the judge—shows that the figure asserted by the father's attorneys was wildly inflated.[67]

None of this helped the mother win a more just decision on appeal. Amazingly, the appellate judge specifically refused to trouble himself with the facts underlying the trial judge's decision condemning the mother and slashing her child support:

> The argument [that the trial judge miscalculated the relevant costs] is a tortuous reassessment of the evidence offered below, recast in light favorable to plaintiff and replete with plaintiff's interpretation. [Apparently the judge meant the plaintiff's arithmetic, since that was the extent of the "interpreta-

tion" involved!] It is an invitation for this court to re-find the facts found by the magistrate. . . . There is no basis for the appellate court to interfere with the facts found by the trier of fact on competent evidence.[68]

This meant, in effect, that the facts no longer mattered: even though the crux of the family court's attack on the mother ostensibly turned on fees and expenses, the actual amounts were no longer important. What mattered was the label the mother carried. She had been called crazy, compulsive, and vindictive. And of course the arguments of a crazy woman need not be taken seriously.[69]

Judges and Their Auxiliaries

This book's discussion of judicial excess against protective parents would not be complete without examining the conduct of the auxiliary figures in the family courts.

"Robed rage" rarely occurs in a vacuum. Instead, we find that it is usually embedded in "explicative transactions"—that is, rulings by which judges intend an exemplary effect on subsequent decisions and (retrospectively) on prior ones. However, Pollner (1979), in his study of explicative transactions in the traffic courts, showed that for rulings to have an exemplary or definitional force—in other words, to be explicative—they usually need to be made "in the presence of onlookers" (such as other defendants). This is because, in the presence of others, the judge is "constituting the situated meaning of the particulars [of each case] to which s/he responds . . . " (pp. 228–229). That is, "the present case [is] considered [in the presence of onlookers] in terms of its capacity to jeopardize or preserve features of already adjudicated cases and its capacity to furnish [or prevent] undesirable precedents" (p. 246).

Other "defendants" (usually called "respondents" in family court) are not present during a protective parent proceeding. The "onlookers" who are necessary for the production of explicative rulings are, therefore, the auxiliary actors—law guardians, caseworkers, mental health experts, and so on—who collaborate in the production of judicial decision making in family courts. That is, family court judges, concerned with the exemplary force of their decisions (as a way of preserving the features of their previously adjudicated cases and preventing unwanted precedents), regularly attend to the interests and opinions of the cadre of auxiliaries.

Former Texas prosecutor Randy Burton, joining two other writers, complained in a 1993 memorandum to former U.S. Attorney General Janet Reno that the close working relationship between judges and family attorneys reached the point of dangerous cronyism. The memorandum expressed particular concern about the judicial appointment of law guardians to represent children in suspected abuse cases. Citing the findings of the Texas Supreme Court Task Force on Judicial Appointments, the authors pointed out that "in some areas of the state, judges use [law guardian] appointment income as a reward or incentive to campaign supporters."[70]

In 1996, a local journalist reported to his editor that the main financial sponsor of a campaign rally for a New York judge was a lawyer then representing a father accused of child abuse in a case before that very judge. The child's court-appointed law guardian was also present at the rally. Both lawyers (the father's attorney and the child's law guardian) made disparaging remarks to the judge about the mother in the case (who was not present), according to the journalist. Soon thereafter, the mother lost all visitation privileges with her eight-year-old daughter. The mother's lawyer, when he learned of the out-of-court comments between the judge and the other lawyers (and their context—a political donor remarking on a case before the object of his largesse), asked the judge to remove himself from the case.[71] The judge not only refused but fined the mother's lawyer $1,000.[72]

Court-appointed mental health experts wield extraordinary influence in family courts. At a congressional hearing in 1992, a New York matrimonial lawyer testified that such "experts" can twist family law procedure into bizarre shapes: "The mother is ordered to submit to a psychiatric exam by chosen psychiatrists . . . [who] then diagnose the mother as . . . paranoid and delusional for believing that her child is being sexually abused by the father. . . . Once this diagnosis is made . . . she will absolutely lose her child."[73] The lawyer prefaced her comments by asserting that "these horrible things happen once these cases land within *the system*" (p. 73, emphasis added), thus consolidating family court judges with the experts they appoint.

Perhaps because family courts operate in a culture that is sui generis, judges are largely unaffected by occasional scrutiny from the press or even from legislators. For example, in 1989, New York's state legislature held an unprecedented two-day joint hearing involving four different committees into aspects of the family court system.[74] Mothers and health care professionals testified to the abuses of the family court system. In fact, Assemblyman Oliver Koppell (who chaired the hearing), after overwhelming evidence was presented against one particular Brooklyn Family Court Judge (Leon Deutsch), was moved to discuss ways of removing a judge from office.

In his courtroom, Judge Deutsch (whose law clerk was present throughout the hearing to take notes on the witnesses, many of whom were litigants before that judge) brushed off the criticism. In one case, he began a court hearing in an abuse case by gratuitously telling the mother, "I have been told [the mother], members of her family and [her attorney] have testified at those public hearings relating to this very case." He did not seem to feel the need to make any further comment. That case ended with the total suspension of the mother's visits with her eight-year-old daughter. Nothing happened to the judge.

Behind Robed Rage: Courtroom vs. Public Forum

One unusual feature of court proceedings concerning alleged child abuse is the cloak of confidentiality (ostensibly to protect child victims) that insulates such proceedings from the general public. This helps to drive a wedge between what judges say about cases in their own courtrooms (comments that are heard only by experienced court auxiliaries, family court attorneys, and the litigants themselves) and what they say about the system when they know their comments will be read by the public at large. Thus, judges who have been asked by reporters to comment on the family court system in general have sometimes made statements that seem quite at odds with their own rulings in particular cases (which were not available to the public).

For example, in 1990, Manhattan family court Judge Jeffrey Gallet told *New York Newsday* that a Hasidic mother's fatal beating of her eight-year-old Hasidic son, after previous attacks had gone unnoticed by authorities, showed that "the whole system has lost its logic, its cohesion, its ability to function . . . there's no oversight, no accountability."[75]

This complaint of "no accountability" came strangely from a judge who, in one case before him a few years earlier, had removed a six-year-old child from her home without even taking evidence, simply because her mother (concerning whom there was no evidence of any sort of child abuse or neglect) had missed an appointment with a psychologist when chest pains had sent her to a hospital instead. A special counsel to an important New York State Senate committee later characterized the judge's actions in that case as illegal and unconstitutional,[76] and later testimony not only revealed very credible evidence of abuse but also established that the child's experiences in foster care had been "miserable," pointing to the fact that the child had been forced to "handle feces."[77]

Judge Gallet's public comments were at odds with his own performance on another issue as well. He told the *New York Law Journal* in 1989, regarding the controversial validator Dr. Arthur Green (who frequently accused divorcing mothers of lying about sex abuse), that "he [Judge Gallet] is concerned that there is a proliferation of unqualified validators [in the family courts] many of whom possess no more than marginal scientific and educational credentials. . . .There is a danger that judges will abdicate their responsibilities to mental health experts . . . [who] often come to their conclusions using incompetent and incomplete evidence, without regard for even the most basic due process safeguards."[78] Yet Judge Gallet himself appointed Dr. Green, and others like him, to make determinations concerning the sexual abuse of children.

How could this same Jeffrey Gallet speak so forcefully of family courts' lack of oversight and accountability, and their reliance on dubious expert witness testimony, when in his own courtroom he seemed so willing to place himself above the law and to rely on the questionable views of controversial mental health experts?

One's first impulse is to set this down to hypocrisy. But perhaps the observations laid out above suggest a different interpretation. Context can alter judgments; the attitudes of the relevant "onlookers" must be taken in account. A newspaper is read by laymen. The family court system, on the other hand, is controlled by an unusual cadre of specialists who, as we have seen (and will see in more detail in the chapters that follow), bring their own brand of justice to actual abuse proceedings. A judge—speaking as a concerned citizen to other concerned citizens—is naturally unwilling to endorse a system that has allowed the killing of a child. But the same judge, in the company of specialists—those family court auxiliaries who are rarely visible to the general public but who are either physically in the courtroom or "virtually" present—approaches an abuse inquiry in the strange way this cadre has evolved, giving no apparent thought to what the general public would think if it knew what was going on.

This example illuminates how judges "situatedly make and manage meaning" for their auxiliaries (both physical and virtual) in the courtroom. However, because meaning is by its very nature a "situated" production (accomplished within the context of the interactional setting), it is subject to change when the "onlookers" consist of members of the public and not the usual cadre of auxiliary actors who constitute the judicial setting in which judges make and manage meaning.

How Mothers Respond to Robed Rage

Protective mothers not infrequently initiate direct confrontations with judges—a phenomenon rare outside family courts. Protective mothers sometimes plead for the return of their children, and sometimes boldly ac cuse the judge and his/her auxiliaries of ethical violations, of conspiratorial behavior, even of corruption. Transcripts of family court cases sometimes contain monologues by protective mothers nearly half an hour in length.

A particularly dramatic example occurred in a California case that unfolded in the late 1990s (and is still not fully resolved). In 1995, the mother had sole physical (and joint legal) custody of her three school-age children, two of whom (two girls, ages four and six) had complained of being sexually abused during visitation with their father. A medical examination carried out at the University of California, Davis, Medical Center showed that the older girl had "thickened folds" of the anus, "generalized increased vascularity" of the perihymenal tissue, and an "irregular, narrow thickened" hymenal wall.[79]

The judge assigned a law guardian and a court-appointed evaluator to interview the mother and her children. However, the law guardian never investigated the charges of abuse (in fact, according to the mother, he flatly "refused to speak to the medical examiner" whose report had supported the charge).[80] As for the evaluator—as soon as his report was given to the court, the judge abruptly transferred custody of all three children to their father and denied the mother any further contact with them.

The main reason for this custody transfer was that the court-appointed evaluator condemned the mother for having taped a thirty-minute video in which the child repeated her reports of abuse by the father. The mother had intended to give the tape to investigators; in fact, the mother would later assure the judge she "had been instructed by a sheriff's detective to tape."[81] But the reaction of the family court system was swift and extreme. The evaluator charged that the mother's making of the videotape (never mind the acts reported by the child *on* the videotape) was "verbally sexualizing and sexually explicit coaching of the child."[82] Surely most outsiders would consider the evidence of abuse by the father in this case more compelling than the evaluator's debatable complaint, which in any event did not point to any abuse on the mother's part. Yet the judge's rulings against the mother read like a judgment of excommunication. Not only did he remove the children from the mother—he denied her all visitation privileges and added a "Stay Away Order" preventing her from attending school events and extracurricular activities and even from contacting the children's schoolteachers. [83]

One afternoon, the mother—on a California freeway during a rush hour traffic jam—saw her children in a nearby car and waved to them. Incredible as it sounds, this drew criticism from the judge at the next court appearance: "I don't want any accidental stuff happening out on roadways, I don't want any waving by Mom to the children."[84]

The mother continued to present evidence that her youngest child had made disclosures to her schoolteacher and to her classmates of sexual abuse. The judge rejected these disclosures without investigation by classing the case as a "type" he claimed to be familiar with. In so doing, he invoked the "documentary method of interpretation" to deflect all the evidence that pointed to abuse (a conclusion he was not prepared to reach); he made sense and order of those same facts by showing how the *particulars* of the case at hand were actually representative of a certain *mold:*

> This case is really just a divorce. . . . If I were not a person, a judge, who has been exposed to these situations of false allegations of sexual abuse several times, I would probably react with horror at the thought that these children had been abused by their father, but I have seen this accusation raised on occasions in other marriages. I am sorry to say to those of you in this room that it appears to be a phenomenon of this county and the adjoining Calaveras County. But this is not the time and this is not the place for witchcraft or anything resembling it.[85]

The next day, the mother's lawyer tried to argue that the judge had refused to hear relevant evidence. The judge, however, did not need evidence to support his made-in-advance reading of the case:

LAWYER FOR MOTHER: What I have tried to assert on September 26th and again yesterday is that you haven't listened to the evidence.

JUDGE: Do you have someone who observed [the father] engage in any act of sexual abuse of these children as a credible independent witness? The answer to that is "no," and you know the answer is no! Now, don't harass this Court any more![86]

In other words, the judge now required the mother to present an eyewitness to an act of sexual abuse before he would even consider evidence that it had occurred—even though the mother had been barred from all contact with her children without a single witness having observed *her* harm the children, simply because she believed her children's reports!

In 1998, the mother, now bankrupt, went before the court as her own representative and passionately demanded an explanation for her continuing isolation from her children:

> There was no legitimate reason in the world that my kids were ever taken away from me in the first place. I'm not a bad person; I've never committed a crime, I've never been accused of committing a crime. You all took one stupid video and you blew it into something. That's not the way it is. That was thirty minutes out of a lifetime. You totally ignored everything else in my lifetime: How I communicated with the kids, the love I've given them, I gave birth to these kids, I nurtured them, I nursed them, I loved them, I never would do anything purposely to harm them. I told this Court over and over again I realize I made a mistake when I made that video, but it was not intentional, it was not something that was designed to hurt my children. You all took that one thing, you just blew it way out of proportion, then you punished me for what I believe in. . . .
>
> . . . Our nation was founded on the ability for people to believe, able to believe what they want to believe and nobody should be punished for that. That's exactly what's happened to me, and the court has actually criminalized me because I believe what my kids told me. You are entitled to your opinion; you are fully entitled to not believe if you want to. I'm not telling [you] you have to, but I'm telling [you] you don't have a right to judge what I can and can't believe and punish me for what I do and do not believe. My children—those are my children, I have a constitutional right to have a relationship with my own children. I'm not a criminal, I mean, I'm not a drug addict, I've never done anything to where my time with my kids has to be monitored. They did perfectly fine with me all these years. I was their primary caretaker. Nobody took that into consideration. You didn't go and ask my kids where they wanted to go, you didn't do that, you didn't want to hear from me, you barred me from testifying. No matter how many times my attorney would ask, you would not let me on the stand. I don't remember— I can't remember what the Appellate Court says, but that is a violation of due process. That's like you putting—you made me into a criminal and with this stupid parent alienation syndrome [sic], which doesn't even exist, you wouldn't even let me on the witness stand to defend myself against it. Just because he [the court-appointed expert] believes in it, it does not make

it true. The American Psychological Association does not believe in it. It has been debunked by every legitimate therapist there is. . . .[87]

. . . This is pointless to have a hearing in front of you; you are totally biased against me. . . . I cannot get a fair hearing in front of you. . . .[88]

. . . I want my constitutional rights to have the free association with my children. I'm not a criminal. Just because [of] that one stinking, stupid videotape, that you've blown into a huge thing, does not make me a criminal, does not make me a bad parent.[89]

It was not only the judge who had penalized this mother for believing her children. A court-appointed visitation supervisor had actually complained in court because one of the children had written to her mother and the mother had written back. The mother assailed her conduct as the judge sat in stony silence:

> It was a violation of my constitutional rights for anyone to ever say my child couldn't write me a letter. . . . She is a child, but she has the same constitutional rights that adults do. She reached out to me and I responded. In a situation like this how do you think my daughter would have felt if I didn't respond to her? The supervisor and I do not get along. We're never going to get along. It's not in the best interests [of the children] to continue seeing the supervisor if she and I can't get along.[90]

The father's attorney apparently spoke for the system when he scornfully described the mother's monologue as having been delivered in an "aggressive, abusive, belligerent, nasty, intolerant tone of voice."[91]

The mother made accusations against the system as well. She even alleged the existence of a "racket" in which the head of the court-ordered supervision program made "hundreds of thousands of dollars off of Parental Alienation Syndrome, which does not exist,"[92] since mothers who lost custody for bringing abuse allegations (and were stigmatized as suffering from Parental Abuse Syndrome) had to pay the court-appointed supervisor to monitor their visitation with their children.

It is illustrative of the dilemma in which many protective mothers find themselves in family court that this mother tried, at various times, to demonstrate her "parental competence" in ways governed by the family court's own procedural and institutional terms. Since, as we have seen, the "mother-as-nurturer" is so easily eclipsed by the situatedly achieved definition of "mother-as-litigant," the protective mother must address the practically reasoned supervening definition of motherhood—the one that revolves totally around her litigation conduct—to convince the court that she is fit to parent her children. But this California mother also, and repeatedly, expressed the fact that parental fitness could not really be defined as the court was defining it.[93]

From the point of view of mother-as-litigant and not mother-as-nurturer, making the controversial videotape was no doubt an error in judgment, since the mother's questions could have "contaminated" the testimony of an impressionable child witness. But the act surely arose from nothing more malicious than shock over what the child had said and concern that her own account of it might not be believed. The family court refused to see it that way. And this is, alas, typical: the mother's attempt to protect her children is itself classified as a form of abuse. In the high-profile case of Dr. Elizabeth Morgan, the cosmetic surgeon who went to jail for over two years while her daughter was in hiding with her parents, the mother's medical photographs of her daughter's injuries—clearly taken with a view toward presenting evidence to ensure her daughter's protection—were described by the family court as "pornographic"!

The mutinous behavior of the California mother described above continued outside the courtroom. During the late 1990s and into early 2000s, the mother met every week with a handful of other mothers on the steps of the state capitol. Together they handed out materials to state legislators and their aides containing a litany of civil rights complaints the mother had suffered at the hands of the judge and his cadre of auxiliaries. They criticized the law guardian, the court-appointed evaluator, and the visitation supervisor who ran a program for court-ordered supervised visits. The mother attracted attention by wearing a T-shirt printed with the judge's name and picture. Above his head, in bold letters, was the word "WANTED."

Chapter 5

Lawless Law Guardians

In most states, a family court dealing with an allegation of child abuse will appoint a legal representative for the child or children. These representatives are variously named in different jurisdictions: "law guardian" and "guardian ad litem" are the two most common.[1] Even though the policy of appointing such "law guardians" is relatively modern, it is now overwhelmingly popular in family courts: Lidman and Hollingsworth (1998) state that more than 1,100 guardians are appointed *weekly*, in custody cases alone, throughout the United States.[2] In theory, these representatives are appointed by family courts to ensure that the welfare of the children is not forgotten in a case involving a charge of child abuse—that is, in a situation in which the adversarial posture of the parents makes it difficult for their lawyers to put the children's interests ahead of their own clients' interests. Unfortunately, however, this benign theory is not always honored in practice. In the real world of family court, law guardians operate under very few controls and consequently are free to follow the unwritten rules of a system that, as we have seen, has its own topsy-turvy priorities.

What happens when law guardians disregard the law? In the previous chapter, we analyzed how family court judges can sacrifice objectivity when they feel their authority threatened by a protective mother. Here we examine a related problem. Since law guardians theoretically speak for the children, they are in a uniquely powerful position to cripple an accusation of child abuse, simply by refusing to credit it. And by the same token, they can quickly become the objects of outrage and parental mutiny when protective mothers believe they are failing to observe their legal duties to protect the children.

Law guardians reflect the priorities and attitudes of the system of which they are a part. Just as family court judges may scrutinize a parent accusing the other of child abuse more closely than the abuse allegation itself, law guardians may expend the better part of their professional energies dogging the steps of parents they suspect will take the law into their own hands. And just as the judicial system can ignore procedural rules and safeguards while it pursues a protective parent, law guardians may also behave like outlaws.

In the cases we have studied, law guardians have committed acts including lying to the family court and to higher courts; suppressing evidence of sexual abuse; and communicating false or incomplete information to state prosecutors and child protective service caseworkers who were trying to investigate claims of sexual abuse.

The particulars of these cases will be discussed below. But first, we should introduce some of the criticism that has already been leveled at "lawless" law guardians by child protection advocates and others.

The Role of Law Guardian Comes under Attack

In the past two decades—that is, during the precise period that law guardians have become fixtures in abuse-related family court litigation—law guardians have also attracted sharpening debate.

One of the earliest critiques of the roles and responsibilities of law guardians appeared in a 1990 treatise on the protective mother problem published by the National Center on Women and Family Law.[3] In *Legal Issues and Legal Options in Civil Child Sexual Abuse Cases: Representing the Protective Parent*, attorneys H. Joan Pennington and Laurie Woods cautioned that "the role of the Guardian Ad Litem, his/her qualifications, rights and duties, and accountability vary from jurisdiction to jurisdiction. Generally, there are no standards, no certification, no requirement of neutrality, and no guarantee that it is the child's interests being represented" (p. 16).

Pennington and Woods's concern was not misplaced. In the years since they wrote, task forces and state legislative committees that have investigated the performance of law guardians have expressed serious reservations. In 2001, the Massachusetts Senate Committee on Post Audit and Oversight, for example, found "system-wide deficiencies in guidelines, standards, training, role definition, accountability, and investigations."[4]

The harshest words have come from an attorney with extensive firsthand contact with law guardians in family court cases. In the *Loyola Journal of Public Interest Law* (2002), Louisiana activist attorney Richard Ducote, who has specialized almost exclusively in protective mother litigation for nearly two decades, actually called for the abolition of law guardians in child custody litigation.[5] Against the theory behind law guardian appointments—that a "neutral" representative can best represent a child's interests while the parents are at loggerheads in litigation—Ducote maintains that "nature has . . . arranged it so that most parents do, in fact, have more invested in the child's welfare than the guardian ad litem du jour," and therefore "it is certainly reasonable to conclude . . . that after two decades of experience and experimentation . . . the GAL's [guardian ad litem's] place in custody cases should be extinguished" (pp. 117, 119).

Ducote supports this position by calling law guardian "neutrality" an "illusion," a dangerous illusion that "invites private dialog between the judge and the attorney" (on the theory that the law guardian is not an advocate for either parent), when in fact "the attorney-guardian ad litem is, in many instances, merely another voice, representing another interested party" (p. 145).

All too often, Ducote argues, the "interested party" to whom the law guardian gives his/her unstinting, unconditional advocacy is the father, who is already implicitly favored by the judge. The law guardian, acting as a mouthpiece for the judge's preconceived position, then provides further "support" for the judge's prejudice, since the law guardian enjoys the presumption of "a level of competence, validity, wisdom, credibility, and objectivity richly undeserved" (p. 119).

Ducote also documents the damage done by biased law guardians: "Children are frequently ending up in the custody of the abusers and separated from their protecting parents," a tragedy that "does not happen in spite of GALs, but rather because of the GALs" (pp. 135–136).

Ducote discusses several cases in which law guardians, "without any authority to do so, want to determine acceptable playmates for the child, insist on screening letters and gifts to the child, and unilaterally alter court ordered visitation schedules" (p. 143). Even worse, Ducote points to a pattern of cover-ups resulting from the unmonitored role of law guardians: "Some GALs insist that children discuss important issues only with them, to the exclusion of the custodial parent, and seek to conceal evidence of abuse from the court under their questionable authority to invoke testimonial privileges on behalf of the child" (p. 143, n. 167).

Ducote argues that cover-ups can reach the point that the

> GAL fights to keep a child in the custody of a parent previously endorsed and exonerated by the GAL, despite mounting proof that the parent is indeed abusive and the GAL erred, often through gross negligence, in the first recommendation. In such instances, GALs have forcefully opposed the in-

troduction of new abuse evidence and instead have increased the blame on the non abusive parent. In this way, the GAL hopes to avoid any judicial finding that suggests his or her incompetence and jeopardizes future lucrative GAL appointments. (p. 146)

In this article—and in conversations with us—Ducote stresses that law guardians can threaten the welfare of innocent children so easily because they, like judges, enjoy virtually absolute legal immunity from the consequences of their official acts (p. 148). Indeed, we are not aware of any mothers who have received money damages after suing their children's law guardians; at most, a few mothers around the country have been successful in getting the law guardian off their cases. Most painful of all, even those mothers have been helpless to change custody or visitation orders issued at the instigation of the hostile law guardians.

Ducote's call for the abolition of law guardians remains a marginal position, in part because federal law, the Child Abuse Prevention and Treatment Act of 1974 (CAPTA),[6] which provides much-needed federal funding to state child protective services agencies, specifically calls for the appointment of law guardians in custody cases that entail charges of child abuse or neglect. In addition, as noted above, many states require the automatic appointment of a law guardian in any custody case—whether or not allegations of abuse or neglect have been made. But Ducote is not alone in his concern about the gap between the high hopes lavished on law guardians and their actual performance.

For example, Ducote points to a 1995 report on the guardian ad litem program from the Minnesota Office of the Legislative Auditor, Program Evaluation Division, which noted considerable confusion about just what a law guardian was supposed to do once appointed:

> Judges differ in how they use guardians ad litem. In some cases, guardians simply gather information and present recommendations to the court. In other cases, guardians may act as custody evaluators, or visitation expediters. Judges, court administrators, and guardians do not always agree on what constitutes the guardians' responsibilities. Judges also differ in their expectations of guardians for communicating and reporting. People told us the multiplicity of the guardian roles can be confusing, especially to parents who may not always understand why guardians are appointed. (pp. 112–113)

Ducote notes that the findings of the Minnesota report "were consistent with the experiences in other states" (p. 112).

Lidman and Hollingsworth (1998) have argued that "the faulty role definition" for law guardians paves the way for overreaching:

> Some individuals thrive in being in a position of power over others. A guardian ad litem can insert herself into a family to structure the interactions among the family members, without having any historic, emotional, financial or physical commitments and responsibility for the consequences. Without the controls and limits which are inherent in the judicial system and which constrain judges, the guardian ad litem, with or without admirable motives is not accountable.[7]

Law guardian "controls" are particularly weak because in most states, although the guardians are practicing attorneys, it is only the judges who appoint them—not the grievance committees of the local bar associations—who generally hear complaints about a law guardian's behavior. As a practical matter, this sort of "supervision" does little good in cases in which the law guardian's bias corresponds to the judge's own attitude.[8] For instance—in a case that will be discussed below in greater detail—when a Long Island, New York, mother filed a grievance against her sons' law guardian for misleading an appellate court about medical findings indicative of sexual abuse, the local bar association to which she sent her complaint referred it right back to the judge who had appointed this law guardian in the first place. The bar association claimed that the judge was the only authority who could monitor the law guardian's conduct, even assuming the law guardian had misled a panel of judges of an appellate court.

Lies and Cover-ups

Perhaps because law guardians are among the most critical auxiliaries of the family court system, they are also among the key instruments of family court madness.

In the most extreme cases, law guardians have engaged in schemes involving the concealment of evidence and courtroom dishonesty. In other cases, law guardians have botched their cases by focusing their suspicions entirely on protective mothers and ignoring all evidence that their children may have been sexually abused.

Sociologists have examined how law enforcement officials sometimes alter "facts" in a courtroom setting in order to fit them to the system in which they operate. Albert J. Meehan's 1997 study of police record-keeping practices (referred to above in chapter 3) argues that to prove "guilt" in a court of law, police often resort to a "transformation of what happened into 'facts' that will appear to conform with proper legal procedure . . . [which may include] . . . a set of 'facts' that are lies" (p. 189).

Among Meehan's examples is a police report that describes youths at the scene of a crime as "screaming and yelling" and "breaking a window," though they did not do this; these fabricated events were presented just to make a case of "guilt" to a judge. Meehan pointed out that the arresting officers strongly suspected the youths, who had a history of drug offenses, but were frustrated by the lack of evidence needed to ensure a conviction. For that reason, the "events as they unfolded . . . [were] clearly altered to create the elements of what the law defines as an offense" (p. 189).

Meehan described the alteration of the "facts" in police reports as the *situated accomplishment* of the arresting officers, who produced their records for what ethnomethodologists identify as "contractual" uses[9]—to serve as a "contract between the organization and the person served." That is, when police records are produced for an "outside" source—a court, for instance—they are carefully constructed around the "outside" source's priorities, even if this means changing the facts (pp. 186–189).

In a similar way, some law guardians produce "records" (both oral and written) in which facts are carefully selected, and sometimes even fabricated, to fit the needs—and often the prejudices—of the family court system. For instance, in courts in which protective mothers are expected to violate orders they disagree with, to evade the court's jurisdiction and so forth—in short, to cause trouble for family court judges—the law guardians often focus their attention on a mother's predisposition to acts of "mutiny" against the court. And if this means ignoring, or even suppressing, evidence that supports the mother's suspicion of child abuse, so be it.

A Vermont mother had two sons, whose disclosures of sexual abuse by the mother's ex-husband was supported by substantial evidence (see chapter 4 above). But the law guardian appointed by a Connecticut judge (after the father, in Connecticut, got a Connecticut court to take jurisdiction of the case) refused to consider any of this evidence, while repeatedly encouraging an all-too-willing judge to treat the mother as a lawbreaker.

The law guardian was the judge's former law secretary, and before she had been on the case for a month she had already absorbed the judge's attitude toward the litigants. At a hearing held before the law guardian had even met either child, the judge stated (without any basis in evidence) that the mother had "lied to the court, apparently she's lied to her attorney who withdrew from the case. And this court has no confidence in her as a cred-ible person." The judge also claimed that the mother's actions, and her accusations against her ex-husband, were "outrageous" and compared her behavior to that of "Bonnie and Clyde."[10]

The law guardian viewed the case through the same one-colored lens. Though in theory she was duty-bound to represent the children's interests, she remained deaf to all evidence that the father was abusing them. And the evidence was substantial: in Vermont, where the mother and her chil-dren lived, a district director of the Department of Social and Rehabili-tative Services wrote that the mother had "acted appropriately to protect her sons from further harm";[11] and a doctor wrote to the law guardian describing the young boys as "hyper-sexualized," reporting that one of them—four and a half years old—was talking about suicide and bluntly concluding that both boys "desperately need ongoing psychotherapy to get them through this stage of sexual child abuse."[12] The law guardian ignored all this.

Indeed, she more than ignored it. She actually urged the judge to move the two boys *into the physical custody of the man accused of repeatedly abus-ing them.* Her only stated reason was that the mother had not brought one of the boys to school—but he was under five years old and not legally re-quired to attend.[13] Obliging the law guardian's preferences (which were ev-idently his own as well), the judge first had the boys placed with the father's sister (who was also accused of abusing the children and adamantly denied all charges against her brother) and later did in fact place both children in the father's custody.

This approach to representing allegedly abused children was not one ec-centric act on the law guardian's part. As long as she remained active in the case (several years), the law guardian behaved as though her real client were the man accused of abusing the boys she represented. In November 1996, the mother appeared before another Connecticut judge with a signed state-ment from the children's doctor stating that the children were in "immi-nent danger" of further sexual abuse from the father and his sister. The doctor also warned that one of the children was suicidal and might kill himself at any time if the boys were not removed from the father's custody. The mother even brought affidavits from police officers and social workers who believed that the father had sodomized the boys; she implored the judge to grant an emergency motion removing the boys from the father's custody, repeating that their doctor considered them "in imminent danger of sexual abuse or death."

The law guardian coolly asked the judge to ignore the mother's pleas because the mother "is to notify me in advance before going to court for any additional orders [and] that has not occurred." The mother denied having seen any order requiring such advance notice, and so—at the law guardian's insistence—the judge refused to listen to anything the mother had to say until a copy of the order requiring advance notice to the law guardian was located in the court's case file, copied, and ceremoniously handed to the mother.

By that time, hours had passed since the mother had come to court. Hoping that the law guardian's procedural sensibilities had now been satisfied, the mother tried again to make her emergency request on the children's behalf, only to be brushed aside once again by the children's legal representative:

MOTHER: I have personal knowledge that there are criminal proceedings being taken by the State of Connecticut, criminal investigation. . . . I have witnesses and—

JUDGE (interrupts): Are you prepared, [law guardian]?

L.G.: Absolutely not, Your Honor.

MOTHER: I have exhibits—

JUDGE: Excuse me, ma'am. The tape recorder can only pick up one of us talking at a time. . . . Yes, [law guardian]?

L.G.: Your Honor, I am not prepared. I just happen to be in the courtroom today. There are other motions in this matter scheduled for which [the mother] has been served. I think [she] could file appropriate other orders . . . I would request that there not be any testimony today and that any additional proceedings be sealed and I will submit a petition to the court concerning that.

The mother watched, speechless, as the judge turned to the father's attorney and asked him, too, if he was ready to proceed. He said he was not. That the father's attorney wanted a delay before facing evidence of his client's alleged abuse was no surprise. But the *children's* attorney, confronted with a physician's letter stating that both children were in imminent peril, did not even want the court to consider the matter! Moreover, she was requesting that further proceedings be "scaled" so that any future accusations against the father, from any source, could be kept secret.[14]

The desperate mother tried once more. Once again, the law guardian was indifferent to any evidence that her two small clients were in imminent danger. She only reacted—and then with sudden fury—when the mother raised a new concern about the father:

MOTHER: Your Honor, I have a statement that my children are in immediate danger of sexual abuse or death as we speak. . . . I have no time to wait. My children—

JUDGE: I am not going to hear it today, ma'am. Do you want a date—

MOTHER: Could you please place them in a neutral zone so that I don't—

JUDGE: I am not going to enter any orders until after I have a hearing and I am not going to have a hearing today. If you want a hearing you can go see Mr. Goetz who assigns hearings for me.

MOTHER: All right. . . . They are declared in imminent danger—

JUDGE: Ma'am, I heard that.

MOTHER: I know, but I have information from the State of New York that [the father]—

JUDGE: You've told me that several times.

MOTHER: No, I have not, Your Honor. . . . I just want on the record that [the father] has been put on New York as an alleged perpetrator of children. . . .

L.G.: Your Honor, this is slanderous! This is perjury and it's slanderous! [In fact, the mother's statement was perfectly true, though New York ultimately dismissed proceedings against the father for lack of personal jurisdiction.]

FATHER'S LAWYER: Your Honor, can I have that stricken from the record?

MOTHER: No, it's real!

JUDGE: We're through.

L.G.: Thank you, Your Honor.[15]

Thus, the law guardian—whose job was to advocate for her young clients' interests and to protect their welfare—seemed interested only in defending the man accused of abusing them, even when a doctor said they might be abused again, or die, at any moment.

A law guardian appointed in a Maryland divorce showed similar priorities—and a willingness to bend both procedural rules and the facts of the case in order to aid a father accused of abusing the law guardian's clients.

The divorcing couple had two small boys. Six months after the couple separated, abuse allegations against the father were reported to authorities. The Maryland court appointed a "guardian ad litem" to represent the children and ordered joint temporary custody pending trial, with the boys to spend roughly equal periods of time with each parent.

The GAL had taken no action at all in response to the abuse allegations against the father. However, less than two months after the parties agreed to yet another temporary custody order, the GAL filed an "emergency" motion against the mother, claiming she presented "a very real risk of flight with the children" and urging the court to restrict her to supervised visits with her children. An emergency hearing was held that same day, but the Maryland court refused to alter the physical custody arrangement and refused to order supervision of the mother's contacts with the children.[16]

However, the GAL refused to take no for an answer. Having failed to persuade the Maryland judge to strip the mother of custody, he crossed the border into the District of Columbia (where the father lived) and urged CPS officials there to charge the mother with child abuse on the theory that she was mentally ill—the "proof" being that she believed her children had been abused. (As we have seen, CPS officials are all too willing to treat a child abuse accusation backed by a mother as an act of child abuse *committed by* the mother.) A few days later, D.C. officials did exactly that: they claimed that the mother was mentally ill, removed both children from her custody, and allowed her to see the children only under supervision at weekly intervals.[17]

Was the mother mentally ill? As the GAL surely knew, the psychologist appointed by the Maryland court to evaluate the parents had reported that "there was no evidence of any pathology on the MCMI [personality test]" he administered to the mother and no evidence of a "conduct disorder" in any of the tests.[18] Another psychologist who examined the mother found no evidence of mental illness or personality disorder of any kind, and wrote a report to that effect. A therapist who reported to the Maryland court had documented that the children reported to her, spontaneously during therapy, that their father had kicked one of the boys in the crotch, tickled his private parts, thrown grass in his face (he was allergic to grass), withheld food from him, ridiculed his artwork, and threatened to kill him and his mother by setting fire to their house.[19] It is therefore hard to believe that the GAL reported in good faith to D.C. authorities that the mother was mentally ill and was making "false" allegations of abuse.

Indeed, the most extraordinary thing about the GAL's action is that he appears to have actually *misstated* the facts of the case to D.C. caseworkers in order to turn their agency against the mother. A D.C. caseworker's memo states that the GAL informed her that an expert evaluator had already found that "sex abuse [by the father] was highly unlikely" and "believe[d] the children are making these allegations to relieve the stress of the mother."[20] The evaluator had not made either statement in his extensive testimony; what is more, in a report, he had stated clearly that he did *not* find the children were being coached by their mother to make their reports of abuse.[21] According to the same D.C. caseworker's memo, the GAL also gravely understated the court-appointed psychologist's diagnosis of the father: he claimed that the psychologist had found him "a little passive-aggressive"[22] when the psychologist had actually found the father suffered from "a moderately severe mental disorder."[23] If the caseworker's memo is accurate, the GAL—who had already failed in one attempt to take the children away from their mother—simply lied to D.C. authorities to make sure his second attempt was successful. And he did so, remember, in an effort to support the father accused of molesting *his own young clients.*[24]

These startling actions on the part of a lawyer supposedly representing two small children who might have been abused show how law guardians in family courts, like police in some criminal cases, can make false statements in a father's defense for the "contractual" purpose of getting the court to remove children from a protective mother's custody. In layman's terms, they have made up their minds from the start that a mother's accusation of sex abuse must be stopped—so the facts of the case are merely the malleable instruments to be turned to that end. What makes the phenomenon so insidious in family courts is that law guardians, unlike police officers, *are presumed to represent the best interests of the children they place at risk.*

A Brooklyn, New York, family court case featured a law guardian whose interests were so close to those of the father—who was credibly accused of child sexual abuse—that he actively denounced the mother for reporting her suspicions to law enforcement officials and then misled district attorney officials in order to prevent a prosecution.

The law guardian's priorities[25] were evident almost immediately, when—without even having met his six-year-old client—he supported the removal of the child from her mother's home and her placement in foster care, even though the mother was not even suspected of causing or threatening harm to the child. (It was her *father,* who did not live with her, whom the girl had accused of sexually abusing her.) The law guardian then claimed that the mother was "mentally ill" and aggressively supported the father's demand for custody, despite the girl's abuse accusations against him. The law guardian even claimed that the mother's belief in the child's abuse reports against the father constituted child "neglect" in itself. In fact, when a psychiatrist appointed by the law guardian found that the mother showed no sign of mental illness, and suggested that the girl should be returned to "the only home she has ever known," the law guardian attempted to prevent the psychiatrist's report from reaching the court record.[26]

The law guardian was prepared to go even further. Immediately after the trial—in which the mother had ended up being accused for having made a "false" accusation—an official from the law guardian's own agency admitted, within earshot of the mother's lawyer, that an incident of alleged sex abuse by the father had in fact occurred. The act of abuse had been witnessed by the girl's grandmother, and confirmed by the girl herself, but had been dismissed by the law guardian throughout the trial as sheer fabrication. Now an official of the law guardian's own agency admitted that the father *had* held the child on his pelvis as he lay on the floor outside the bathroom, and had gyrated under her. Furthermore, when separated, both father and girl were "wet." The only questions, the official said, were whether the father had acted for sexual gratification and whether the liquid on them was the father's semen or the girl's urine. In other words, the girl's lawyer had knowingly denied the truth about an abuse accusation made by his own client—the child.[27]

Ironically, the law guardian—who acted as though his job were to prosecute the mother—was incensed when the mother tried to take her case to actual prosecutors. When he learned that the mother had contacted the district attorney (DA) in New York's Ulster County (where the alleged sex abuse took place, although the case was litigated in Brooklyn Family Court), the law guardian reportedly called the district attorney's office to state, falsely, that the child had recanted her charges.[28] He also sent the DA a psychological report that was critical of the mother, but failed to send the more favorable report *that had been requested and obtained by his own agency.* He also fulminated to the mother's lawyer, who told her that her effort to have the father prosecuted "was going to hurt [her] bad . . . real bad" in the family court proceedings.

In an Idaho case in the early 1990s, the court-appointed law guardian, just days after his appointment and *without even having consulted his clients,*[29] recommended that two small boys be removed from their divorced mother's home and placed in foster care, after one of the boys—and an older sister—reported that the father had sexually abused them. In the face of a pediatrician's testimony supporting the boy's report, the law guardian told the judge that the "parties" (read: the *mother*) needed to be taught a lesson for having passed on the boy's charges to the court: "I think if we do that [remove the young boys from their mother's home] that maybe we'll impress upon both parties that this isn't going to be tolerated by the Court, because if we don't get the lesson through, we are going to be back in this courtroom or some other courtroom the rest of our lives."[30]

That one of his clients had reported being abused was not the law guardian's priority; it was the mother's having reported this, and having brought a medical witness to support the charge, that he insisted could not "be tolerated by the Court." The judge promptly granted the law guardian's request and ordered the boys into foster care. The law guardian was not finished, however. As it turned out, his real goal was to place the boys with the man one of them had accused of abusing them.

Just before a court hearing held about a month after the boys were removed from their mother's home, the law guardian informed the mother's lawyer, for the first time, that the foster parents (who had been specifically picked by the father) were going on vacation and the boys needed a different place to live as a result. At the hearing, the law guardian made a surprise recommendation that the boys be transferred *into their father's custody*.[31] After the family court judge complied with his wishes, the law guardian even opposed allowing the mother to be with her children during the day, while the father worked.[32]

The law guardian defended the father even as more evidence of abuse continued to surface. Over two years after the boys were placed with their father—on the law guardian's recommendation—a clinical psychologist who interviewed the boys concluded that "these boys were sexually abused by their father . . . in [the younger boy's] case, particularly, the abuse was ongoing."[33] Once again, the law guardian's reaction to the news was not an expression of concern for his young clients; rather, he set out anew to punish the mother—this time, for bringing the children to a psychologist.[34]

In a Colorado case, the mother had observed several troubling symptoms in her young daughter, including persistent vaginal discharges, masturbatory behavior, and nightmares. She also appeared "very clingy."[35] The child disclosed to doctors, social workers, psychologists, and even her teachers that her father fondled her genitals and "it hurts."[36]

Two separate medical exams, including a colposcopic examination of the girl's genitals (using a special kind of microscope to see into the vagina), found details consistent with sexual abuse trauma. The first exam showed that the child's external genitalia revealed "a crusty yellowish discharge in the perivulvar region" and an "approximately 1 mm. vertical laceration on the posterior fourchette"; it found the child to be "erythematous [reddened] and tender to touch over both vulva."[37] The second exam found the girl had "a generous vaginal opening with an abraded area from 3 to 5 o'clock," and concluded, "[I]t is worrisome that this child's genital examination has undergone marked changes in one year."[38]

The mother was understandably worried about her daughter's safety. But the law guardian appointed by a family court judge had her own agenda.

The law guardian chose mental health experts (approved by the court) who diagnosed the mother with a "hysterical personality disorder." The law guardian then openly supported the father's demand for sole custody of his daughter.[39]

In fact, the law guardian was so committed to the father's case that she did volunteer work on his behalf—a step she herself told the court was "unusual." First, "on her own time," she studied the works of Dr. Richard Gardner, a highly controversial expert whose theories about Parental Alienation Syndrome (which blames the mother who reports sex abuse for "alienating" the child from the father) have been widely discredited by his peers. (Gardner's theories are discussed in more detail in chapter 7.) Not content with reading Gardner's work, she then paid $300 of her own money for a long-distance consultation with Dr. Gardner, whose New Jersey office was thousands of miles away from the Colorado court.

The law guardian's use of Gardner's dubious theories was particularly questionable in this case for two reasons: no expert witness had placed the theory of Parental Alienation Syndrome before the court; and the theory assumes the "brainwashing" of children by mothers, while the child in question was probably too young to have the cognitive skills on which "brainwashing" depends.

Yet the law guardian, after going to such lengths to place her young client in the custody of a man credibly accused of abusing her—and to find a way to duck the physical evidence that tended to support the charge—actually asked the court to reimburse her for the money she had spent in contacting Dr. Gardner out of court![40]

It is no wonder that in conversations between this mother and one of us, over a period of several years, the mother repeatedly blamed the law guardian, even more than the family court judge, for destroying her family life.

A case involving allegations of child abuse that reached the Kentucky Court of Appeals provides another example of unaccountable behavior on the part of a law guardian—behavior condoned, unfortunately, by two of the three appellate judges who heard the facts. The exception was Judge Michael O. McDonald, who wrote a scathing dissent in which he criticized the family court judge, and his colleagues on the appellate panel, for depriving a mother of custody of her son because she had made sexual abuse allegations against the father.

And Judge McDonald had particularly sharp words for the boy's guardian ad litem, whose appointment he attributed at least partly to judicial cronyism, noting that the law guardian had been "a campaign contributor" of the judge who appointed him and had a "professional relationship" with the father's "good friend and the godfather of the child."[41]

The sex abuse allegations against the father, Judge McDonald wrote, deserved serious attention from the child's lawyer (and the court): the boy's "treating psychiatrist . . . first raised the possibility of sexual abuse . . . due to symptoms [the child] was experiencing"; then, a "forensic pediatrician" examined "the child's anus and [found] significant scarring [and] concluded the child had been sexually abused."[42] Unaccountably, wrote McDonald, "the court *upon the guardian ad litem's ex parte urgings*,[43] ordered that the child be released from Ten Broeck Hospital, where he had been placed by his treating physician [for problems related to the sexual abuse], and further ordered that the child's physician be restrained from having any contact with the child."[44]

The guardian ad litem clearly took his cue from the family court judge, who had called the mother on the record "an extremely manipulative, calculating, and vindictive individual."[45] But the judge's attitude was no excuse for the guardian ad litem's cavalier representation of his five-year-old client in the face of serious abuse allegations, in Judge McDonald's view:

> [The guardian ad litem] began advocating for a position on behalf of the child prior to having any opportunity to review the record or discuss the case with the experts involved. This is evident from comparing the date of his court appearance to those on his itemized bill that he had personal knowledge of the case and was lined up with the appellee [father] from the time of his appointment should have been apparent to the trial court. That the trial court allowed [the guardian ad litem] to needlessly berate and demand the appellant [mother] in his questioning of her, particularly over the issue of his fees, a collateral issue, constituted a shocking display of favoritism by the trial court.[46]

McDonald later told the *Lexington Herald-Leader* "that the handling of a controversial Hardin County custody case made him 'sick' and helped motivate him to retire."[47] He also criticized the Kentucky Court of Appeals' decision not to publish the case in its law journal,[48] voicing the suspicion that the court did not want his dissent to appear in public "because he 'desecrated the temple' by criticizing the trial court judge for being biased and ignoring evidence of a child's sexual abuse." He added, "I was taken aback by the way the case was dealt with. . . . In my opinion it was an impact case and it very much needed to stand for something."[49] Unfortunately, as he himself sadly noted in his dissent, the case was certain to stand for something even without being published—though without his published dissent, it could not stand for the truth:

> I am uncomfortable with the majority's closing thoughts [Judge McDonald wrote]. That the "system" cannot "require certainty" does not excuse the manner in which this case was allowed to proceed. In my opinion we have not only failed the appellant and the child, *but every other custodial parent who may not be able to convince the trial court that his or her child is the victim of abuse.*[50]

Thus, this tragically bungled case, like so many others in family courts, continues to have "explicative meaning"—that is, it affects how cases like it are likely to be handled in the future. So far, the lawlessness of the Kentucky law guardian remains unreproached by the justice system and largely unknown to the legal profession—though it was recognized for what it was by one appellate judge who preferred retirement to family court madness.

Law Guardians—Accountable to Whom?

Law guardian misconduct is particularly damaging to protective mothers because, no matter how law guardians misbehave, it is next to impossible to trigger disciplinary proceedings against them. Although in theory all lawyers—including those appointed to represent minor children—are subject to the oversight of statewide supervisory agencies, many protective mothers have found that law guardians are exceptions to the rule. They are virtually unaccountable for their actions to disciplinary committees, to concerned parents, and even to their own clients.

Such was the experience of a Long Island, New York, protective mother who tried to lodge one of the most serious complaints possible against a law guardian: that he had lied to a court about critical evidence that his clients (her sons) had been sexually abused.

In November 1993, the law guardian appeared before a New York appellate court to oppose the request of the mother's counsel for a stay of a twenty-day jail sentence a family court judge had imposed on the mother for "contempt of court." The mother's offense was that she had failed to send the boys on a visit with their father. Her lawyer told the panel of appellate judges that her client had been justified in barring the visit due to her fears that the father had sexually abused them. Moreover, she said, those fears had been partly substantiated by a medical report made at a hospital where the mother had taken the boys for treatment, in which doctors at the hospital had found "possible sexual abuse" in the older child (age seven) and an "enlarged (purple) vessel" and a "large rectum for age" in the four-year-old.

According to the mother, the law guardian then rose and told the judges that "he had personally checked with the doctors" at the hospital and was told by the medical staff "there was no evidence of sexual abuse."[51] Relying on the law guardian's representations, the appellate court denied the mother's request for a stay of her jail sentence.

The mother reacted by filing an official complaint with New York State's Grievance Committee for lawyer misconduct, accusing the law guardian of having violated his professional responsibilities by misleading the appellate court. Astonishingly, however, the committee responded that law guardians, although members of the bar like other lawyers, are solely "under the control of the court which appoints them." That is, only if the judge who appointed the law guardian finds "that the law guardian engaged in misconduct" can the grievance committee take any action. Otherwise, "this Committee cannot intervene or otherwise substitute its judgment for the Court."[52]

This meant that the mother would have to complain about the law guardian to the judge—that same judge who had appointed the law guardian, who the mother says was related to him by marriage, and who had communicated privately with the law guardian during her case. Only to *him* could she complain about the conduct of a lawyer who had allegedly boasted to the mother, "I bicycle ride with Don [the judge] several times a week."[53]

Not surprisingly, the mother chose not to press her complaint to the judge. She ended up losing custody and all visitation rights with the two small boys.

Giving the family court judges who appoint them sole authority to review the conduct of law guardians actually feeds the system of family court madness, as the collaborative achievement of judges and law guardians supports the bizarre status quo. That essentially precludes any possibility of redress. Yet this is exactly what the system appears to do.

And the situation is no more promising to the children themselves if, upon reaching majority, they seek redress for wrongs allegedly committed by their court-appointed lawyers.

Alanna Krause, an eighteen-year-old college honor student, may be the first such child actually to file a lawsuit against her former law guardian for ignoring her abuse by a parent. Ms. Krause had accused her father of abusing her and had nevertheless been forced by a Marin County, California, judge—with her law guardian's approval—into her father's custody. Years later, her father pleaded "no contest" to criminal child abuse charges filed in another county.

Once the facts of her abuse had finally been admitted, Ms. Krause decided to take legal action. Her 2002 lawsuit alleged that her law guardian had conspired with her father to commit fraud, to interfere with the presentation of evidence, and to make false statements to the family court. She also complained that the law guardian had billed nearly $17,000 for her "services" and had taken some of that money, illegally, from her mother's family support.

Remarkably, a federal court dismissed the lawsuit against the law guardian without even considering Ms. Krause's evidence against her. The reason? The court claimed that the law guardian was entitled to "quasi-judicial immunity," a doctrine that protects court officials from civil liability when they carry out a judge's orders or perform functions equivalent to those of a judge. The court ruled: "Under governing California law . . . therapists, guardians and court-appointed attorneys, are accorded quasi-judicial immunity . . . attorneys for children in child abuse actions are granted immunity from damages claims."[54] The court apparently did not see the irony of placing an attorney who had allegedly defrauded a court, improperly enriched herself, and helped to make her own client suffer abuse in the same class with a "therapist" in the eyes of the judicial system.[55]

For children who have been the victims of grossly negligent or even malicious law guardians, the reasoning of courts like the one in which Ms. Krause filed suit means that if the law guardian inexcusably, or even deliberately, puts a child he or she is supposed to represent through a life of hell, the child cannot sue for malpractice. In other words, the law guardian is lawsuit-proof—unlike any other attorney representing any other sort of client in a court of law.

This leaves children who have been victims of negligent or unscrupulous law guardians helpless to obtain justice, even when the law allows them to speak for themselves. As Ms. Krause put it in a column she wrote two years before filing her lawsuit:

> We children have no choice and no recourse when those adults [who represent us] have their own agendas. . . . My father . . . is an abuser, and living with him was a mental and physical hell. . . . Yet . . . [t]he lawyer appointed

to represent my "best interests" . . . spent her allotted time with me parroting my father's words, attempting to convince me that I really wanted to live with him. She ignored my reports of abuse. . . .

. . . I couldn't replace my lawyer with one who would speak for me nor could I speak for myself in court. I couldn't cross-examine the court evaluators or therapists and their claims were thus untouchable. I felt like I was witnessing the proceedings from the wrong side of soundproof glass.[56]

The View from Higher Courts

Family court cases rarely receive close scrutiny from higher courts, who usually reason that a judge who has personally heard testimony and observed the parties and witnesses must know what he is doing when he makes decisions concerning matters such as child abuse or custody. (In nearly all family courts, unlike criminal courts, the parent accused of abuse—or accused of having made an unfounded accusation—has no right to a jury, so that the case is decided on all issues solely by the judge.)

It is noteworthy that when appellate courts do closely analyze a family court case—usually because the case presents some novel feature—they sometimes express surprise at actions taken by law guardians that went completely unnoticed, or were actually encouraged, by the family court judge. This helps to underscore how much law guardian lawlessness depends on the unique culture of the family court system.

Take the famous "Baby M" case, which brought national attention to the issue of surrogate motherhood. A New Jersey mother (Mary Beth Whitehead) "contracted" to produce a baby for an infertile couple but then changed her mind after the baby was born. She and her husband sought permanent custody of the child while the infertile couple likewise sought custody (and ultimately obtained it).

The New Jersey Supreme Court, though concluding that the child's best interests would be served by placement with the infertile couple, reacted with some astonishment to the conduct of the law guardian (and the family court judge) in that case, writing that Mrs. Whitehead had been unfairly maligned by both of them. The court was particularly puzzled by the law guardian's harsh request that Mrs. Whitehead not even be granted visits with the child she had given birth to "at least until Baby M reaches maturity."[57] The child was less than two years old at the time and would have had to wait another sixteen years before seeing her biological mother if the law guardian's recommendations had been followed. As noted above, a biological parent's visits are seldom barred unless they are actually dangerous to the child—yet here was a law guardian seeking a complete ban on visits for sixteen years, with no evidence that Mrs. Whitehead posed any sort of threat. What was commonplace in family court was surprising, understandably, to the justices of a higher court unaccustomed to the vagaries of protective mother cases.

Unfortunately, few protective mothers—with cases involving only sexual abuse, not a novel public question like surrogacy—ever obtain a hearing before judges outside the family court system.

Lawless Law Guardians and the "Displaced Mother Syndrome"

For protective mothers, the offense of law guardian misconduct is compounded by the law guardian's usurpation of the mother's role. Whether or not family courts actually intend it, the fact is that the appointment of a law guardian—particularly one who is hostile to the mother—means that the law guardian begins to function in many respects as if the guardian, not the mother, had parental rights, forcing the mother aside. Certainly this is how many protective mothers have experienced the astonishing intrusions carried out by law guardians, with the complete approval of a court system that is supposed to protect families, not rupture them. We have dubbed this experience the "Displaced Mother Syndrome."

Displaced Mother Syndrome has very tangible causes. In some cases, law guardians have instructed schools not to communicate with their clients' mothers, not even to give the mothers report cards. Other law guardians have ordered mothers to keep away from school plays and commencement exercises. In one case (discussed in more detail below), when a protective mother whose visits had been terminated learned that her daughter's case was before a "Fatality Review Panel," CPS officials refused even to tell her whether the child was alive or dead, because the law guardian had instructed them that only he was to be informed of developments involving the child.

After experiences like these, displaced mothers confront feelings of grief and loss as their caretaking role is taken away from them. In place of the busy days of getting the children off to school (or day care), planning dinner menus, and reading nighttime stories, they face an empty house and a vacuum of knowledge. Many of them have formed support groups.

Many of the displaced mothers we spoke with said they no longer visited parks or other places where many children are found. They avoided "normal" mothers tending to their children. Many stopped attending church services and community affairs. Other mothers said they felt "unfeminine"—as if they were no longer women, since they were no longer recognized as mothers. One mother told one of us she could not even get herself to her annual ob-gyn exams, stating she was "so far removed from feeling like a woman." She described herself as "legally sterilized" by the family court.

Maternal displacement, however, can be more than just a set of psychosocial reactive symptoms. The displacement may have drastic legal and administrative consequences.

For instance, the law guardian in one high-profile New York case directed the medical staff at a hospital where an allegedly abused child was being treated for life-threatening anorexia nervosa (which she acquired while living in her father's custody) not to talk to the mother, claiming that she was "mentally ill," although the law guardian's own expert witness had reported otherwise. As a result, the doctors refused to give any information to this anguished mother about her daughter's condition—even though, as later testimony showed, the doctors were not even certain the child would live.

Through some bizarre administrative twist, the child's case was later placed before the New York City Child Fatality Review Panel. For days, her mother begged the agency officials to tell her if her child had died. She was repeatedly told that information could be given only to the law guardian, as it was "confidential" even from the mother herself. The mother's attorney made several calls to the law guardian to find out if the child was alive—all her calls went unanswered. Although this was an extreme case, many protective mothers have had great difficulty even getting their children's pediatricians to talk to them once a law guardian intervened in their families.

The role of "displaced mother" is the "situated achievement" of protective mothers—continually interpreted, negotiated, shaped—who have been driven out of the lives of their children by law guardians. We elaborate on two characteristic cases below.

Will This Holiday Be the Last with My Children?

First we consider the case of the Idaho mother, referred to above, who confronted a law guardian's insistence that the family court punish the mother for believing her son's reports of abuse by the father. As shown above, this mother suddenly lost two of her minor children into foster care because she made a report of sexual abuse with the support of a pediatrician. For a time the children were returned to her home—after she was forced to agree not to charge her ex-husband with abuse—but under the pressure of his constant, aggressive litigation, she watched her custodial rights gradually erode. Finally the boys were placed in their father's exclusive custody, and the mother was allowed visits only when the father agreed to permit them.

The contorted legal proceedings proved a perfect breeding ground for Displaced Mother Syndrome. The mother saw her viability as a caregiver shaken to its core. First, the law guardian urged the court to punish her for reporting her son's disclosure of abuse—thus compromising her right to protect her child. Then, when the children were forced into foster care in the summer (on the law guardian's recommendation), it was the law guardian—not the mother or her lawyer—who knew in advance that the children's foster parents would not be able to keep the children throughout the late summer and fall. And it was the law guardian who recommended, out of the blue, that as a result the children should be placed with their father—even though one of the boys reported having been abused by him. Years later, the law guardian made no objection when the father sought confidential records of his alleged victim's visit with a psychologist, despite the obvious violation of the privacy of the child—the law guardian's own client. Finally, with the law guardian's approval, the mother lost custody altogether.

Throughout all this, she practically accomplished her role as a "displaced" mother, particularly on family holidays. In the days before each Easter and Thanksgiving, she told her friends she feared that this would be the last holiday she would have with her children. She took dozens of snapshots of her children sitting around the dining room table—pictures she expected, even while she was taking them, to be her only contact with family holidays in the future. Her motherhood had come to be situatedly defined as a tenuous, threatened existence that could be preserved only in a photo album. Meanwhile, she feared that her family would be "torn apart by a knock at the door from a process server."[58]

Her ex-husband, perhaps sensing her fears, had her served with a custody-transfer petition on the day before Thanksgiving 1998. That wave of litigation ended with the boys being transferred to their father's custody and the mother threatened with a jail sentence if she did not hand over one of her son's confidential psychological records to the man he had accused of abusing him. In the end, the mother was proved right. Her family life was torn apart, with the cooperation of a lawless law guardian. And the final assault was timed to coincide with a family holiday.

Mother Commits "Irrational" Act

The most tragic reaction to "Displaced Mother Syndrome" occurred in a Rockland County, New York, case in which a protective mother—an attorney—killed her child, and herself, when it appeared a family court would transfer her four-year-old daughter to the custody of her ex-husband, who had been accused of sexually abusing her.

Much of the mother's anguish arose from the conduct of the girl's law guardian, who treated the mother with unwavering hostility. *New York Newsday* columnist Carole Agus, writing about the case after the double fatality, complained that the law guardian was "permitted [by the court] to function as the husband's attorney, rather than the child's." For example, when the father was serving a jail sentence for failure to pay child support (a penalty imposed by a judge in a different court), the law guardian petitioned the family court judge to arrange visitation for the father at the jail.[59] In fact, the law guardian's advocacy for the father and opposition to the mother—despite solid evidence of child abuse—went so far that the day after the mother filed an abuse complaint against the father with the police after a weekend visit, the law guardian actually demanded from the family court (and got) an order removing the child into foster care on the grounds that she had been unable to reach the mother by telephone![60]

That order was stricken by an appeals court when the mother took prompt legal action. But the experience terrified her. Amy Neustein, who had followed the case for almost a year, spoke to the mother just a few hours before she killed herself and her child. What the mother disclosed in that conversation shows how deeply she had been affected by the law guardian's conduct.[61]

She said she had just come from court and suffered "a very serious defeat." That day, Rockland County Family Court judge William Warren had ruled against the CPS lawyer, who had maintained that the father was guilty of sexually abusing his daughter. As a result, Judge Warren ordered a resumption of unsupervised weekend visitation between the four-year-old girl and her father. These visits were to begin in just two days.

Throughout the trial, the law guardian had strenuously supported the father—despite the position of CPS and a court-appointed social worker's testimony that "[the child]'s presentation is entirely consistent with that of a sexually abused child,"[62] which supported her report to the court that the "sexual interaction [between the father and the child] included vaginal fondling, vaginal penetration, and at least attempted anal penetration."[63]

Now, the mother said, the law guardian—on hearing the judge reject the claims of sexual abuse—had confronted her in the courtroom and coldly warned her that she was about to face "the custody battle of her life." This threat, coming from an attorney who had already bent the law out of shape to have this mother's daughter removed from her home, convinced the mother that she could not win. She was certain, she said, that her daughter would be lost to her forever if the litigation continued. A few hours later, she and her daughter were both dead.

Judge Warren told the *National Law Journal,* "I cannot explain irrational acts."[64] But shocking as the mother's actions may have been, they were not without historical precedent. Henrietta Buckmaster, in a study of the "Underground Railroad" for escaping American slaves, reports that "resistance to slavery took many forms other than escape . . . [including] . . . killings by mothers of their children when they heard they were to be sold apart [and] in repeated suicides."[65] Writings that have survived from medieval pogroms similarly show that Jewish parents sometimes killed their children—and then themselves—rather than allow the children to be forcibly converted to Christianity (which to them would have meant a radical rupture of family and social bonds as well as a religious violation). In other words, parents who fear the complete displacement of their parenting roles may sometimes, in despair, behave just as this protective mother did.

Judge Warren—and the father's supporters—naturally stressed that child murder cannot be justified under any circumstances. But what about the visceral threats that had driven this sensitive woman to such an extreme? Were *they* justified? Do we ignore the evils of slavery or pogroms because the desperate victims of both sometimes took their children's lives— seeking a gruesome escape from the intolerable?

The mother's suicide note (addressed to two adult children from a prior marriage) clearly suggests her internal struggle and sense of hopelessness:

Dear Jason and Marisa:
    Please forgive me for any pain I have caused or will cause you in the future. You are my children and I love you more than myself. Abigail is also

my child. I cannot knowingly allow her to be sexually abused. I have no choice. I hope you can understand. Be kind to each other. I'm sorry I had to leave you alone.

Love Forever, Mom[66]

Judge Warren's answer to the reporter—that no explanation would be valuable in light of the mother's "irrational" act—is clearly not adequate in the face of such anguish. In fact, it is actually not too difficult to reconstruct the intolerable dilemma that tore this mother apart. As she steadily lost the power to protect her young daughter from alleged sexual abuse, and faced "the custody battle of her life," she knew all too well that she risked being utterly "displaced"—being a mother who would live to see herself driven out of the life of her child by court rulings.

Thus, in a last-ditch attempt to (situatedly) fulfill the role of mother— rather than standing back and watching the child drift away into the hands of an accused molester—this mother took the radical, final step by which she removed the family court, and the tormenting law guardian, from her child's life.

Chapter 6

Anti–Social Services

C hild protective services (CPS) is the generic name for the state social services agencies entrusted with protecting child welfare, including the investigation and prosecution of cases of suspected child abuse. Obviously, therefore, CPS functions as an important auxiliary in the family court system. Unfortunately, it also helps to re-constitute as an ongoing practical accomplishment, the madness of the family courts. CPS agencies are charged with the responsibility of assisting families in crisis and protecting abused children. When, in fact, they do just the opposite, it seems to us that they deserve to be called "anti–social services."

When does that occur? CPS agencies can display quite a few kinds of anti–social behavior when it comes to protective mothers. First, they can bring bogus petitions against the mother, charging her with "brainwashing" her child into believing he or she has been sexually abused; then the agencies can come to court and argue so vigorously against the mother that she will lose custody to the ex-husband, even when substantial evidence exists that he sexually abused the child. Second, when child visitation is in CPS's control, the agency can arrange for supervised visitation between the mother and child that is so restrictive and confining it becomes almost meaningless. A third kind of anti-social behavior is search and seizure: CPS agencies can claim for themselves the right to make unannounced visits to the home of a protective mother, supposedly to "observe" but often to comb her personal belongings for such damning "evidence" as books dealing with child sexual abuse—which can then be cited in court as "proof" that the mother is inventing the abuse charges.

Whatever tack an agency may take, the depressingly common bottom line is that when CPS is out to get the protective mother—as happens all too often—the mother's experience of the legal process is apt to be Kafkaesque. She may be accused in formal legal papers by people she has never met, charged with things that are not against the law, and yet find herself fighting to keep her rights to her children—or even her right to visit them—against not only a hostile ex-husband but a powerful government agency. She may even find that the agency is more committed to punishing her than to determining the children's welfare.

Many protective mothers have found, to their dismay, that when CPS agencies inject themselves into a case involving allegations of child sexual abuse, the outcome can be worse for the mother than if no agency had been involved in the first place.

In fact, CPS agencies' anti–social behavior can have effects that last long beyond the end of a trial. Protective mothers in the grip of hostile CPS agencies can be so affected by the agencies' treatment that their life choices—a future marriage, decisions whether to have more children, where to live—come to revolve around their perceived status as "neglectful" mothers, regardless of how they made decisions before being involved with an agency.

Bogus Petitions

CPS agencies are entrusted by state governments with the responsibility of investigating child abuse reports. If the agency believes a report is well founded, it files a formal petition with a family court, supported by a sworn affidavit from an agency employee, asking the court to declare the child in question "abused" or "neglected" so that the court can take appropriate steps to assure the child's safety. This, at least, is how the system is supposed to operate.

But our research of family court cases shows that CPS agencies often abuse the process, filing petitions simply to inject themselves into divorce litigation whether or not they believe a child has actually been abused. In many protective mother cases, they file their petitions in order to gain control of the accuser, who thus suddenly finds herself at the mercy of the very agency that is supposed to exist for her children's benefit.

Examples of bogus petitions appear later in this chapter, but there are certain common patterns that deserve mention here.

First, petitions against protective mothers may be based on allegations that do not constitute child abuse or neglect as defined by the law—they simply reflect CPS's desire to take control over a woman and her children. Allegations that a mother "conveyed false information" to doctors, that she made an abuse report that "was not totally true," or that she failed to "insulate" a child from the legal proceedings are some of the claims by means of which CPS has removed children from their mothers.

Second, CPS petitions may contain statements that are simply false. CPS agencies are permitted by law to include allegations in their removal petitions that are based on suspicions, "tips," or other less than reliable claims. These claims are rarely questioned by the family court judges to whom CPS turns for orders removing children from their mothers' homes. The mother—who might be able to disprove the charges—need not be informed in advance if the agency claims an "emergency," which it often does. By the time the mother even knows what she is being accused of, a CPS caseworker can be at her door with a signed court order calling for her children's removal—and a police officer to see to it that the order is enforced. Even when the allegations are transparently inaccurate, they are usually good enough for family court. In one case, for example, a mother was charged with "child neglect" after the child accused her divorced father of sexually abusing her during a visit at her mother's home while the mother was away and the child's grandmother was caring for her. The mother was charged on one of two alternate grounds: either she had failed to protect the child from abuse, or she had made a false abuse report. Both claims were literally impossible, the first because CPS's own case notes showed that the mother had been absent at the time (the child had been left temporarily in her grandmother's care), the second because CPS's notes showed that it was the grandmother, not the mother, who had actually phoned in the abuse report. But this did not prevent the child's removal.

In fact, in many cases, CPS removal petitions are sworn to by someone other than the caseworkers who investigate the facts—almost as if CPS officials want to ensure that those who sign can always claim ignorance of the truth if a rare family court judge actually holds them to the requirements of perjury statutes.

Third, CPS agencies can fall back on the "get the kids first, explain later" approach. In these cases, CPS claims an "emergency" that justifies an immediate removal without the usual legal procedures. They may not even file a petition with a court. Once the children are removed from their home, CPS caseworkers grill the frightened, disoriented children for some evidence of maltreatment. When did they last see a doctor? Do they ever play in the street? Does Mommy ever hit them? Shout at them? Is someone watching them at literally all times? Are they dirty? If CPS can make it appear, from such interviews, that there is any possibility of sustaining a child abuse or neglect charge, the illegality of the original removal will generally be overlooked.

Nonvisit Visits

CPS generally performs the supervision of visits when such supervision is required by a court order, after a petition alleging child abuse is filed or after a child has been determined to have been abused or neglected. As we have mentioned, protective parents are often the targets of such petitions. When children are removed from the custody of protective mothers, the *mothers* find their visits under the same CPS supervision usually enforced against alleged offenders.

Supervision of visits is meant only for the protection of the children. But supervision can mean much more than that to a hypervigilant CPS agency. It gives the agency unfettered discretion to make visits torture for parents and children.

Restrictions imposed by CPS in many of the cases we have studied include the following: parents are not allowed to whisper or speak softly to the children; parents are not allowed to give or receive written notes; parents are not allowed to hold their children in their lap; parents are not allowed to touch the children at all; parents are barred from bringing plastic utensils to eat cake; parents are not allowed to make any reference to the caseworkers; parents are not allowed to say anything about the case, even if the children ask about it; parents are not allowed to correct their children if they repeat false statements about their parents they have heard from caseworkers.

In addition, caseworkers often intimidate parents by busily writing notes during visits—notes they routinely refuse to share with the visiting parent but will share freely with a hostile law guardian or judge. These notes are often written with a predetermined agenda in mind and detail the "inappropriate" behavior of the visiting parent, such as whispering, "excessive" hugging—even the expression of "too much" love (which caseworkers can say is an application of emotional pressure).

Search and Seizure

CPS can claim even more extraordinary powers over a parent's life. Besides supervising visits, CPS has the power to inspect a parent's home (without obtaining a search warrant). This means that caseworkers may arrive at any time (announced or otherwise), inspect anything, and then make reports that will later appear in court. They can also subject a mother to endless mental health examinations and have broad license to invade her privacy by demanding releases for personal information such as medical reports, therapist's reports, and the like.

CPS home inspections may concentrate on mundane details such as the tidiness of a home (untidiness on the part of a protective mother may be treated as if it suggested child neglect) or on more specialized issues such as the presence of books describing sexual abuse and sexual abuse allegations (which may be presented as evidence that the mother is manufacturing allegations or is obsessed with concerns about abuse).

However CPS goes about creating an unflattering record of a protective mother's life, habits, and character, the targets frequently find that the process is very hard to stop—it has a life and logic all its own. Once a protective mother becomes "known" to CPS, she has a "record" within the agency that is more than just a paperwork trail. Such records are "running records"—oral instruments that function as selective dossiers (which are based more on the "line" or "rumors" trailing a person than on the substantive facts)—that can be invoked at key points in a case. Such running records fill in where the facts leave off; consequently they may be used to paint a picture of "neglect" or "abuse" even when the facts do not justify it.

Unchecked Power, Secrecy, and Control

CPS malfunction stems from its very nature. Of particular concern are its wide-ranging powers and the secrecy within which it operates.

These factors—already touched on above—contribute to a third problem, which is an attitude among CPS officials that they alone should control the decisions and behavior of the families they deal with. In 1992, Lucy Billings, former director for Special Litigation and Training at Bronx Legal Services, a state-funded program that provides legal representation to indigent clients (and now a judge in the Civil Court of the City of New York), testified before the U.S. House Subcommittee on Select Education of the Committee on Education and Labor. In her testimony, she described how CPS agencies misguidedly make unilateral decisions for a child by excluding the mother from that process:

> [A]gencies mistakenly act as if they have been given total control over the daily life and future of the child and, without parental involvement or consent, arrange for evaluations, services, and the sharing of information. It is common for a contracting agency [a foster care agency] to perform psychi-

atric assessments of children in foster care without prior discussion with the parent, her consent, or fully briefing her as to the outcome. Thus, in addition to not involving the parent in decisions and not obtaining consent, agencies presume it is their right to determine what to share with the parent. Psychiatric examinations of children performed by the agency employees are not discussed with the parent in advance nor after completion. These reports, however, contain information regarding her children that she has every right to know.[1]

Billings also pointed out how CPS misapplies the *confidentiality* (read: secrecy) rules:

> When family members are trying to address the family matters to which the Child Welfare Administration records on the family pertain, the CWA employees, without legal basis, resist disclosure. In contrast, CWA employees freely divulge such information to third parties who have no business or need to know all that is disclosed.[2]

In other words, "confidentiality" works selectively: mothers are barred from information about their own children that is freely shared with strangers—even when the strangers have no need to know it.

Furthermore, Billings identified a problem that is almost unique to the family court system: mothers are denied information by *everyone* concerned in a family court case; it is not unusual that even a mother's own attorney, on instructions of the court, will withhold, for example, psychological reports on the mother written by court-appointed experts. Similarly, mothers in family court cases have frequently complained to us about conferences between a judge and the lawyers, during which the mother herself is kept waiting outside while important decisions about custody and visitation are made in her absence. In no other specialty of law is a client likely to be treated this way.

Playing Judge

CPS's casual assumption of unchecked power has several practical results. One is the ease with which CPS "plays judge." That is, CPS agencies whose involvement in a case is governed by a court order will often assume powers beyond those actually in the order. In some cases, CPS has imposed restrictions on mothers not only in excess of a court order but even in violation of the statutory guidelines that regulate social service agencies—as when CPS prevents a parent from writing uncensored letters to her children, or arbitrarily denies parent-child visits.³ For instance, in the late 1980s, CPS prohibited an Oregon mother from writing letters to her nine-year-old daughter while the girl was in foster care, even though there was no order from a court to that effect.

Visit supervision by CPS calls forth some of the greatest agency creativity in imposing harsh and excessive conditions. We have already mentioned the "no whispering" rule imposed on many protective mothers during visits with their children. In one case, CPS barred a mother from holding her young children in her lap, for fear that she might bend over and whisper into a child's ear. Such orders are seldom stated by a judge or even mentioned in court—but CPS can generally count on family court judges to rubber-stamp their rules whenever called upon. When a Long Island, New York, mother complained at a court hearing in early 2000 about CPS's "no whispering" rule, the judge issued a written order on the spot prohibiting whispering—although there had been no such prohibition to begin with.

CPS prohibitions can border on the bizarre. One New York protective mother, for example, in a case from the mid-1980s, was barred from taking her six-year-old daughter into a bathroom stall without a caseworker present. This was not a case involving allegations of physical abuse against the mother; instead, the caseworkers claimed that if the mother was alone with the child in the bathroom stall she might use the "private" time to "brainwash" her child. In the same case, CPS imposed strange restrictions even on the child's maternal grandmother, who was denied visits with the girl (no reason was ever given on the record) and was sternly instructed not even to touch her. One day, when the grandmother had accompanied the child's mother to the family court building where supervised visitation was about to take place, she saw the child enter the room with a caseworker and leaned forward, smiling. The bailiff who monitored the visitation room rushed over and angrily told the grandmother, "If you move forward one more inch you'll be arrested, ma'am!"

Supervised visitation not only provides a setting for draconian restrictions—it also gives CPS a golden opportunity to manufacture evidence that serves to prejudice the mother in court. Her word is rarely of much value against caseworkers' reports.

For example, in a 2001 New Jersey case, a mother's visits with her children were supervised by CPS caseworkers who were openly hostile to the mother. At the end of one supervised visit, the caseworker could not find the children's coats. Immediately, in front of the children, she confronted the mother and accused her of taking the coats. The mother denied having taken them, but the caseworker angrily persisted in her accusations until the mother actually ran down the stairs to escape her. One of the boys started to follow his mother and was pulled back by the caseworker. The caseworker reported this to the family court judge—blaming it all on the mother, though it was never proved that she had anything to do with the missing coats. The judge obligingly wrote in an official decision that the mother "took the boys' coats and wouldn't return them" during a visit. He even claimed the mother had "forced" the caseworker "to chase after her with the boys in tow." This went far beyond the evidence. But it is rare for family court judges to challenge the CPS version of such events. Indeed, in this case, this incident was specifically cited by the judge in his determination that the mother had "emotionally neglected" the children.[4]

It is common for caseworkers and their supervisors to hover over a mother with legal-size notepads, obsessively taking down everything she says to her child (and CPS employees) or what the caseworker thinks she in fact "meant" to say. Some social service agencies have hidden tape recorders in the visitation room so that not a word of what the mother says will be missed. But this attention is not meant to build an objective record, as one New Jersey mother discovered when her daughter, during a supervised visit, made comments the mother thought suggested manipulation by the father. She asked the CPS caseworker who was taking notes to make sure those comments were written down. The caseworker told her that she had no say in what was recorded and that if she made any other comments about the note-taking she would not be permitted visits at all.[5]

One almost obsessive priority CPS usually brings to supervision of protective mothers is the fear that the mothers will abscond with their children. It takes very little to trigger this fear. For example, the New York protective mother who was supervised even in bathroom stalls was allowed once—exactly once—to take her six-year-old daughter to her home for a visit, a setting she and the child both preferred to the bare office at the agency building where visits had been conducted for more than a year. When she returned her child to the agency after the visit, the caseworker promptly said to her supervisor, "Well, we don't have to get that arrest warrant for her after all." The mother never knew exactly what she had done to move CPS so close to seeking her arrest, but this was the last "normal" visit the mother was allowed to have with her daughter. At CPS's insistence, the family court ordered that the mother never again be allowed to take her child home, even for a visit.

One particularly excruciating aspect of living in the CPS fishbowl is that its complaints about a mother it dislikes can change whenever a new charge better suits CPS's convenience. For instance, in one case, CPS repeatedly accused the protective mother of making hostile comments about the father during her supervised visits with the child. CPS used this accusation to try to persuade the judge to terminate the mother's visits altogether. To disprove the allegation, the mother began bringing her own minicassette recorder to the visits, unobtrusively taping the visits by keeping the recorder inside her jacket. When CPS found out about this, it stopped accusing the mother of denigrating her ex-husband—but immediately condemned her for invading the child's privacy by taping her.

CPS also flexes extralegal muscles during home visits to inspect the "living conditions" of protective mothers. A New York mother with two young daughters, who alleged being subjected to repeated sexual abuse during visits with the father, was herself subjected to weekly "surprise" visits by CPS caseworkers. On one occasion the caseworker found books on sexual abuse in her bedroom drawers. Though there was certainly nothing illegal (or even surprising) about this, the caseworker confronted the mother on the spot with the suspicion that she was "planting" sexual content in the minds of her daughters. This mother eventually lost all confidence in the system and fled, along with her girls.

A Brooklyn, New York, mother suffered a different sort of intrusion. Apparently because the mother believed that her daughter had been sexually abused (and was therefore, by definition, a flight threat), a caseworker was assigned to follow the mother whenever she traveled from one borough to another. At other times, the same caseworker would park her black sports car outside the mother's home for hours, sometimes for half a day, while closely observing who was going into and out of the house.[6] The mother had not been accused of neglect and had no criminal record, but she found herself under the sort of surveillance normally reserved for dangerous criminals.

Some mothers get a taste of how CPS can "play judge" even before their cases get to court.

For instance, in 2001, a West Virginia mother's three-year-old child came back from a visit with his father exclaiming, "My daddy hurt my pee pee; put medicine on it!" The mother contacted the Department of Human Services to seek the filing of an abuse petition against the father.

Instead, according to the mother, once CPS officials met with the father (and his lawyer) the CPS caseworker assigned to the case solemnly told her that "people can lose their children for making up stories" and added, "it would be best to just drop the whole issue" as "it would be a 'shame' if she were found to be the problem." The mother told the authors she definitely heard this as a warning, "a very clear message to shut up and not make any more waves."

Playing God

CPS agencies can do more than play judge. As Lucy Billings (now New York City Civil Court Judge Billings) commented in testimony quoted above, CPS can take upon itself the authority to reshape a protective mother's family, to make all her decisions, even in some cases to make judgments that judges themselves cannot make. In other words, they play God.

In 1993, Dr. Marta Lundy, then assistant professor of social work at the University of Illinois' Jane Addams College of Social Work, was surprised to receive a formal letter summoning her to a meeting with the commissioner of the Illinois Department of Children and Family Services. She soon found herself the object of high-pressure treatment by CPS. Her crime? She had made a report of child sexual abuse to the department.

Dr. Lundy had been conducting research under a federal grant into the hidden costs (for example, financial, vocational, and relational) to protective parents and their families that resulted from their reporting of sexual abuse to authorities.[7] During an interview conducted by one of Dr. Lundy's research assistants as part of the study, a child disclosed that she had just been sexually assaulted by her father.[8]

Since Dr. Lundy, a social worker, was required to report incidents of sexual abuse under child abuse reporting laws, she phoned the child abuse hotline and reported what the child had said. That was when she received her summons.

When she appeared before the CPS commissioner, she was sternly warned that she was not allowed to report sexual abuse disclosed by that child, because "the local family court judge forbade any CPS investigations in this case."

In other words, Dr. Lundy was told that the mandatory reporting laws were in practice overridden by "higher authorities"—namely, a family court judge and CPS—when they considered it undesirable to hear any more about a particular allegation of child sexual abuse. What was more, CPS had thought so much of its power to override reporting laws that it had issued a written summons to the social worker to ensure that the reporting laws would not be followed in that particular case. Dr. Lundy has told us she found it "utterly shocking" that a social worker could be "reproached" by the commissioner himself for "fulfilling her responsibilities in the first place" to "report child sexual abuse."[9]

This event prompted Dr. Lundy and her coinvestigator, Dr. Carol Rippey Massat, to redefine the extent of their study so as to include the phenomenon that is the subject of this book—that is, the "penalization" of mothers, and others, for reporting sexual abuse.[10]

Less than a year later, after Drs. Lundy and Massat had seen several cases in which CPS penalized mothers for making good-faith reports of sexual abuse, Dr. Massat took the extraordinary step of writing to George Burgasser, then acting chief of the Child Exploitation and Obscenity Section of the U.S. Justice Department, to apprise him of this disturbing pattern: "The findings of a preliminary study funded by NCCAN showed a consistent pattern of punitive responses [to the nonoffending parent] to the reporting of child maltreatment . . . a pattern of obstruction of investigations . . . in apparent contradiction of the legal requirements of CAPTA."[11]

Dr. Massat told one of us her personal reason for writing to the Justice Department. Just as a researcher may be moved to take action during a study when it reveals public health dangers, she said, what she had seen of the penalization of protective mothers warranted some action, such as a Justice Department investigation. (The Justice Department did not respond.)

Another story reveals a similar pattern of overreaching by CPS. In January 1996, the *New York Post* reported that New York City's Child Welfare Administration (CWA) had suspended Rosalie Harman, a senior-level supervisor, for purportedly "violating the agency's press policy."[12] But according to the *Post*, "agency sources said Harmon [*sic*] has been a target of retribution by CWA officials since 1993, when she testified without permission before a state Senate panel about a bitter custody battle" (p. 4).

That "bitter custody battle" involved a child who was abruptly removed from her mother's custody and placed in foster care for nearly a year and half because the mother had allegedly made a "false" report of sexual abuse. (In fact, mental health professionals confirmed the girl's credible disclosure of sexual abuse, which had originally been reported by an eyewitness—not the mother.) The case attracted public and legislative attention when the

then eight-year-old girl nearly died of anorexia nervosa after being transferred to her father's custody. Harman, who heard about the case after a
fresh report concerning the child's alarming emaciation, obtained CWA's
file on the case in an effort to learn how the child's condition had deterio-
rated to such an extent. What she found in the file prompted her to write,
in a sworn affidavit:

> The Brooklyn field office worker pressed for a physical examination of the
> child . . . [and] the father maintained he did not want to be investigated for
> child sex abuse. For some inexplicable reason the case was closed. . . . The
> sex abuse protocol therefore was incomplete.[13]

Senator David A. Paterson, who chaired a New York Senate hearing that
investigated the agency's misconduct in this case, told the *Post* that at the
time Harman testified before his committee about her agency's mishandling of this case, she expressed a fear of retaliation. Thinking back on it,
Paterson said, "I should not have allowed her to testify. I have always wres-
tled with my conscience about the peril I exposed this woman to within
her agency" (p. 4). Paterson was one of several who believed that Harman
was being punished because of her testimony—that is, because she had
told the truth about a mishandled investigation of alleged child sex abuse
in which the father was given preferential treatment and the child's welfare
was jeopardized.

A week after Paterson shared his suspicions with the *Post,* he repeated
them in a letter to Lee J. Radek, then bureau chief of the Public Integrity
Division of the U.S. Department of Justice:

> A key whistle blower at my 1993 investigative hearing into the [name with-
> held] case made headlines last week when she was suspended without pay.
> The penalization of this whistle blower came as no surprise to me in that I
> had been apprised of the fact that she had been reproached [by her superior]
> in front of several of her colleagues for [making] inquiries into the [name
> withheld] case. I, too, as an elected state official have met only with the most
> severe form of resistance each time I've attempted to investigate malfeasance
> of agencies and judges over the handling of the [name withheld] matter.
> Quite honestly, I found the reaction of agency officials, judges and elected
> officials to be formidable and frightening. My concern is that the punish-
> ment of this whistle blower will have a chilling effect on other potential in-
> formants unless there is a concerted effort made to crack open this case once
> and for all.[14]

One final way in which CPS agencies play God in protective mother cases is by assuming the power to redefine a case's facts and legal procedure in order to change its outcome.

A District of Columbia case illustrates how CPS officials can do this, playing judge *and* God at the same time. The mother in this case lived in Maryland, where she was litigating a divorce from a man she believed had sexually abused her two boys, aged four and seven. The Maryland court heard "emergency" allegations from the law guardian that the mother represented "a very real risk of flight with the children," urging the court to restrict her to supervised visits with her children. The judge, however, refused.

But the law guardian was in simultaneous contact with a "higher" authority: the CPS agency of Washington, D.C., where the father lived. Even as the Maryland court was hearing actual evidence, and deciding that no emergency existed, CPS caseworkers, based entirely on hearsay and guesswork (without even a pending D.C. case to give them jurisdiction), were already deciding that they knew better.

Before the Maryland court had discounted the charges against the mother, a caseworker for the District of Columbia CPS had already written a memorandum stating that her agency wanted to "bring the case into DC Courts" in order "to have the visitations with the mother changed to SUPERVISED."[15]

To accomplish this result, CPS did not hesitate to rewrite the facts of the case that was proceeding in Maryland. The caseworker's memorandum contained several serious inaccuracies:

- The caseworker stated that the "children are continuing to be placed in the middle of the parents' battle." In fact, two separate evaluators had already *refused* to conclude that the mother was coaching or manipulating the children.[16]
- The caseworker wrote: "It is feared that the mother may kidnap the children and run or harm the children in some way." This is precisely what was alleged in the Maryland court, but no evidence was ever presented to support the charge, and the only court that heard the charge rejected it.
- The caseworker claimed that an evaluator appointed by the Maryland court had said that the mother "has no rational thoughts at this time," that she "is getting worst [*sic*]," that her "disorder is hard to treat," and that she "fired 4–5 of her attorneys." *Not*

one of these statements appears in the evaluator's extensive testimony.

On the very day the Maryland court signed an order refusing to find an emergency or to limit the mother's custody or visitation, CPS in the District of Columbia filed its own petition—thus commencing the case all over again in a new jurisdiction—and seized the children, refusing the mother access to them. CPS restricted the mother to supervised visits of two hours per week and even cut off her telephone contact with the children. The father, meanwhile, was given custody and completely unrestricted access to them both, despite the abuse allegations against him.

The allegations against the father did not lack evidentiary support. A therapist documented that the children reported to her, spontaneously, that their father had kicked the elder boy in the crotch, tickled his private parts, withheld food from him, and threatened to kill him and his mother by setting fire to their house. She also reported that one of the elder boy's teachers had observed him flinch when the teacher placed his hand near the boy's head. The boy said he was afraid to visit his father.[17]

But CPS appeared quite ready to leave the facts behind. For example, its petition charging the mother with "neglect" claimed that the Maryland court had already given the father primary custody. That was untrue: the parents had shared equal time and custodial rights with the children.[18] The petition also claimed that the children had "changed their story" about the alleged abuse by their father in January 2001 to be "consistent with [the mother's] account of events"—a very suspicious-sounding circumstance. Yet this claim, too, is not supported by the record.

As the months wore on, and the mother struggled in vain to have her children returned to her, CPS's claims against her—which, as we have seen, had never had much connection to reality—became increasingly bizarre. Eventually a D.C. police detective assigned to the case claimed in a sworn deposition that the mother posed a threat to the children because the "thought crossed my mind" that the mother "would enter into a murder suicide pack [*sic*] . . . with her and the children" if she lost custody to the father. As for how the detective came to believe this danger existed, she admitted she had not consulted a psychiatrist but said, "You know, you hear about it in the news all the time."[19] Perhaps she believed herself capable of reading the mother's mind—which is less surprising than it sounds, since CPS had already proved itself capable of reinventing facts and moving a case from one court system to another to achieve the results it wanted.

False CPS Records

We have seen (in chapter 5) that law guardians can produce records that are selective, or even false, in order to serve the "contractual" purpose of persuading a family court judge to punish the mother. Anti–social service agencies can do the same thing. In fact, the unchecked power and secrecy that characterize CPS agencies make them a perfect breeding ground for false or misleading records. Facts are easily distorted in an environment isolated from scrutiny.

Suppose a CPS agency files a petition against a mother that contains provably false statements. In theory, this should be easy to correct. In practice, even patently false statements in a petition can have very serious consequences for the protective mother. For example, a false "tip" that a mother is mentally ill and dangerous may prompt a judge to order psychological evaluations before anyone bothers to check the accuracy of the charge. The evaluators, knowing from the petition what CPS wants to find, can then determine that the mother has a "histrionic" or "narcissistic" personality, or is overly "enmeshed" with her children, or suffers from one or another of the vague diagnoses favored in family courts. This, in turn, gives the judge a rationale for removing the children from the mother, even if it turns out (as it often does) that the original "tip" was completely baseless.

False records can become "true" in another way as well. Certain actions, such as child custody, can become self-justifying over time. That is, after a child has been removed from its mother and placed with the father, the child will gradually accept its new environment (even if originally he or she vehemently objected to it), so that after enough time with the father CPS can resist a return to the mother's custody by claiming this would needlessly "uproot" the child. Similarly, when a young child is placed in foster care and is told repeatedly that the only way out of a stranger's home is to live with the father, most children, after sufficient time, will choose that alternative over foster care. In this way, false statements that result in children being removed from protective mothers gradually become "factoids." The mother may prove them false and still never recover her improperly removed children.

To make matters worse, there is really nothing to stop caseworkers from making false statements in the first place, whether in case note files or in sworn documents submitted to the court. This is because caseworkers generally enjoy legal immunity from lawsuits, even if their inaccurate statements in agency records or court documents wrongly cause a child to be removed from an innocent mother. We explore this issue—and possible reforms in the law—in greater detail in part III, chapter 11.

Spurious Neglect Petitions

We have already seen that the formal complaints, or petitions, by which CPS agencies seek the removal of children from mothers may be more factitious than real. It is appropriate at this point to examine this phenomenon more closely.

The laws governing family courts throughout the country, though they differ in some details from state to state, provide a generally consistent definition of child neglect. New York law defines a neglected child as one "whose physical, mental or emotional condition has been impaired or is in imminent danger of becoming impaired as a result of the failure of his parent or other person legally responsible for his care to exercise a minimum degree of care."[20] In Colorado, a parent is guilty of neglect if he or she "has abandoned the child or has subjected him or her to mistreatment or abuse or . . . has suffered or allowed another to mistreat or abuse the child without taking lawful means to stop such mistreatment or abuse and prevent it from recurring."[21] Similarly, California law defines child neglect as "the negligent treatment or the maltreatment of a child by a person responsible for the child's welfare under circumstances indicating harm or threatened harm to the child's health or welfare."[22]

It is noteworthy that none of these definitions includes the making of unfounded sex abuse allegations as a kind of child neglect. Indeed, even to the extent that these definitions embrace psychological harm to a child, they certainly seem to require much more than a showing that a mother suspects abuse by the father. The District of Columbia's definition of "psychological abuse" is typical: it requires a showing that a mother suffers from an actual, definable mental illness and, *in addition,* proof that this mental condition poses a real threat to the well-being of the child.[23] In *all* the statutes cited above some actual danger to the child's health or welfare is required in order to reach a finding of "child neglect."

Statutes authorizing a family court, at the urging of CPS, to remove children from their homes *before* the completion of a court proceeding— that is, before a parent has been found guilty of abuse or neglect—are even more strictly drawn. States must show that "removal is necessary to avoid imminent risk to the child's life or health" (New York);[24] that "continuing the child's place of residence or in the care and custody of the person responsible for the child's care and custody would present a danger to that child's life or health in the reasonably foreseeable future" (Colorado);[25] or that "[t]he child would be subjected to an imminent threat to life or health to the extent that severe or irremediable injury would be likely to result if the child were returned to or left in the custody of his parents . . . and . . . there are no alternatives less drastic than removal of the child from his home which could reasonably and adequately protect the child's life or health pending a final hearing" (Virginia).[26] Again, these statutes represent the norm throughout the fifty states.

In practice, however, CPS applies extremely elastic definitions to these laws, making it possible for mothers to lose their children—even before a trial or hearing—for reasons such as the following: (1) spending too much time litigating; (2) failing to "insulate" children from the legal proceedings (even when the children are too young to understand the process, let alone to be brainwashed); (3) making an abuse report that is"not totally true"; (4) changing therapists for her child without first obtaining permission from a family court.

It is evident that none of these claims fits the statutory definitions of neglect, let alone of an "emergency" justifying removal of children. Yet for each of these reasons CPS has sought—and obtained—the removal of young children from their mothers' homes.

In fact, in some cases we have examined, CPS's accusations were apparently not even believed by CPS. For example, a Brooklyn, New York, neglect petition charged the mother with having made a false report—but also charged her with having failed to protect her child from the reported abuse and charged the father with abuse as well! Obviously not even CPS could have believed all these allegations. And many of the cases we studied included allegations against the father that CPS never bothered to investigate fully. Evidently, it suits CPS's ultimate agenda in many cases to allege the unfitness of *both* parents; after all, that makes removal to foster care that much easier to justify. And once children are in foster care, CPS can exert considerable control over them (control that can yield statements from the children in support of CPS's case) by making it clear that their release from foster care depends on their accepting the home CPS has chosen for them—as we will see in more detail below.

Of course, CPS agencies would not generate spurious petitions if these were not generally accepted by family court judges. In practice, few judges demand that CPS agencies adhere to the legal standards set for them (and those who do, such as the New York family court judge described in chapter 2, are likely to find themselves driven out of the system altogether). Not only is there widespread judicial tolerance of improperly founded petitions and removal orders; judges sometimes even *press* CPS to file a neglect petition on the flimsiest of grounds.[27]

Below are a few case histories involving spurious petitions for neglect and the ensuing orders removing a child or children from the mother's custody. They are typical of many similar cases.

THE "FALSE REPORTING" MOTHER

In 1993, a young British-born Brooklyn, New York, mother fled to a battered women's shelter with her three-year-old son. She told workers there that her husband had been abusing her and the boy. (A health professional confirmed, anonymously, her suspicion that the father abused the child.)[28]

In September 1995, the boy disclosed that he had been abused in his father's apartment—nicked on his penis by his father's apartment mate, then beaten savagely with a belt by his father—"because of the blood he had to clean up," according to the mother. Twice that month, she reported her suspicions to the CPS "hotline," which found enough support for her charges to list them as "indicated," child welfare jargon for "substantiated." Their reports noted a "small cut" under the boy's penis and bruising on his buttocks.[29]

The mother had particular reason to be concerned: a hospital report made in 1994 described the father as "chronic paranoid type," displaying at times "acute mania, with paranoid, agitated, violent, irritable behavior."[30]

A Brooklyn court appointed a law guardian and an evaluator. But visits between father and son continued, and the mother, feeling that nothing had been done to protect her son, turned to the district attorney's office for help. She met with a "counselor" for domestic violence and child abuse complaints, but still no progress seemed to result.

Then, in May 1996, the case took a new turn when the mother brought the child to a hospital following further disclosures of sexual abuse. The hospital found no physical evidence of abuse this time, although the child reportedly said that he had been fondled on his genitals. But now the "counselor" at the DA's office, who had brushed aside the abuse reports, swung into action—against the mother. More than seven months after the mother's first visit seeking help, she suddenly found herself summoned, with her son, to the counselor's office for a second interview. The same day, the counselor finally phoned CPS with her own abuse report—seeking action against the mother.

CPS was more than happy to oblige. The next day, its officials filed papers in Brooklyn Family Court accusing the mother of child neglect and seeking the boy's "emergency" removal from the mother's home. A family court judge issued the order, and the mad family court merry-go-round was off to a typical start.

No one who has read this far will be surprised to learn that the allegations used to obtain this "emergency" removal were wildly inaccurate. For example, CPS's petition against the mother stated:

> Since approximately March 1996, the respondent mother has made several *false reports* of child abuse/neglect to the State Central Register alleging injuries to the subject child. On several occasions [the mother] has sought medical attention for the child and made *false accusations* of abuse or neglect to the medical staff.[31]

These sworn statements were untrue: as CPS must have known, the mother's charges had been at least partly substantiated. The reports were at most unproved; they were not "false."

CPS was not finished. The petition concluded: "The respondent mother has previously been diagnosed with mental illness and has exhibited homicidal tendencies."[32]

These allegations were clearly intended to establish an "emergency" sufficient to justify the child's removal. But they were untrue: no mental health professional had ever diagnosed the mother with any mental illness, let alone with "homicidal tendencies"![33] This was a critical inaccuracy.

Paradoxically, having charged the mother with making false reports, CPS rounded out its proof of an "emergency" by charging the father with, among other things, having "beat[en] the subject child with a belt" and standing silent while his roommate "cut the subject child on his penis, causing him to sustain a laceration." (In other words, the mother had falsely reported abuse, but the abuse had occurred.) This charge was intended only to justify the child's removal into foster care, however; once the boy was away from his mother, CPS forgot all about the charges against the father.

As is usual in family courts, the falsity of the charges against the mother did not attract undue attention. The law guardian sided with CPS, telling a reporter that removal had been necessary because the mother "was making a series of accusations that . . . were unfounded." (As shown above,

New York law requires an "imminent" threat to the child's health or welfare to justify removal; how making unfounded accusations, even if this had actually occurred, could constitute such an imminent threat is anyone's guess.) Family court proceedings dragged on for more than a year before the mother even got a chance to challenge CPS's claims—during which time she was allowed only two hours a week of supervised visitation with her son. This occurred despite the fact that the court-appointed evaluator's written report did not even describe the mother as dangerous.[34]

The mother told a reporter that the law guardian and CPS repeatedly pressed her to agree to give the father unsupervised visits; if she did that, she said, they would agree to return the child to her custody. She held her ground for months, insisting that only supervision could adequately protect the child when in contact with the father. Eventually, however, she was forced to compromise. In exchange for continuing supervision of the father's visits, she agreed to leave the child's *legal* custody with the state, though she was given primary physical custody. This meant that the state had ultimate supervisory control; CPS had the power to "monitor" the mother for another eighteen months or longer.

During this time, the mother was subject to unannounced home visits by CPS at any time, and required to attend "therapy" sessions—always with counselors who worked for CPS or were recommended by the agency. She also had to report regularly to a CPS caseworker.

When CPS originally removed this mother's son from her home, the agency had claimed she had a mental illness and "homicidal tendencies." As we have seen, these claims could never have been taken seriously, and were in fact used only to obtain the removal and to keep the child under CPS control for over a year thereafter. Besides, the father quickly seemed to lose interest in visiting his son (and any visits were supervised), so there were rarely opportunities for additional abuse reports that could be claimed as evidence of the mother's "illness." But with the child officially in CPS's custody, even while living with his mother, CPS hit on a different set of allegations for the next step.

CPS's constant interviews, "therapy" sessions, and unannounced visits gave the caseworkers ample opportunity to observe the mother's weaknesses as a homemaker. The mother has described herself as suffering from Attention Deficit Disorder, and she often had difficulty completing several household tasks at once. Though no one had previously attacked her fitness as a mother—a CPS caseworker who visited the child at his mother's home early in the case "observed child to be calm" and noted that he "appearance [sic] well"[35]—caseworkers now began to describe the mother as "forgetful" and "sloppy." They filled their case notes with references to her confusion at home, her unwashed dishes, the appointments she missed or was late for. Quickly, the mother achieved a new "running record": as a mother so sloppy, distractible, and overburdened that she could not care for her child.

This sounds almost comical, but it was not funny to the mother: she described her life as "constant pressure" and worried daily about the next CPS visit. She had doubts about her own competence. CPS, she was sure, would find something wrong with her house again. What would it be this time? What would happen to her? Could they take away her child again? What if they found something undone, something out of place? Needless to say, the mother's anxiety did not improve her performance.

Meanwhile, CPS caseworkers were not content with criticizing every aspect of the mother's homemaking. They also steadily pressed her to place her child in foster care, even if just for a weekend. Between the constant criticism, the helpless sense of living in a fishbowl, and the repeated urgings to place her child in foster care, the mother began to give way. After months of urging from the CPS, she agreed to place her son in a foster home—only temporarily, she thought.

CPS pressure did not stop there, however. Eventually the caseworkers persuaded her to relinquish her parental rights altogether (and to have her child placed for adoption) lest she face a long, difficult court battle trying to prove her parental fitness.

We have dwelt on the details of this case, which bear repeating—if only in summary—because they show how CPS intervention, through the family court process, can effectively reshape reality. The case began with some unverified and inaccurate entries in a CPS file; it passed into false statements in a needless neglect petition; it ultimately became a war of attrition against a mother whose child had already lived more under the control of CPS than of his mother. After seeing the child welfare system take her son, hold him for over a year, place her under constant supervision, and threaten her with more attacks, the mother was unable to resist what had become, by then, a self-fulfilling prophecy. Even though she had fought vigorously to keep her son, she could not fight forever against an adversary that could change the rules whenever it chose.

THE MOTHER WITH NO "ENERGY AND TIME LEFT FOR PARENTING"

In 1989, a New Mexico mother whose ex-boyfriend may have sexually abused their four-year-old daughter found herself charged by CPS with "neglect." The reason? CPS alleged that the mother "invested so much energy and time in the legal issues" that she "may not be able to have energy and time left for parenting."

How could a woman's commitment to "legal issues" such as attempting to protect her child from an apparently abusive relationship constitute child neglect? Here is how CPS built a catch-22 for this particular mother:

During custody litigation between the couple (who were never married), the couple's child reportedly showed signs of having been sexually abused. CPS records show that sex abuse "referrals" were made to the agency by two psychologists, one of whom was the child's therapist. CPS also acknowledged that the girl "had intermittent vomiting and diarrhea following visits with the father," as well as "sleeping problems, fear of the dark and weight loss."[36] The mother's attempts to persuade CPS to start official proceedings against the child's father were unsuccessful; CPS claimed that the reports of abuse were not substantiated by physical evidence. However, CPS did offer the office of a "Court Clinic" for visits in an attempt to neutralize the "conflict" that was clearly taking place between the parents.

The mother told us that the father would "erupt" whenever he saw her. An affidavit submitted by the child's attorney confirms that the parents fought during visits. However, when the mother refused to bring her child for a scheduled visit, telling the clinic that she did not want to expose the child to any more of her father's outbursts, she was arrested and jailed for contempt of court.

Not long afterward, the clinic decided that supervising these visits was too difficult. At that point, CPS immediately sought the child's removal into foster care. CPS claimed this was necessary because "the Court Clinic does not have the staff to provide the necessary monitoring" and because "both parents have invested so much energy and time in the legal issues that they may not be able to have energy and time left for parenting."[37] A family court judge promptly removed the child from her mother's home.

In other words, CPS justified the removal of a four-year-old child from her mother because the mother attended to "the legal issues" and because of conflicts with the father that she says were not her fault and that in any case could have been contained by supervision! Just as amazingly, CPS's petition did not allege any actual deficiency in the mother's parenting abilities as a result of her attention to the case.[38]

Family court placed the girl in the custody of the State of New Mexico Human Services Department. She stayed in a foster home for several months. And now CPS's true goal emerged. Had its complaints been genuinely directed at "both" parents, as its papers claimed, it would never have recommended placing the child in her father's custody.

But that is what CPS did. Having achieved its goal of removing the girl from her mother, CPS never actually pursued the charge against the father; like the charge against the father in the previous case, this one was evidently only a means to get the child into foster care. Instead, according to the mother, CPS urged that the child be placed with the father, who gained sole custody of the girl after a three-month interval of foster care.

Ironically, the charge of "excessive litigation" then became a self-fulfilling prophecy, as the mother waged a two-year political campaign to regain her daughter, reaching out to support groups, news media, and politicians. CPS saw all this merely as "proof" of the mother's unfitness, and eventually it recommended—successfully—that even her visits with her child be suspended.

Having lost her daughter entirely to CPS, the mother finally, painfully began to rebuild her life. But the effects of the agency's campaign against her remained for years. Increasingly suspicious, the mother hesitated to date; in fact, she told one of us that she feared having another child, worrying that CPS would take the new one away just as it had the first.

THE "BRAINWASHING/COACHING" MOTHER

In 1986, a California case began hopefully for a protective mother when local CPS officials filed a petition against the father of a three-year-old girl, charging him with (among other things) "cutting" the "minor's perineum [between the vagina and the rectum] with a knife."[39] A caseworker testified in support of the charge. The child also made consistent reports of abuse and repeated them to a family court judge.[40] In response to all this, the judge ordered that the father's visits be supervised by CPS, and he scheduled a hearing for a later date to determine whether visitation should continue to be supervised.

But before the next court date, according to the mother's later testimony (submitted in writing to a congressional committee), the father applied for—and received—a transfer of his case to another court some thirty miles away. Immediately he began an aggressive campaign to take custody of the child from the mother.[41]

A new CPS worker was assigned to the case. According to the mother, the new worker *withheld* from the judge her colleague's petition accusing the father of child abuse—along with forty-seven pages of supporting documentation.

In August 1987, CPS, citing the recommendations of the court-appointed family therapist, filed a petition seeking the child's placement in foster care.[42] Ignoring the existing record of abuse by the father, CPS claimed that removal was necessary because of "the custody dispute." Weirdly, CPS complained that the child—who had reported being abused by her father on several occasions—was "forced to play roles . . . in an attempt to please or appease her mother." The agency also complained that "the minor's mother behaves 'almost as if she is obsessed' with the belief that her daughter has been molested" and accused her of "coaching" the child to make reports of abuse.[43] Without further questions, the judge ordered the child placed in foster care for several months.

Thus, in classic family court fashion, the mother was judged more by her running record—the "party line" on her case, shared by auxiliary agents in collaboration with the judge—than by the facts.

In this hostile environment, battling CPS and an "expert" who did not believe her, the mother struggled to protect her daughter from what appeared to be continuing abuse. The child returned from visits with burns, scratches, and bruises.[44] CPS turned a deaf ear, refusing to investigate at least eight reports of alleged child abuse made by doctors and the child's therapist.[45]

When the child was released from foster care four months later, the father and mother were given joint physical custody, with legal custody retained by the state. The child continued to show symptoms of sexual abuse, including "genital warts, urinary tract infections, various vaginal infections, bruises on various places on her body and vaginal area [including] cuts, abrasions and lacerations."[46] But the reports were still ignored by CPS.

Finally, in February 1988, the child complained again of molestation by her father. Once again, the mother reported the disclosure to CPS, whose officials called her "irrational." Desperate, the mother took the girl out of state, in defiance of a court order forbidding her to do so (since the child was legally in the custody of CPS). Freed from CPS's restrictions concerning which doctors the mother could consult, the mother arranged for the child to be brought to a pediatric gynecologist in Oregon for testing. A colposcopic exam of the child's genitalia revealed a dramatic fact: the girl had a sexually transmitted disease. In her report, the examining physician noted, "After what appeared to be condyloma lesions . . . on the perineum, a biopsy was taken in the right lower perineal area [showing] definite condyloma infection." She summed up: "At this point, the conclusion has to be noted that the patient probably has contracted a known sexually transmitted infection, and therefore, the reasonable conclusion is that she has suffered sexual abuse."[47]

The pediatrician also told the mother that if these condyloma lesions had not been removed, the child would have run the risk of pelvic inflammatory disease and ensuing sterility.

The mother later told one of us that when she received this medical report, she was certain that CPS would have no choice but to prosecute the father for abuse and that the child would soon be given back to the mother's custody. Given the Oregon doctor's conclusions, who could blame her for believing that?

But she was wrong. A member of the mother's family contacted CPS and sent the agency a copy of this new medical report—showing that the young girl had a sexually transmitted disease—in the hope that the mother and child could return to California and that the child would be properly protected. The caseworker she spoke to, however, was unmoved. She insisted that the mother had "brainwashed" her child to believe she had been molested. Even physical evidence apparently meant nothing to an agency that had already made up its mind.

The family court judge had a federal warrant issued for the mother's arrest. She remained in hiding for four years, until she and her daughter were caught in 1992. While she was in jail, awaiting trial on parental kidnapping charges, a friend testified before a Congressional subcommittee in her support. She told a panel of congresspersons that "during the continuing processing by CPS," what should have been a straightforward abuse case "became convoluted and distorted."[48]

The mother was acquitted of the charge of parental abduction after she persuaded a jury that she had had no other choice under the circumstances but to abscond with the child in order to protect her from abuse. But incredibly, despite all the evidence that the child had been abused, the family court heeded CPS and eventually awarded custody to the father. On the day the court ruled in his favor, CPS "yanked" the child, according to her mother, "kicking and screaming," out of school to take her to the father's home. The child, then twelve years old, hardened by her experience in the "Underground Railroad," fled within a few months to a "safe house" connected with the Railroad.

This did not mean a reunion with her mother, however. The "safe house" operator, to protect the child from discovery and the forcible return to her father that might ensue, advised the mother against visiting her, with the result that she did not see her daughter until the girl reached the age of eighteen and was at last free of the family court's control.

By then, the years of futile court battles, oppression by CPS, and life as a fugitive had all taken their toll. The child had never received a formal education. The mother, not yet forty, was disillusioned and bitter. She told one of us: "I've suffered tremendously and I have very, very little expectation for society to ever reconcile with how cruelly the family courts treat sexually abused children."

Significantly, she perceived her own case not as an anomaly but as part of a larger picture. This fact deserves some consideration. What it illustrates, to an ethnomethodologist, is that the mother—through her own efforts to make practical sense out of the actions of the family court system—invoked the "documentary method of interpretation." In so doing, she saw her own case as "documenting" or "pointing to" an underlying social problem, namely, society's failure to grapple with how the courts treat sexual abuse. And in defining that problem, the mother had particularly harsh words for the behavior of the CPS agency that had been charged with protecting her daughter and had instead torn her from the parent who had tried to protect her: "CPS just shook my beliefs in democracy and freedom in America."

THE MOTHER WHO COMMUNICATED "FALSE INFORMATION" TO THE DOCTOR

In 1991, a divorcing New York mother of two young girls, a registered nurse, was awarded sole custody of her two daughters, aged three and seven. Several months later, after a weekend visit of both girls with their father, the mother made a report to CPS, claiming a suspicion of sexual abuse. CPS took no action; the father then persuaded the family court to move the children to his custody, claiming the mother was unstable.

About a year later, while the mother was litigating for the return of her daughters, the younger child complained to her of pelvic pain. She also had a high fever. The mother took her to a hospital, where doctors were baffled by the symptoms. The mother suggested the child might be suffering from "pelvic inflammatory disease" (PID), and explained that such inflammation could have resulted from sexual abuse. The mother went on to complain to the doctors that CPS had not told the family court all it knew about the medical evidence of her daughter's alleged abuse.

Thanks to the information given by the mother, the doctors made a report to CPS that child sexual abuse had been alleged.

A few days later, the mother was stunned by the arrival of a formal petition accusing *her* of neglecting her daughter. She was particularly mystified by the specifics of the accusation, which were based entirely on her attempt to aid in her daughter's diagnosis and her criticism of the agency. Evidently CPS believed that this amounted to a form of child abuse:

> Upon information and belief, on or about February 1, 1993 the Respondent [mother] caused false information to be given to representatives at Nyack Hospital resulting in the filing of a report of alleged child abuse or maltreatment [against the father] which alleged, inter alia, that the child has been sexually abused "regularly" by [the father]. Specifically, the report contained the false statement provided by the Respondent or her representative, that "child has a history of pelvic inflammatory disease;" and that the local Child Protective Services "withheld information from Family Court, given to her from [a child abuse expert], in which there was medical evidence that the child was sexually abused. . . . "[49]

CPS also cited the mother's efforts to publicize her children's plight as further evidence of "child neglect": "Upon information and belief, in or around January and February 1993, the Respondent distributed a 'flyer' in and around [the child's school], and Nyack Hospital while [the child] was a patient . . . alleging, inter alia, that her daughter without specificity has been sexually abused by [the father]" (p. 3).

The filing of this neglect petition was enough to prevent family court from returning the girls to their mother's custody. After all, how could a judge give children back to a mother who had been charged by a state agency with "neglect"? But the charges in the petition were baseless: the evidence indicates that the mother gave a full and accurate medical history. And how could her attempts to enlist support in her effort to protect her daughter amount to "neglect"? Nevertheless, CPS used the wording of the petition to serve its "contractual" purpose of convincing the family court not to restore custody to the mother.

A few months later, when the mother picked up her daughters for a visit, the elder girl complained of pain in her vagina so severe she wanted to be taken to a hospital. The mother did so. This time, the medical evidence of abuse prompted officials to report that there had been "sexual offenses" against the girl, including "aggravated sexual abuse in the first degree . . . in the second degree . . . and/or rape in the second degree."[50]

Confronted with this new evidence of abuse, CPS began to change its tune: now it too accused the father of abuse, and had both children placed in foster care instead of in the father's custody. But even then, CPS's attack on the mother did not abate. Now the agency charged the mother with neglect, not for giving "false" information to the doctor, but for "failure to protect" her children from abuse. In other words, when CPS disbelieved the mother, she was guilty of neglect because her information alleging abuse was "false"; but now that it was considered true, she was as guilty as if she had never reported it at all! This patently baseless allegation against the mother was used, like other charges we have discussed above, to persuade a family court to place the children in foster care rather than back in their mother's custody.[51]

In fact, CPS's new attitude was only a facade. Hardly had the children been placed in foster homes when CPS dropped the charges against the father, while still maintaining that the mother was "neglectful." Now the stage was set for the father to regain full custody. CPS bowed out of the case, having taken no action of any kind, throughout its long involvement, to protect the children from abuse.

Having been the target of one false CPS petition after another, the mother turned to activism. Despite being placed under a gag order by the court forbidding her to speak out about her case, she marched every weekday in front of the family court for a month, together with about thirty other women, carrying placards denouncing CPS and family court. She also went on a week-long hunger strike to seek an investigation of the family court system.[52] As her protests continued, she received support from an important official, the chief medical examiner for the county where the litigation had been taking place. He told *New York Newsday:*

> This could be one of those cases where mistakes were made down the line. I have reviewed all the records. . . . I wrote an affidavit to the court. But I have run up against a brick wall. . . . There is much in this case that is suspicious, but it's been screwed up.[53]

Yet, in spite of the public support for this woman and the public criticism from the chief medical examiner, the mother—who had already lost custody—lost all visitation rights with both daughters as well.

After years of failed attempts to protect her children, this mother found peace in the belief that final salvation was at hand. As part of her daily routine, the mother read from Revelation those verses dealing with the Last Days. Her critiques of the family court system became almost biblical in tone: she has said she "strongly" believed that a few "token children would first have to die" as a "sacrifice" to the "evil system" before it improves.[54]

In 1986, a mother in Brooklyn, New York, lost custody of her six-year-old daughter for allegedly failing to protect the girl from abuse that, according to CPS, never happened.

The couple had divorced in 1983, and the mother—who, by agreement, had full custody of the couple's only child—took the child to live in her parents' Brooklyn home. In May 1986, during a visit by the girl's father, the child's grandmother saw the father holding the six-year-old girl tightly on him as he lay on his back, his pants open, his pelvis gyrating underneath her. When the grandmother separated them, she saw that the father and the girl were both "wet." The girl later confirmed that her father had played this "game" with her several times, and that she did not like it.

The girl's mother had not been present during the visit, but when she learned what had happened she agreed with her mother that the father should not visit the girl, or at least not without supervision. He then filed an action against her, seeking full custody of the child.

The Brooklyn Society for the Prevention of Cruelty to Children was the agency assigned, under state and city contract, to investigate (and pursue) child abuse cases in Brooklyn at that time. The girl confirmed her grandmother's eyewitness account of sexual abuse to BSPCC's investigator. But after a cursory investigation—during which the father refused to be interviewed—the agency filed a petition that charged *both* parents with child abuse or neglect.[55] The charges against the father arose simply enough from the eyewitness report of his mother-in-law. Those against the mother, however, contained an Orwellian ambiguity. She was accused either of failing to protect her daughter from abuse or of endangering the girl by reporting a "situation" that was "not totally true." In other words, she was guilty of neglecting her daughter whether or not her ex-husband had abused her. *He* might be innocent; *she* was guilty under any circumstances. And yet no one (apart from CPS) had ever accused her of any mistreatment of the child whatsoever!

CPS's petition (like others we have examined here) was sworn to by a person who knew nothing of the facts. That was natural, perhaps, considering that it contained critical misstatements. The mother was absent from the house when the alleged abuse occurred (and so could not have prevented it); and she did not make the report (and so could not have made a false one). Yet, with a bizarre double standard we have seen in other cases above, CPS was prepared to condemn her based solely on charges made against her ex-husband.

The mother appeared for a court-ordered psychiatric examination and produced her daughter for examination as well. On October 17, 1986, before the results of any tests were available to the court, and no evidence of any kind suggested any danger to the child while in her mother's home, a Brooklyn Family Court judge threatened the mother that if she did not undergo a second, psychological, evaluation within fourteen days, the girl would be removed from her home and placed in foster care. This threat was all the more remarkable because the judge claimed, falsely, that the mother had agreed to such an evaluation and that the father had already had a psychological evaluation. (He had not; nor was there any earlier agreement that either parent would have a psychological exam.) CPS's lawyer, who knew full well that these statements were not true, stood silent.[56]

CPS's real agenda became clear at once. The mother made an appointment for a psychological evaluation the business day immediately following the court's order. But on the way to the evaluation, she suffered chest pains and checked herself into a hospital, fearing a heart attack. Doctors concluded she was suffering from anxiety—hardly to be wondered at, under the circumstances.

That was enough for CPS. The very next day, without even giving notice to the mother or her lawyer, CPS's lawyer demanded—and got—an order from the family court removing the young girl into foster care. CPS's lawyer angrily complained that the mother was "resistant" to the psychological evaluation—even though she had agreed to the appointment and had only missed it for medical reasons—and went on to say, brutally, that even if the father *had* sexually abused the girl ("What he did or didn't do to this child, that may or may not amount to sexual abuse, I do not know"), her daughter should be removed forthwith from her mother's home, because "if she [the mother] has anxiety attacks, then maybe she can't care for the child, and maybe the child is suffering the same anxiety attacks she is suffering."[57] He also accused the mother, falsely, of refusing to obey court orders.[58] (She had not violated any court order.)

As a result of CPS's misstatements, Brooklyn Family Court removed the girl from her mother's home. By contrast, the father, who had been accused of abuse by an eyewitness (and the child victim), had refused to be interviewed by CPS, and had not been seen by a psychologist, got red-carpet treatment from CPS, which would soon drop the charge against him altogether.

It is worth noting that the removal caused by CPS was not only unnecessary and cruel—it was illegal. First, it was made without a constitutionally required hearing. Second, the removal violated New York law, since there was no showing of overriding necessity.[59] Finally, the removal violated the family court's own order, which had granted the mother fourteen days to have the psychological evaluation, of which only four had elapsed when the judge signed the removal order.[60]

CPS had not finished with its attacks on this mother. When the mother's lawyer sought the dismissal of the charges against her, based on the obvious factual errors in the petition, CPS simply rewrote the petition to allege that the mother had caused the girl to develop symptoms of abuse by wrongly believing the abuse had occurred. When it was pointed out that no expert who had evaluated the child, or the mother, had ever made such a claim, CPS and the family court judge quickly located another expert— the notorious Dr. Arthur Green—who (after talking to the judge and being told that no abuse had occurred) obligingly diagnosed the mother as suffering from a "circumscribed psychosis" that enabled her to transmit symptoms of abuse to the child. (This sort of bizarre mental health diagnosis, seldom encountered anywhere but in family courts, will be discussed below in chapter 7.) CPS's lawyer also told an evaluating psychologist (as he later admitted during trial) that the mother was "paranoid" because she believed her daughter was going to be put up for adoption while in foster care. Yet this fear could hardly be called "paranoid"—it was, in fact, completely justified: an official of the foster care agency itself admitted in testimony that he had told the mother her daughter would be adopted.[61] To CPS, anything the mother said or believed, even when it was true, was proof of "mental illness."

As in other cases we have discussed, once CPS had secured the child's removal into foster care, it abandoned the charge against the father. It also abandoned the factual claims made against the mother and amended the petition no fewer than three times in order to ensure that the mother would never regain custody.

The plan worked. The mother never regained custody; in fact, family court ultimately awarded the allegedly abusive father full custody of the child. Almost at once after going to live with him, the girl (then eight years old) declined into anorexia so severe that her life was threatened; a treating physician called her "by far the worst case of emaciation I have ever seen."[62] The mother rushed her daughter to a hospital for emergency treatment (the father, a physician, had refused either to hospitalize her or to monitor her condition with necessary blood tests), an act which, according to later testimony, may have saved the girl's life.[63] How did CPS respond? It refused to investigate the father either for continuing sexual abuse (severe anorexia in a girl so young is often a symptom of sexual abuse) or for medical neglect (for failing to treat his daughter's life-threatening condition). Family court then condemned the mother for giving the child medical treatment without the father's consent and cut off the mother's visits and telephone contact, even barring her from writing the child letters.

This mother turned to activism, appearing on dozens of television and radio programs to publicize what had happened in her case and others. On several occasions, when CPS learned of an upcoming appearance, CPS's lawyer contacted the show's producers and maligned the mother to them.

This mother, like some of the others whose stories have been told here, bore long-lasting scars from the senseless destruction of her relationship with her daughter. For years, she did not buy new clothes or date men. In fact, she did not even go for gynecological examinations. She told family members that she could not think of herself as a woman, let alone as a mother. And the thought of having another child was terrifying: what if this one, too, should be taken away?

Conclusion

The case histories summarized above are representative of a national problem. When sexual abuse allegations are involved, CPS agencies make crucial decisions about the fate of children without any apparent concern for the children's interests. Accusations seem to be made, instead, with another agenda in mind: the desire to remove a child from a protective parent, to place the child in foster care, and then to take whatever final steps are necessary to make it appear that no abuse could ever have occurred. If this means basing neglect petitions on rumors, baseless tips, unfounded "diagnoses," or even outright untruths, CPS will take that step. Unchecked power and unqualified secrecy give CPS agencies the power to do virtually whatever they please.

In recent years, the child welfare system has come under attack for letting children die or suffer serious maltreatment in their homes. CPS's defenders have replied that the agencies are understaffed and overworked. The eagerness of the system to remove healthy children into foster care for the ultimate purpose of placing them in the custody of men credibly accused of sexual abuse is, therefore, particularly outrageous in the context of a CPS system supposedly too "overburdened" to protect children from real abuse.

For instance, from *Child Maltreatment 2002,* the annual report prepared by the National Child Abuse and Neglect Data System (NCANDS),[64] we learn that "approximately 1,400 children died of abuse or neglect during the year 2002, a rate of 1.9 children per 100,000 children in the population."[65] Perhaps the time that CPS spends "rehabilitating" relationships between sexually abusive fathers and their child victims could be better spent preventing child fatalities.

All in all, it should be clear that the madness of today's family courts would be impossible without the assistance of CPS agencies, which use precious resources to pursue false charges against innocent mothers who have reported suspicions of sexual abuse.

Chapter 7

Mental Health Quackery

In 2003, New York matrimonial attorney Timothy Tippins published in the *New York Law Journal* a cautionary article on the use of mental health theories in family courts. Tippins, former chair of the New York State Bar Association's Family Law Section and Task Force on Family Law, first stated the obvious: "the role of mental health opinion in court has proliferated in recent decades and nowhere is its impact more profound than in child custody litigation." Then he gave this warning:

> Mental health opinions can spell the end of the line for the disfavored parent because of the indicia of authoritativeness they have come to carry . . . that emanates from the assumption that the opinion rests on scientifically reliable and valid principles and procedures. Sadly, that assumption is unwarranted. . . . [S]ome courts are deeply influenced by these opinions and reach custodial decisions unaware that scientifically they stand on feet of clay.[1]

If the reliance of courts on meretricious "science" poses a problem for "the disfavored parent" in ordinary custody litigation, it is downright dangerous in cases involving child sex abuse allegations. In these cases, pseudoscience regularly does serious damage to mothers who raise such allegations and to the children who may be victims. In fact, hostile epithets posing as scientific "syndromes" have played a central role in the backlash of the family courts against protective parents. Branded as "vindictive," "calculating," "manipulative" and/or "hysterical," "narcissistic," or "paranoid" on the basis of one questionable theory or other, women lose custody of their children—and in many cases all visitation rights as well.

The importance of these pseudoscientific labels in a closed system like the family courts can hardly be exaggerated. They establish a "running record"—an informal history that is invoked at critical points in the decision-making process, eclipsing every other feature of the case, including evidence that the mother in question is functional and rational. They may even overshadow objective evidence of possible sexual abuse to a child. Mothers dogged by these court-generated "running records" find that nothing they say is taken seriously—except as further "evidence" against themselves. Yet their only "sickness" may be their attempt to protect their children from abuse.

Specious "mental illness" labels applied to protective mothers can corrupt the judicial process in several ways. For one thing, they can cause family courts to overlook evidence of abuse because that evidence dovetails with "symptoms" of one of the mental health theories whose effect is to discredit accusing mothers. Second, they allow courts to punish mothers for making sex abuse allegations that are determined to be *unproven* as if the allegations were found to be *maliciously fabricated,* by labeling the accusation as part of a mental illness that will supposedly cause the mother to continue a "pattern of denigration" if she is not deprived of custody and otherwise penalized. Third, they can feed a system that is already suspicious of protective mothers "psychological" reasons to believe that the mother will kidnap her children and flee the jurisdiction, reasons such as claiming her personality is "grandiose" or "paranoid." Fourth, such theories can cause courts to do precisely what is most dangerous to abused children—that is, they can cut the children completely off from the parent who believes them and wants to protect them from the abuse they report.

Most of all, perhaps, mental health quackery functions as the theoretical glue that holds together all the elements of malfunction we have been examining: judicial overreaching, unregulated law guardians and social service agencies, misplaced priorities, systemic prejudices, and unchecked power.

Genuine experts have already noted some of the dangers inherent in introducing psychological theories into domestic litigation. Psychiatrist Jonathan W. Gould, in *Conducting Scientifically Crafted Child Custody Evaluations* (1998), specifically cautioned judges against overreliance on an expert's opinions, giving undue weight to the personal opinions of a witness offered within the guise of "scientifically based opinion."[2] But in spite of the caveats expressed by Gould and others, mental health professionals enjoy an expanding role in family court litigation. Not only are their opinions given great weight in evaluations of abuse charges—in some cases, their role extends even beyond the evaluative stage. For example, they can act as court-appointed visitation supervisors (supervising a mother's visits with her children) and as court-appointed family counselors, even after the litigation is over. They can also serve as consultants to child protective services, which means that they can recommend that charges be filed against a mother they deem "paranoid" or "delusional." These various roles multiply the effect of the theories that such "experts" carry into each particular case.

We can see, then, that family court madness depends critically on the theories of psychologists who function within the system—theories that, significantly, have little or no life outside the family courts, seldom passing muster under the accepted standards of mental health professions. And by applying ethnomethodology, we further learn how it is that mental health experts in their day-to-day work—giving undeserved diagnoses to protective mothers—reflexively *re-create* a mad system that in turn deems their practice an acceptable mode of operation.

In this chapter we examine the foundations of quack theories masquerading as mental health theories in the family courts and the effects they have on judicial decision making.

The Theories

In chapter 2, we touched on the most prominent of the questionable mental health theories used in family courts. A brief recapitulation will be useful here.

New Jersey psychiatrist Richard A. Gardner's "Parental Alienation Syndrome" (PAS) is perhaps the best known, and most widely used, of these family court theories. Gardner claimed that he had identified a "disorder" in which "children, programmed by the allegedly 'loved' parent, embark on a campaign of denigration of the allegedly 'hated' parent." Extensive criticism of Gardner's work by mental health professionals, legal scholars, and some judges has done little to diminish the popularity of PAS in the family courts.

In a 1998 law review article thoroughly analyzing Gardner's theory, Kathleen Niggemyer pointedly observed that although PAS

> has not been subjected to peer review or accepted by experts in the fields of psychology or child advocacy . . . some courts have used Gardner's PAS theory to quickly diagnose PAS, abruptly remove a child from a custodial parent who alleges abuse, and place the child in the custody of the allegedly abusing parent simply because the custodial parent has alleged that the non-custodial parent was abusing the child."[3]

In 1996, the American Psychological Association's Presidential Task Force on Violence and the Family, in a report titled "Violence and the Family", had specifically rejected Gardner's theory. Criminal courts have done so as well. For example, in 1999, a New York court refused to admit evidence of PAS in defense of a man accused of criminal child abuse, finding that PAS was not "a generally accepted concept with the professional community."[4] More recently, a California appeals court upheld a criminal court's exclusion of testimony about PAS on the ground that "the testimony was not scientific enough to satisfy the '*Kelly-Frye*' rule," which is the "gold standard" for the admissibility of evidence.[5]

But the reception given to Gardner's theory by family courts has been astonishingly different. Indeed, although Richard Gardner died in 2003, PAS continues to have an amazing influence in the family court system both in the United States and abroad.[6] For example, several months after Gardner's death a mother lost custody of her two sons, aged nine and eleven, in an Israeli court that based its decision on Gardner's theories. An Israeli newspaper that covered the trial quoted Dr. Paul Fink, a professor of psychiatry at Temple University and past president of the American Psychiatric Association, on the impact of Gardner's theories in this case: "This is junk science. . . . Dr. Gardner should be a rather pathetic footnote or an example of poor scientific standards."[7] Obviously, this was not the opinion of the court that made its custody decision on the strength of Gardner's theory.

Until his death in 1998, Dr. Arthur Green was, like Gardner, a highly popular evaluator in cases of alleged child abuse. Like Gardner, Green thought protective mothers should be carefully examined for evidence of "brainwashing." For instance, Green advocated closely watching the mother-child interaction when a child reports abuse. He opined that if the child looks at his mother while describing being sexually abused to a professional, this indicates a "brainwashed" child. He also argued—as we shall see, with fateful consequences—that a protective mother may be paranoid and delusional with respect to an allegation of sex abuse while remaining completely functional, without any trace of mental illness, in all other areas.

Both these (typical) claims of Dr. Green have been strenuously criticized by his colleagues outside the family court system. One outspoken New York judge, Jacqueline Silbermann, harshly characterized both Green and Gardner in 1991 after the two of them teamed up[8] to condemn a protective mother in a case litigated before her. In deciding the case, Judge Silbermann stated:

Dr. Green and Dr. Gardner's testimony was that of the worst hired guns, each showing a willingness to opine on virtually anything petitioner [the father] requested them to. Each was willing to criticize every other professional in the case, and yet neither of them verified any information or any history given to them by petitioner.[9]

But Silbermann's repudiation stands alone; Green remained a popular and prestigious expert witness until he died in 1998. What is more, his methods are still used by other family court evaluators.

Psychologist Ira Turkat, writing along the lines laid down by Gardner and Green, has named "Malicious Mother Syndrome" (MMS) to identify "mothers [who] not only try to alienate their children from their fathers, but are committed to a broadly based campaign to hurt the father directly."[10] The use of this theory in family courts has been severely criticized by women's advocates. For instance, Smith and Coukos (1997) stated: "Courts should be vigilant in evaluating any psychological expert testimony that claims to be able to discern false from true allegations, or that can be used to explain away or cover up abuse," concluding that the "most well-intentioned judges may be completely unaware of how they [judges] view protective parents until they are presented with empirical information about . . . child abuse."[11] This advice, however, has not been heeded by many family court judges.

Below we dissect the significant elements of these suspect theories and discuss as well how they actually function in family courts.

Why Do Family Courts Use Quack Theories?

Family courts are charged with an extremely difficult and often unrewarding task in cases involving child abuse allegations. Such charges are very difficult to prove, and available evidence is often available only in the form of opinion. Complicating the matter is the fact that the opinions of experts may easily conflict in the same case. One expert may find a child's disclosure of abuse persuasive—another may have doubts about it. To make matters even more difficult, repeated interviews of the child—which are nearly always necessitated by the court process—make evaluation more difficult as the child's utterances become less spontaneous. And yet no judge can conscientiously ignore charges of child abuse. So the family court judge in such cases is repeatedly called on to make a Solomonic choice, poised between the knowledge that a rush to judgment may devastate an innocent parent and the fear that failure to find abuse when it is actually occurring will betray everyone involved, especially the child. And the judge must often make such a choice with very little real help.

The difficulty of evaluating children's disclosures accurately is well recognized in the relevant literature. In 1987, in the *Journal of Interpersonal Violence,* psychiatrist David Corwin, along with other researchers, pointed out "the well-known tendency of abused children to utilize denial and dissociation in defending against their memories of abuse [which] could create a range of unpredictable and seemingly paradoxical reactions."[12]

Roland Summit, professor of psychiatry at the University of California (Los Angeles), has introduced the term "Child Abuse Accommodation Syndrome" to describe a number of behavioral responses to sexual abuse trauma—low self-esteem, helplessness, depression, and self-blame. Dr. Summit emphasizes that, as part of this syndrome, children may "recant" their allegations of abuse and even show signs of affection toward their abuser.[13]

Researchers S. E. Palmer and R. A. Brown, in a 1999 study of 116 cases of child sexual abuse that had been confirmed by a perpetrator's subsequent guilty plea or conviction (or by highly consistent medical evidence), found that 72 percent of the child victims actually denied the abuse when they were first questioned about it. The Arizona Coalition against Domestic Violence, in its 2003 study of protective mothers, cites the Palmer and Brown study to show that "victims don't disclose [abuse] because of fear of the consequences, self-blame, lack of awareness and difficulty in talking about the abuse."[14]

Yet honest family court judges are expected to sift these paradoxical, inconsistent facts and statements and make decisions that will radically alter a family's life. It must be admitted that the judge's task in such cases is not enviable.[15]

Compared with such daunting responsibility, it is fatally easy to blame the accuser. This not only disposes of the case   obviously there is no child abuse if a "delusional" parent says there is—it eases the conscience of a judge who might otherwise worry about making the wrong decision. If a mother is crazy and "vindictive," then the court's obligation is clear. That the course taken by the court in such cases—silencing the accuser, cutting off contact between the child and anyone who believes abuse is occurring— is precisely what will protect a father who really is guilty of abuse rarely seems to trouble judicial minds.

Thus, family courts have come to rely on psychological theories that, however poorly substantiated scientifically, do a fine job of diverting the court's attention from the alleged abuse to the personality of the mother. New Jersey psychiatrist Richard A. Gardner, one of the most notorious critics of protective mothers in child abuse/custody litigation until his suicide in 2003, provides an excellent example of this. In his writing, Gardner set forth some extraordinary characterizations of mothers who made what he termed "false" reports of abuse.[16] For example, in *True and False Accusations of Child Sex Abuse* (1992), he stated that "mothers who fabricate a sex abuse allegation are often hysterical and/or exhibitionistic. They typically exaggerate situations, 'make mountains out of molehills,' and will take every opportunity to broadcast the abuse."[17] It can readily be seen that when such a theory is applied to a mother—any mother—who believes her child has been abused, her anger ("hysteria"), anxiety about possible repetition of the abuse based on whatever evidence she may have ("exaggerating situations"), and repeated calls for help ("broadcasting the abuse") can quickly type her as a "falsely accusing" mother.

Another controversial evaluator, Dr. Arthur Green, fits the same blame-the-accuser model. In 1986, for instance, Green advocated closely watching the mother-child interaction when a child reports abuse to a professional, claiming "delusional and vindictive mothers often control the child by monitoring his or her responses through eye contact and subtle facial expressions. The 'brainwashed' children respond by 'checking' with their mothers before proceeding."[18] The application of this theory, too, can easily stamp *any* disclosure of child abuse a "false" one. Indeed, many of Green's colleagues sharply disagreed with the approach set out in this article. Two years after it appeared, Graeme Hanson, assistant clinical professor in psychiatry and pediatrics at the University of California, San Francisco, and eighteen cosigners published a letter in *Journal of the American Academy of Child and Adolescent Psychiatry* in which they stated: "In our experience, children who are anxious . . . 'check' with their mothers for reassurance before proceeding. This does not invariably indicate brainwashing."[19]

Green's insistence that a mother's "subtle" encouragement of her child's sex abuse report marks her as "delusional and vindictive" is particularly ominous because many children are reluctant to disclose abuse, even to professionals, without a certain amount of encouragement. In a 2001 study of sixty-four nonoffending mothers of children believed by researchers to have been abused, Deblinger and coauthors reported that most abused children will not talk about sexual abuse if they are not specifically prompted to do so (as in, for instance, a discussion about "good touch" and "bad touch.")[20]

This means that a protective mother, confronted by an evaluator like Dr. Green, faces a Hobson's choice: since abused children are unlikely to initiate a conversation about abuse, a worried parent must in some sense "prompt" the child by introducing the topic of abuse. But this will open the mother to a charge that she "coached" her child into fabricating sex abuse. And if a Dr. Green has his way, she is likely to lose custody.

Indeed, both Gardner and Green sometimes went to astonishing lengths to discredit protective mothers' allegations of sexual abuse. For example, they argued that sex abuse accusations endorsed by a mother during a contentious divorce actually express her *own* sexual problems—including her alleged sense of sexual deprivation.[21]

Gardner never produced any evidence to support this peculiar theory, but he was perfectly clear about what he meant:

a mother . . . who cannot allow herself to accept the fact that she still may harbor the desire for sexual activities with her now-hated spouse, may project these feelings onto her daughter and develop the delusion that her husband has sexually molested the child. It is as if each time she entertains the pedophilic fantasy (of her husband molesting her daughter), she satisfies vicariously (by projecting herself into her daughter's position) her own desire to be the recipient of her spouse's sexual overtures.[22]

Green made a similar claim. In describing the characteristic situations that breed false disclosures of sexual abuse by a child, he stated:

[T]he child is influenced by a delusional mother who projects her own unconscious sexual fantasies onto the spouse . . . the allegations of incest usually begin shortly after the marital separation, while the child is visiting the father. The object loss inherent in the separation and impending divorce acts as the catalyst for this pathological process.[23]

Here, clearly, is an argument that attributes any abuse accusation surfacing during divorce to unresolved sexual problems of the mother—not the accused father!—and thus turns the normal sex abuse inquiry on its head. Indeed, such attacks on protective mothers, posing as sober scientific insights, illustrate a particularly pernicious aspect of family court quackery: precisely those things that tend to appear in meritorious sex abuse allegations can be used, in light of these theories, to discredit them.

As a matter of fact, a large body of peer-reviewed literature shows why

sexual abuse incidents are likely to occur at the time of the divorce—a phenomenon that cannot be explained away as the "projection" of fantasies by
a sexually frustrated wife.

For example, as David Corwin and his coauthors have argued, "the losses,
stresses, and overall negative impact of separation and divorce may precip-
itate regressive 'acting out' by parents, including child sexual abuse." The
authors further explore the correlation between divorce and sex abuse by
suggesting that

> it is possible that the adult character traits and behavior problems frequently
> associated with the sexual abuse of children are more common in people
> whose marriages break up. Included in this list are narcissistic traits . . .
> paranoid ideation . . . antisocial tendencies, impulsivity . . . sexual difficul-
> ties . . . and substance abuse. . . . [24]

Maryland psychologist Dr. Mary Froning, in a September 1988 letter to
the *Journal of the American Academy of Child and Adolescent Psychiatry,*
cited Professor Kathleen Faller's published work to stress

> three factors that seem to contribute to the risk of sexual abuse in divorces,
> especially when the abusing parent resisted the divorce. First, is the loss of
> structure of family life; second, the feelings of devastation and loneliness on
> the part of the offender, which cause him to turn to the child for emotional
> support and then lead to sexual interaction with the child; and third, the
> tendency of the perpetrator to express some of his anger toward the spouse
> indirectly by sexually abusing the child.[25]

Corwin and coauthors also noted that "abused children may be more
likely to disclose abuse by a parent and to be believed by the other parent
following separation and divorce." They explain: "[W]ith the breakup of
the parents comes diminished opportunity for an abusing parent to enforce
secrecy as there is increased opportunity for the child to disclose abuse sep-
arately to the other parent."[26] In other words, sex abuse is more likely to be
disclosed by the child who feels safe enough to talk about the abuse when
the abuser is already out of the house.

In light of all this published work pointing to the greater likelihood of
abuse disclosures during divorce, it is clear why Green's and Gardner's
theorizing—which goes so far as to blame such disclosures on an unstable,
vindictive, and sex-starved ex-wife—is likely to turn judicial inquiry in an
abuse case onto a course diametrically opposed to its proper object. Sadly,
that is precisely what makes such theorizing popular in family court.

All Mothers Suffer from the Same Illness

The psychological theories unique to family courts have several unusual features. These features deserve analysis because a detailed examination helps to explain the damage these unsubstantiated theories can do in cases involving child abuse allegations.

The first odd feature of the theories we are examining is that they place *all* mothers the theorists wish to stigmatize as "false reporters" in the same procrustean bed. In the population at large there are many kinds of mental illness, each consisting of basic pathological conditions with a wide range of accompanying features. In the family courts, however, mothers across the country are diagnosed as suffering from the *same* genre of mental illnesses. This of course defies statistical probabilities and common sense.

Protective mothers are described by these "experts" in highly predictable language. In lay terms they are "self-absorbed," "manipulative," "calculating," "rigid and judgmental," and "overly opinionated." In psychiatric terms they are "*paranoid-delusional*," with "*narcissistic*," "*histrionic*," and "*exhibitionist*" features, and display "*grandiose*" self-assessments. Many mothers trying to prove their charges of sexual abuse are found by mental health experts to be living in a "fantasy" world where they feel compelled to superimpose *their* beliefs on everyone around them.

These terms reappear with depressing frequency in "expert" evaluations rendered in family courts. It should be borne in mind that a mother who believes her child has been abused is likely to be emotional; that if the charge is not readily acted on, she may well tend to suspect (often, alas, with good reason) that officials connected with the case are favoring the accused abuser; that in order to protect her child she is obliged to try to make other people accept her belief that a danger exists. Thus, a mother with a well-founded suspicion of abuse may easily be pigeonholed as "mentally ill" if family courts accept these boilerplate evaluations, as they all too often do.

"Mental Illness" That Is "Circumscribed" to One Topic

A particularly strange feature of family court mental illness theories is that they provide for mothers to be "paranoid" and "delusional" about one issue—their suspicion of sexual abuse—while showing no trace of mental illness in any other connection. Mothers have been found "paranoid" by court-appointed experts solely because of their belief in their children's abuse. Yet in many of these cases, the "paranoid" mother is embarrassingly devoid of some of the most common symptoms of paranoia, such as intense and irrational mistrust or suspicion (which can bring on a sense of rage, hatred, and betrayal), a preoccupation with hidden motives, a fear of being deceived or taken advantage of, and the inability to relax. True paranoids are argumentative, abrupt, stubborn, self-righteous, and perfectionistic. Protective mothers often display little or nothing of this clinical profile.

Arthur Green, the New York psychiatrist whose theories drew sharp criticism from his colleagues (discussed above), dodged this fatal objection by claiming in a 1986 article that such mothers suffered from a unique sort of "paranoid psychosis" that was "circumscribed" or restricted to a single topic. He illustrated this so-called diagnosis with an account of one case in which he had served as court-appointed evaluator.[27]

About a year later, Green claimed to locate just such a "circumscribed paranoid psychosis" in another case. The mother in question, whose "paranoia" consisted in the fact that she believed her mother's eyewitness account that her six-year-old daughter had been sexually abused—an abuse incident that one of New York's most prominent abuse evaluators found "strong reason to believe" after interviewing the girl—had already been examined by a psychiatrist and found to have no mental illness. Green himself, in a report submitted to the family court, admitted that the mother was "fully adjusted" and "performing successfully" in her professional and personal life. He even admitted that she did not suffer from any delusions—except for her beliefs concerning her daughter.[28] Nevertheless, he did not hesitate to label her belief in her daughter's abuse a "circumscribed psychosis." In his 1986 article, Green had given the same diagnosis to "Betty C," the mother whose case he had used to illustrate a "false" allegation of sexual abuse. She too was a competent professional woman who demonstrated a high level of functioning.[29]

The legal danger of pronouncing a single belief a sign of paranoia, without considering the possibility that this particular belief may be justified, should be obvious. Green's offense in this case was particularly egregious because (as discussed in more detail below) he concluded no abuse had occurred not from an examination of evidence but simply because the judge told him privately that it had not (while the judge, in turn, claimed to base his conclusions on Dr. Green's evaluation!).

But even Green's clinical assumption—that a "circumscribed psychosis" is a legitimate sort of diagnosis in a wide range of family court cases—is untenable. In truth, a "circumscribed" psychosis—a psychosis narrowly restricted to one topic—is an extremely rare occurrence. Most clinicians consider it nearly impossible for the same individual to have "delusional" or "paranoid" thinking about one particular topic while showing no distorted thinking about other topics. A psychiatrist consulted by an investigator for a New York State legislative committee interested in family court malfunction explained to one of us that the kinds of psychotic illnesses that cause delusional and paranoid thinking cannot "freely discriminate" among topics, "choosing one thing to be paranoid about and not another."[30]

Yet Dr. Green has attributed this rare condition to many mothers in family court litigation across the country. Four of these mothers later gave compelling firsthand testimony at both state and federal legislative hearings on the devastating effects of such diagnoses on their cases.[31] But Green's many followers still find a willing audience for this theory in family courts.

Mental Illness That Can Be "Induced"

Another claim almost unique to family courts is that mothers who suffer from an "illness" that makes them believe their children have been abused are able to *induce* that same mental illness in their children. Mothers are accused of *inducing* paranoia in their children, who join their mothers in thinking "crazy" thoughts. Faller, Corwin, and Olafson (1993) trace this strange idea back to 1981—and to a family court case, naturally. Two researchers (S. Kaplan and S. Kaplan)[32] studied the case of two children whose mother had made allegations of sexual abuse. Believing the charges to be false (even though they were confirmed by the children themselves, who testified consistently to the abuse over many court sessions), they proposed "the possible dynamic of *folie à deux* (folly of two) as an explanation for the children's allegations" of sexual abuse.

Faller, Corwin, and Olafson emphatically deny that such an application of the notion of folie à deux is clinically acceptable. They point out that Kaplan and Kaplan offered their diagnosis "despite the fact that there was no delusional thinking diagnosed in either child, the mother, or the maternal grandparents. . . ."[33] That is, for a child to be susceptible to "paranoid" and "delusional" thinking, both the child and the mother must have an underlying *psychosis*. No such psychosis was found in the case studied by Kaplan and Kaplan.

In spite of the deeply flawed foundation of this theory, however, the folie à deux concept has gained wide acceptance in the family courts. In the 1980s, Dr. Richard Gardner used it as part of his "Parental Alienation Syndrome"[34]—"a disorder in which children, programmed by the allegedly 'loved' parent, embark on a campaign of denigration of the allegedly 'hated' parent," whereby the "sex abuse accusation emerges as a final attempt to remove him [the father] entirely from the children's lives."[35]

It is easy to see why Gardner embraced folie à deux, however rare such a phenomenon might actually be in the circumstances encountered by family courts, to buttress his "syndrome." Gardner claimed that sex abuse allegations were being manufactured by hysterical *mothers*. However, he was faced with the embarrassing fact that in most cases in which courts consulted him the *children* also described having been abused. What was more, the children's reports appeared sincere and credible. Gardner avoided the difficulty by introducing folie à deux, arguing that the children's reports must have resulted from mental illness *induced* in them by mentally ill mothers.

In fact, Gardner's theory forced him to go even further than that. He claimed that mothers could not only induce paranoid psychotic thinking in their children (that is, they could "program" children to believe they had been abused)—they could even induce such psychosis *in their children's therapists!* "[T]here are some [therapists]," wrote Gardner, "who are indeed man haters, and who do indeed partake in a folie à trois [folly of three] relationship with their patients."[36] In Gardner's world, a child, mother, and therapist do not necessarily all confirm an abuse report simply because it is true—this might, instead, occur as the result of a strangely contagious mental condition.

Law professor Carol Bruch, in a critique of Gardner's theories published in 2001 in the *Family Law Quarterly*,[37] points out two obvious flaws in Gardner's argument. First, she notes that folie à deux or shared psychotic disorder—a "disorder in which a second or further person in a close relationship with a primary person comes to share delusional beliefs of the primary person, who already had a Psychotic Disorder, most commonly Schizophrenia—is rare."[38] Second, she points out that for such disorders to "occur in primarily *young* children is also contrary to the literature."[39] Yet Gardner's cases mostly involved young children, and he claimed to find "induced" mental illness in case after case of alleged child abuse.

Another theory of "induced" mental illness that has flourished in family courts is called "Munchausen Syndrome By Proxy." This strange theory has become, according to one prominent matrimonial attorney, the "classic" countercharge to an abuse allegation in family court litigation.[40] Yet, as used in family courts, it rests on a distinctly flimsy foundation.

Munchausen Syndrome, named after the eccentric writer Baron von Münchausen, is a mental illness characterized by a need to attract attention and sympathy by assuming symptoms of strange illnesses or similar conditions. In 1977, a British pediatrician, Roy Meadow, first identified a variant of this syndrome that he named "Munchausen Syndrome By Proxy." In this syndrome, a parent—usually a mother—uses her *child* as the "proxy" by which she attracts the attention of health care professionals. Such mothers constantly subject their children to unneeded and sometimes dangerous medical treatment and will even induce symptoms in their children in order to keep doctors' attention. The illness is considered rare but is also considered very dangerous by psychiatrists, particularly because it is difficult to diagnose: mothers who suffer from the disease generally appear to be highly conscientious caregivers.

Evidently, a theory that can stigmatize a mother who seems to be an excellent parent was too good for family court theorists to resist. The theory of Munchausen Syndrome By Proxy (MSBP) has gradually developed an offshoot that rarely appears outside family court litigation—but can be devastating within it.

Perhaps the first step in the growth of this branch of the theory occurred when Herbert A. Schreier, a Florida psychiatrist, argued that it was specifically a women's disease. We have noted above that most diagnosed cases of MSBP do involve mothers—but Schreier insisted that there were special reasons why MSBP (also referred to as "factitious disorder by proxy") should occur in mothers. In *International Pediatrics*, Dr. Julio Apolo cited the work of Schreier and his cowriter, J. A. Libow, for the proposition that *mothers* with a history of "emotional neglect in their early childhood especially by their fathers" turn to the physician "as the longed-for father figure and, by inducing or falsifying illness, the child is used to relate to and control the physician."[41] Of course, this hypothesis, which blandly assumes that "the physician" is always male, overlooks the large percentage of physicians today who are women—in pediatric medicine in particular as many as 50 percent in the United States are women—but this was only the beginning.

In 1986, British psychologists Sinanan and Haughton argued ominously that "the probable range of variations in the presentation of Munchausen syndrome is likely to develop in parallel with the evolution of medical and social services,"[42] implying that the increased availability of services to sex abuse victims would result in a larger number of false claims by an adult that a child has been molested.

Sinanan and Haughton did not claim to have actually observed any such cases. But by 1993, in *Issues in Child Abuse Accusations,* California psychologist Deirdre Conway Rand was claiming to have identified a "contemporary" form of MSBP that occurs "when the mother creates the appearance that the child has been abused by someone else, generally the father in a divorce and custody or visitation dispute."[43] Rand had already argued, in a 1990 article, that this peculiar affliction, like Gardner's PAS, could be induced in a child, who would then act "as a confederate of the mother, with the two involved in a sort of folie à deux, a pattern that might be perpetuated even after the child reached adulthood."[44]

Apart from its reliance on the faulty folie à deux principle, there are important theoretical objections to this approach to MSBP. Kathleen Faller, professor of social work at the University of Michigan School of Social Work, argued in a 2002 PowerPoint presentation to the Seventh Annual Northern New England Conference on Child Maltreatment that MSBP is misapplied in protective mother cases for several reasons. For example, the classic MSBP mother "wants to be seen as super-mom . . . while moms in divorce are not seen as super-moms." In addition, classically defined "MSBP moms do not accuse someone [of abuse]." Faller concluded that the improper use of MSBP diagnoses in custody cases "is just another way to prevent mothers from protecting their children."[45]

The wisdom of Faller's objections can be seen by examining an application of this "contemporary" MSBP theory to an actual family court case. One example will suffice here.

A Long Island, New York, mother whose seven-year-old daughter was diagnosed at birth with spina bifida, a congenital condition that causes a child to be born with a partly exposed spinal column and results in permanent damage to certain nerves, lost custody of her child primarily because she was diagnosed with Munchausen Syndrome By Proxy. But she was not even suspected of this "illness" until she brought sexual abuse allegations (confirmed by the child) to the attention of the family court.

For seven years, the mother was the child's primary caretaker, working extensively with doctors and nurses in treating her daughter's complex and chronic condition. Not one health care professional ever so much as hinted at the presence of MSBP in this mother. On the contrary, the child's regular pediatrician—who treated her from birth until shortly before the mother lost custody—wrote to the court:

[T]he mother . . . was always compliant and gave appropriate medical care. [The child] has multiple problems including hydrocephalus, seizures, spinal cord problems, and bladder problems. [The mother] always had objective findings and . . . was appropriate in bringing [the child] into the office or hospital as the situation warranted.[46]

Only after the mother had accused the child's father of sexually abusing the girl did court-appointed experts produce a diagnosis of Munchausen Syndrome By Proxy.

A court-appointed evaluator, a Ph.D. in psychoanalysis, reported to the family court judge that the mother was making "false" allegations of sex abuse and that this might justify a diagnosis of mental illness, including MSBP:

The false allegations of sex abuse can be seen as part of the divorce syndrome and ultimate goal of alienating the children from the father. Additionally, it could be a part of a Munchausen by Proxy Syndrome. There is reason to speculate that [the mother] has created or exaggerated medical symptoms with regard to [the child]. The current forensic evaluation does strongly speculate that the sex abuse allegations fit into a contemporary type of Munchausen by Proxy Syndrome.[47]

Note that this was the first time, in the child's seven years of intensive medical treatment, that anyone had suggested that the mother had either "created" or "exaggerated" any of the child's medical symptoms. In fact, the "expert" herself claimed only that there was "reason to *speculate*" along these lines, and any such speculation contradicted the direct observation of the child's pediatrician. Significantly, this court-appointed evaluator appeared to consider the creation of such symptoms in the child an important element of the MSBP diagnosis.

The same expert who labeled the mother as a case of MSBP because of her sex abuse allegations curiously, however, admitted she did not have the basic knowledge or expertise to assess whether the mother had overused the health care system to treat her daughter's spina bifida condition. In her written report to the court, she explained that in order to determine this a "full review of the medical records . . . would need to be done by two medical doctors, a pediatric specialist and a psychiatrist." In her testimony, she likewise told the court that she rested her diagnosis of MSBP on the sex abuse allegations, since she did not "feel comfortable with the medical aspects" of the daughter's case to render an MSBP diagnosis based on those.[48]

Thus, the mother was diagnosed as having a mental illness that forced her to seek constant attention from health care professionals through the manufacture of symptoms—and yet no one ever determined that the mother had induced or exaggerated any of her daughter's medical symptoms, even though her condition gave the mother ample opportunity to do so.

The psychoanalyst explained this peculiar application of MSBP by itemizing ten of the mother's personality characteristics that she considered consistent with MSBP: in particular, the mother was "a pathological liar," had "a great need for adoration," was "manipulative and charming," and was "obsessed with the child's illnesses, among other things."[49]

Yet, *even in support of her sex abuse allegations,* the mother had never taken her daughter for an invasive medical exam, nor was she accused of having her daughter undergo any unnecessary treatment for abuse, such as extensive psychological counseling—nearly always a principal symptom of MSBP.

Despite the shaky evidence of mental illness in this case, the court-appointed expert did not hesitate to recommend the extremely harsh step of transferring the child's custody immediately to the father. In fact, she went further, recommending that the mother be limited to strictly supervised visits. To support this step, she evidently thought her diagnosis insufficient; she invoked instead the all-too-common specter of parental "mutiny," telling the court the mother should have *only* strictly supervised visitation to "prevent her from taking the children [*sic*] from the jurisdiction or possibly doing damage to herself or the child."[50] It is not clear what was supposed to give rise to this concern: the mother had never attempted to take the child out of the court's jurisdiction and had never done any harm to the child. Moreover, as we have seen, MSBP was never clearly applicable to this case in the first place.

But this was family court. The mother had made a sex abuse allegation; the allegation had not been proved; therefore, the mother required punishment. The mental diagnosis was needed only to supply a cog in a well-oiled machine.

Mental Illness That Grows in a Vacuum

Another suspicious feature of family court mental health diagnoses is that many of the alleged conditions appear to grow in a vacuum. None of the mothers we studied who were given mental illness labels in family court had any prior history of mental illness. None had any history of substance abuse or sociopathic behavior. In fact, many of these mothers admittedly functioned well in their jobs and in their personal lives (serving as Little League coaches, active in PTAs, taking a leadership role in their churches and synagogues). They became "mentally ill" only when they accused their children's fathers with acts of abuse.

But, according to most experts, this is not the way mental illnesses work. True, sudden trauma can cause certain short-term, episodic mental illnesses, such as "situational adjustment disorders" or "reactive clinical depressions"—but these are very different from the "psychosis" that family court experts claim to find in protective mothers. What is more, these mental illness symptoms are usually evident over a significant period of time and affect the person's daily activities.

In fact, at a conference cosponsored in 1999 by the National Alliance for the Mentally Ill on the effects of mental illness on employment, it was agreed that 85 percent of people with serious mental illnesses are unemployed—or, if employed, are working at jobs that are "poorly paid and sporadic."[51] By contrast, protective mothers, supposedly too "ill" to care for their children, are in most cases gainfully employed and reasonably well paid. Thus, it is very unlikely that so many of them can in fact be "mentally ill."

Only in family court does "mental illness" mean something sharply different from what most people, professionals and others, understand it to mean. An aide to a state senator, concerning the case of a certain protective mother, told one of us, "I just know that mother is not mentally ill in spite of what the court says. I just know [because] she's so easy to deal with." In fact, this mother was "mentally ill" only because she believed eyewitness testimony that her daughter had been abused.

Mental Illness That Requires Harmful "Treatment"

Another damning feature of these theories is that the "treatment" recommended for the "illnesses" they propound is exactly what is worst in cases of actual child abuse.

What do the believers in these theories recommend? Isolation of the child from anyone who believes in the abuse the child is reporting; supervision of the child's contact with the protective parent, so that the child is discouraged from describing abuse; forcing the child into the custody of the very parent he or she fears. A better prescription for intimidating genuinely abused children, forcing them to hide their painful truth while punishing the parent who has tried to protect them (and incidentally rewarding the abuser), can hardly be imagined.

Richard Gardner, for example, wrote emphatically that "the most potent therapeutic measure that one can utilize for PAS children is the reduction of their access to the alienating parent," claiming "there was a significant reduction or even elimination of PAS symptomatology in all . . . of these cases."[52]

Significantly, Gardner reached this radical conclusion—with appalling implications for any parent who suspects abuse, and for any child who needs a parent's belief and protection—after just one telephone interview (lasting no longer than twenty to thirty minutes) with each of several parents who had been accused of sexual abuse and now had full custody of the allegedly abused child. According to Gardner, these parents claimed that PAS completely disappeared after custody was awarded to them, particularly when their child's visits with the other (formerly accusing) parent were limited. (How Gardner could have expected the alleged abusers to report anything different from this is not explained.) Since no other researcher ever interviewed these parents and since Gardner did not even attempt to use objective criteria that could be reviewed by other scientists, it is hard to see why these self-serving statements from some accused parents deserve any professional consideration at all. But Gardner was convinced— he wrote without hesitation: "This study [sic] provides confirmation of my longstanding observation that the most potent therapeutic measure that one can utilize for PAS children is reduction of their access to the alienating parent."[53] He might have added: It is certainly the most potent measure for ensuring that a child who has reported sex abuse by a father will never report it again.

Psychiatrist Jonathan Gould (mentioned above) clearly had such radical proposals in mind when he cautioned that "experts have often been criticized for overstepping the bounds of their expertise, providing opinions of a personal nature couched in the aura of empirical science."[54] Gardner's methods do even more than that, since on the basis of his personal opinions he was willing to recommend steps certain to be devastating to children who have actually been abused. The same is true of approaches similar to Gardner's. Only in family courts do such theories flourish.

An Unhealthy Symbiosis between Mental Health Professionals and Judges

The theories we have been examining are not only questionable as mental health diagnoses. Used in family courts, they have the dangerous effect of blurring the line between judge and psychologist. The fact-finding process in an abuse case, which is supposed to be the responsibility of the judge (abuse cases in family courts are almost never tried before a jury), is subverted by a mental health expert who claims to be able to determine that a mother's personality makes her accusation incredible. Similarly, judges are encouraged by the use of such theories to play the role of therapist, prescribing remedies meant to "treat" a mother while in fact they involve the court in abuses of its judicial power. This unhealthy symbiosis corrupts the legal process. It also helps to explain some of the stranger aspects of custody-related abuse litigation.

DOCTORS PLAY "JUDGE"

It is a fundamental principle of family court jurisprudence that courts may not delegate their fact-finding authority to anyone, including evaluators or mental health practitioners, in any matter pertaining to the welfare of a child.[55]

However, as we have seen, some of the mental health theories used in family courts have precisely the effect of short-circuiting the judicial function. This is particularly likely—and particularly wrong—when a purported mental health theory places great stress on the legal context of a sex abuse allegation. Such theories seem tailor-made to allow an evaluator to judge the fundamental question in a sex abuse case based on his own (nonprofessional) prejudices. It comes as no surprise that some of the experts whose approaches we are examining here seem convinced that if a sex abuse allegation is raised in the context of divorce and custody it *must* be false—even though this contradicts much of the published research. When such experts perform evaluations of accusing mothers, they tend to base their diagnostic conclusions on "legal" factors—the presence of a pending divorce/custody action, or the posture taken toward the case by a family court judge—rather than on the clinical features of the mother's personality functioning, though the latter are the only things the evaluators are professionally competent to evaluate.

A single case illustrates this point. A Brooklyn, New York, protective mother was accused by CPS of "brainwashing" her daughter to believe she had been sexually abused by the child's father (even though an eyewitness had reported the abuse incident). A psychiatrist, who was board certified in child and adult psychiatry and neurology, was asked to evaluate the mother for mental illnesses—and was pointedly told the legal "line" on her case: that she was paranoid, believed she was being conspired against by CPS and family court, and had fabricated the sex abuse charge.

The psychiatrist's report illustrates the correct way to handle an examination for mental illness in such a case. She noted that the mother's allegations of a court conspiracy to cover up sexual abuse seemed difficult to believe. On the other hand, she found no evidence of psychotic disturbances in the mother. She reported:

> [The mother's] current clinical picture presents a complex diagnostic question. Some of her behavior could be classified as "paranoid" given the themes of being conspired against, maliciously maligned. . . . However, she does not present any history of social isolation, seclusiveness or eccentricities of behavior. She does not show restricted affectivity and in fact, can show genuine warmth with interest in the person she is interacting with. . . . All in all, you are left with an academically and professionally successful woman, who . . . had been successfully raising her daughter prior to [the time of removal].[56]

The expert also specifically indicated (on Axis II of the "Diagnostic Impression" chart contained in her report) that the mother had no mental illness. Thus, she limited herself to a clinical evaluation, based on the facts available to her, leaving to one side the court auxiliaries' claim that the mother was "delusional." She not only concluded that the mother had no mental illness but urged the court to immediately return the child to her.[57]

This, however, was not the result desired by the law guardian, who had selected the psychiatrist. In fact, the law guardian actually refused to present the expert's report to the court or to call her as a witness.

The family court judge later ordered an evaluation of the mother by the controversial Dr. Arthur Green. Green's evaluation recklessly did what his predecessor had carefully refrained from doing: he mixed the roles of judge and evaluator, using legal proceedings whose propriety he had no way of judging to control his psychiatric diagnosis. First, he told the mother that no amount of evidence would persuade him that the alleged abuse had actually occurred; after all, he said, the judge, the judge's clerk, and others involved in the case had already told him it did not![58] He also told her (at their very first session) that because of what the judge had told him, he already knew that she was "paranoid" and "delusional." He thus effectively made his diagnosis before even examining his client. (Interestingly, Green claimed he was able to reach his conclusions about the alleged abuse because the "finding" that it had not occurred, and that she had invented the charge, was "the law of the case." He thus not only invoked a legal doctrine to justify a psychiatric diagnosis—he *misapplied* the doctrine, since no such formal findings could have been made while the trial was still proceeding. Green, a nonlawyer, clearly did not understand this.)[59]

Throughout his report to the court, Green referred to the mother's attitude toward the case against her as the basis for his diagnosis of "paranoia," writing: "She [the mother] expresses an abundance of projective and paranoid mechanisms. She maintains that there is a conspiracy against her. . . ." In fact, Green noted specifically that "[a]side from [the mother's] delusional beliefs concerning the judges, [agencies,] and myself, there is no evidence of disorganized thinking, or hallucinations, or other behavior which might be associated with a Schizophrenic disorder." Thus, he based his diagnosis of paranoia squarely on issues he could not, as a clinician, legitimately resolve.[60] In this respect his approach was directly opposed to that of the former evaluator, who based her diagnostic impression on her own clinical observations rather than the "running record" built up by hostile court officials and law guardian and social service agencies.

Green's evaluation formed the basis of the family court's decision in the case. Yet it was clearly flawed as a psychiatric diagnosis, not only because it assumed the existence of a "circumscribed psychosis" (a peculiar thing indeed), but also because Green relied, for his diagnosis, on determinations by judges and agency lawyers that he, as a mental health professional, could not evaluate (and that were, as we have seen, legally premature). As a result of Green's evaluation, the mother lost custody. She eventually lost all visitation, too, including the right to write letters and make telephone calls to her daughter.

Another problem caused when the evaluator takes over the judge's role—a problem virtually unique to family courts—is that an evaluator may take it upon himself to *predict* legally significant acts, such as a mother's defiance of a court order, before they occur. This can have fateful consequences. We have already discussed a case in which a mother was limited to supervised visitation because a mental health expert claimed that her "illness" might cause her to kidnap the child. This is unfortunately not rare in family courts. It is not unusual for family courts to impose restrictions on mothers who have never violated a court order, simply because a psychologist has claimed that she conforms to some sort of a psychological "profile" of a runner. Experts have made such assessments based on brief interviews, and have made them whether or not the mothers have stated any plans to go "underground."[61]

"GUILTY" BY REASON OF INSANITY

Another unhealthy feature of the mental health theories we are examining is that they encourage evaluators—and judges—to eliminate one of the elements of proof required by the law before a protective mother can be punished. In this way, these theories actually erode a protective mother's legal rights.

This occurs when mental health evaluators claim that a mother's sex abuse accusations, though not malicious, must be treated as harshly as if they were, because they are assumed to be the products of mental illness—and therefore will continue unless restrained. The legal significance of this is worth a bit of explanation.

Under ordinary circumstances, a mother who makes an accusation of sex abuse—even if that accusation turns out to be impossible to prove or legally unfounded—cannot be punished for doing so unless her accusation was intentionally false. If she acts maliciously against a child's father in deliberately inventing a charge against him, she is alienating the child from the father and is subject to penalties for doing so. Such penalties may include loss of custody, if a court concludes that this is the only way to prevent her from turning the child against his or her father.

But if she is simply mistaken in her suspicions, no penalty may be legally applied to her. We have mentioned above (chapter 4, note 15) a New Jersey appellate court that ruled a family court cannot punish a mother for her subjective beliefs about a child's sexual abuse, even if the court does not ultimately endorse them. This ruling reflects fundamental legal principles.

But this, of course, assumes that beliefs are not automatically translated into action. That is, a woman who knows her belief that sexual abuse has occurred was not ratified by a court can refrain from alienating the child from the father once she knows she is legally forbidden to do so. This is the assumption the law makes of all ordinary people. It must do so; otherwise a great many people could be treated as guilty until proved innocent.

But exactly this assumption is challenged when a mother's belief that sexual abuse has occurred is translated by a mental health theorist into a product of mental illness. The mentally ill do not enjoy the benefit of the assumption of a distinction between belief and action. Illness is not controllable; the woman who suffers from it will continue to act, uncontrollably, no matter how forcefully she is told not to. If she believes, "pathologically," that a man has sexually abused her child, she will continue to intervene between that man and that child no matter how many times a court rules against her. There is no way to prevent this—unless the court deprives her of the opportunity by removing the child from her custody, supervising her visits, and so forth.

Therefore, the woman whose accusations are said to result from Parental Alienation Syndrome, or Munchausen Syndrome By Proxy, will be treated just as harshly as if she were actively fabricating the accusations that, in fact, she is making sincerely.

This gives family courts a dangerously appealing excuse to treat protective mothers as guilty until proved innocent. If they are said to be mentally ill, they are automatically malicious—or, rather, they must automatically be treated as if they were, because their thoughts supposedly spill over into action. In truth, actual malice is difficult to prove. Sex abuse charges are rarely exposed as intentional fabrications. But the substitution of "mental illness" for malice in the lexicon of family court quackery allows courts to ignore the need to prove guilt—and to punish protective mothers without the same degree of proof they demand before punishing accused fathers. In short, these theories serve as legal maneuvers that circumvent the burden of proof that would otherwise be required to stigmatize an accusing mother, and as a result they can turn an entire sex abuse case legally upside down.

JUDGES PLAY DOCTOR

While family court evaluators play judge, family court judges often find it convenient to appoint themselves mental health experts in order to couch their criticisms of mothers in what looks like "expert" language.

When, for instance, a judge tells a custody evaluator that the mother is "crazy," the judge acts as the arbiter of her sanity, when he should defer to the clinician to make such a diagnosis.

A Texas judge in 2001 played doctor when he removed a two-year-old girl from her mother's custody on the strength of his own "diagnosis." An entry in the judge's handwritten log on the case, made a few days before he removed the child, used the phrase "parental alienation." Yet the custody evaluation later written by the court-appointed expert contained no reference to parental alienation of any kind.[62]

In a Brooklyn, New York, case, both the CPS case supervisor and a CPS psychiatrist expressed concern that an allegedly abused six-year-old girl showed "sexual provocativeness" during interviews, spreading her legs in front of both men and, according to the psychiatrist, watching for his reaction when she did so. Both professionals considered this a possible symptom of sexual abuse.[63] The judge, however, evidently determined that there should be *no* evidence of sexual abuse in the case, decided to substitute his judgment for the psychiatrist's: he had seen the same movements when he interviewed the child privately in chambers, he wrote in his decision, and "I found this to be not at all sexually provocative, but merely the nervous movements of a child too frequently interviewed." Nor was that all. A psychiatrist retained by the child's law guardian had concluded that the mother had no mental illness; the judge impatiently substituted his own conclusion for the expert's, claiming (contrary to the psychiatrist's own findings) that her "report reveals a seriously disturbed person."[64] Another psychiatrist found no evidence that the mother was mentally ill; the judge concluded that the psychiatrist "really does not understand the nature of the proceedings here in Court."[65] Yet another mental health expert, after administering a full battery of personality tests to the mother, concluded during "lengthy" testimony that the mother would be a proper custodial parent; the judge dismissed this expert conclusion as "quite plainly wrong."[66] He even offered his own "diagnosis" of the mother's courtroom behavior, claiming she was "histrionic and grandiose" while testifying. [67]

Unfortunately, playing doctor in this fashion is not at all uncommon in family court. In one New Jersey case, the mother was subjected to three separate court-ordered psychiatric evaluations over a nine-month period. Not one of these psychiatrists made a diagnosis that she was mentally ill or unfit. In fact, all three recommended that she have custody of her three children.[68] Nevertheless, the family court judge did not hesitate to refer to the mother's "illness" in stating his findings.[69] He awarded custody to the father and found the mother guilty of "emotional neglect."[70]

UNHEALTHY CONSEQUENCES OF THE SYMBIOSIS

It can clearly be seen that the use of family court quackery corrupts the legal process by short-circuiting the proper legal inquiry into whether an alleged act of abuse actually occurred or not. This results directly from the nature of the theories themselves, which encourage psychologists to dodge the factual complexities of an abuse case and "resolve" it without evidence.

Dr. Richard Gardner provides a very clear example of the way in which psychological "evaluators" have crossed over into a judge's role on the strength of questionable theories. In fact, Gardner's published work proves again and again that he could not offer an evaluation of Parental Alienation Syndrome (as he did in hundreds of cases) without reaching a conclusion that no abuse had actually occurred. Although he generated a very detailed list of symptoms to describe Parental Alienation Syndrome (for instance, poor bonding with the accused parent, overt hostility toward the accused parent that can spread to the alienated parent's extended family, and weak or absurd rationalizations for the deprecation of the accused parent), he claimed that *all* these symptoms can be disregarded if the abuse really occurred.[71] In a 1998 article he was equally emphatic: "I have repeatedly stated that when true abuse is present, then the PAS [Parental Alienation Syndrome] diagnosis is not applicable in that the children's animosity is justified."[72] Yet Gardner *never* explained on what basis he was able to reach a conclusion as to whether or not abuse actually occurred. One must conclude that every one of his diagnoses of PAS included a factual determination that no clinician in Gardner's position can be competent to make (and that Gardner himself never justified).

Indeed, Gardner seemed to don a judge's hat in family court litigation more often than he wore the hat of a clinician. In 1998, Professor Faller (mentioned above) carefully critiqued a large body of Gardner's work. She concluded that he "does not provide any research findings to substantiate his assertions about proposed characteristics and dynamics of the Parental Alienation Syndrome."[73] In fact, Faller pointed out that Gardner's book *Sex Abuse Hysteria: The Salem Witch Trials Revisited* (1991) dismissed the idea of "proof" in clinical matters: "The term scientific proof is not applicable to most of the issues discussed here. . . ." Gardner, she wrote, even "goes on to refer to the standard and accepted practice of citing support for professional opinions in existing literature as 'specious buttressing.'"[74] If that is true, however, then on what "proof" were so many mothers condemned as suffering from PAS, with the result that their allegations of abuse were not only ignored but were turned against them? How did Gardner "prove" that their children had not actually been abused?

When a clinician wears a judge's hat, even the law can be rewritten by a psychologist. In one case a clinician actually took it upon himself to rewrite the legal definition of what constitutes child sexual abuse.

This occurred in a case in Buffalo, New York, that arose in the mid-1980s. A court-appointed expert testified as to his understanding of what constitutes child abuse:

LAWYER FOR MOTHER: If a seven year old *consented* to sexual touching, then that would not be sexual abuse in your definition?

PSYCHOLOGIST: I would say that's inappropriate. I would not call that sexual abuse.[75]

In fact, under New York law, an adult is guilty of *first degree sexual abuse*—a felony—whenever "he or she subjects another person to sexual contact" when that other person is less than eleven years old; the law further defines "sexual contact" as "any touching of the sexual or other intimate parts of a person not married to the actor," including "the touching of the actor by the victim, as well as the touching of the victim by the actor."[76] In this case, the father had allegedly touched the girl's genitals and placed her hand on his genitals. Since she was only seven, these acts clearly constituted child abuse under the explicit language of the law. (In fact, they constituted a felony.) Thus, the expert in this case actually overruled state law in positing his own definition of sexual abuse! The judge, however, accepted the expert's definition over the statutory one and awarded the father accused of sexually abusing his daughter full custody of his seven-year-old child.[77]

"Parental Alienators"

Here we show in more detail how the theories described above work in actual family court cases. Here are the stories of three different women diagnosed by court-appointed experts as "parental alienators" because they supposedly fabricated charges of sex abuse in an effort to turn their children against their fathers.

A SEX ABUSE ALLEGATION AS PROOF OF THE MOTHER'S "FANTASY"

In 2000, a Georgia protective mother was suddenly called into court for an emergency hearing (held at the law guardian's request) in which she lost custody of two young girls, aged six and eight, that very day. This emergency hearing was prompted by a court-appointed mental health expert's report on the mother, written the day before. According to the report, the mother suffered from "impaired reality testing and tendency to use fantasy to excess."[78] In interpreting the psychological tests given to the mother, the expert made the following claim:

[This mother] tends to use fantasy excessively. The Rorschach findings indicate that in situations of stress she is likely to "defensively" substitute fantasy for reality. This is a form of denial that provides some temporary relief in that it may replace an unpleasant situation with an unrealistic but more manageable situation. This tendency usually results in a dependency on others to solve problems. In other words, people that do this often think that external forces will resolve a situation if they can avoid the problem long enough. This is a particularly destructive stylistic tendency for [the mother] given her problems in thinking. This increases the likelihood that her fantasies will involve considerable distortion of reality.[79]

None of this appeared to suggest an "emergency"—but at the hearing the next day, the expert played her trump card, claiming that the mother "is implanting false memories [of sexual abuse] and she is alienating both of these children from their father."

Then, putting on a lawyer's hat—situatedly achieving her role as "therapist turned lawyer"—she used the occasion to advise the court concerning its proper legal course. She told the judge, "I don't believe anything short of a *dramatic intervention by the court*—and even that might not be effective—is going to have any impact on this [the children's hostility toward the father]."[80]

Significantly, the expert disregarded the children's statements to two other psychologists, one of whom had made an oral report to the state's child abuse hotline that the father had "fondled" the children while they were in bed at night.[81]

These two psychologists had interviewed the children a number of times and concluded that "the children did not appear coached" and, indeed, showed the proper "affect associated with this disclosure [of sexual abuse]." They had also found that the older child "appeared distressed in a way that would be consistent with that kind of [sexual abuse] disclosure."[82] Nevertheless, the court's expert was not only convinced the abuse was a "fantasy" of the mother but was prepared to demand the isolation of the girls from their mother.

Louisiana attorney and national child abuse advocate Richard Ducote, in a memorandum on this case addressed to the Cobb County Bar Association and to the Metro Atlanta Board of Mental Health Professionals, alleged that the expert had been misled by the child's law guardian, her "good friend," who had "'assured' her that the sexual abuse allegations were false."[83] Once led to believe (through this unofficial persuasion) that the charges could be ignored, the evaluator found many of the criteria of Richard Gardner's Parental Alienation Syndrome present in the two girls. In her report claiming an "emergency," she noted "the following features of parental alienation":

1. a campaign of denigration against [the father];
2. weak, frivolous or absurd reasons were given for the deprecating feelings and statements;
3. a lack of normal ambivalence toward the parents (all good and all bad);
4. child's opinions are independently initiated [in one child only];
5. automatic support for the favored parent;
6. almost complete lack of empathy for the feelings of the alienated parent;
7. borrowed scenarios or "adult wording."

But had the expert not assumed the falsity of the allegations, these same symptoms could have been very differently construed. Similarly, had the expert not assumed the allegations were false, the mother would not have been diagnosed with "impaired reality testing" and a "tendency to use fantasy."

Besides basing her entire diagnosis on an assumption about the falsity of sex abuse allegations (reached unofficially, *not* after a judicial inquiry), the expert abused her clinical role by telling the court, in her report, that the mother "has discussed with the Examiner taking the children and going underground."[84]

As we have seen, such a claim is almost always designed to enrage a family court judge. It encourages the court to treat the mother as if she were in violation of court orders and guilty of parental kidnapping before she has done any such thing. We have also seen that this is a corruption of the role of a mental health evaluator, who cannot properly predict on psychological grounds that a protective parent—simply because she is a protective parent—will defy the law. In this case the claim was doubly cynical, because it was virtually an invention: when the evaluator was cross-examined by the mother's lawyer, she admitted she could not recall when the mother, who had been seen four times over the course of four months, had made such a statement. Nor could the expert recall any specific details. In fact, she finally conceded that the mother's supposed mention of the underground did not cause her to believe it was "serious enough or compelling enough" to be an "emergency."[85] But that was precisely what the evaluator had claimed—when she needed a reason to have the children removed from their mother.[86] She had even recommended harsh specific measures to be taken to prevent a parental kidnapping: "Additionally, it would be imperative to notify both girls' school that their mother was not allowed to visit [and] not to take them from school without expressed written permission by [the father]."[87]

The unhealthy combination of a legal prejudgment and an accusation of future lawbreaking, masquerading as psychology, had the desired result. The abuse charges were never fully investigated, despite the substantial evidence supporting them. The children were immediately removed from their mother as a result of the "emergency" claimed by the evaluator, though (as we have seen) no real emergency could have existed. This mother never regained custody of her two daughters. In fact, she has not been allowed to see them for over four years.

A MOTHER FORBIDDEN TO EXPRESS LOVE TO HER CHILDREN

In 1995, a California mother who had been divorced for about a year became another woman accused of being a "parental alienator." Several months later she lost custody of all three of her children (a boy, aged ten, and two girls, aged four and seven) to her ex-husband. In addition, she was cut off from any contact with the children for almost half a year; thereafter she was limited to strictly supervised visitation for another four years.

The court battle, which began several months before the mother lost custody of her children, was precipitated by the girls' disclosures of sexual abuse. The parents were sharing joint custody, with the children spending weekends with their father. When the girls told their mother they had been sexually abused at their father's home, the mother asked the family court to suspend the father's visitation until the charges could be fully investigated.

The mother's concern that her children were being abused was supported by several facts. First, both of the children's therapists strongly suspected sexual abuse. The four-year-old's therapist reported that she showed features "in her spontaneous play that are consistent with a child who has experienced trauma."[88] The other girl's therapist reported, in a sworn statement, that when asked to write (symbolic) letters to her father the child wrote: "I wish you would stop touching me in my privates. Stop doing that because it hurts! Why didn't you stop when I told you to stop?"[89]

Second, a medical examination of the older girl showed genital abnormalities that raised the question of sexual abuse. The girl had been examined with a colposcope that showed "a narrow irregular thickened hymen," and "generalized increased vascularity" of the perihymenal tissue.[90]

Third, the older girl was interviewed by the Multidisciplinary Interview Center (MDIC), a team of forensic scientists used by the local district attorney's office. The girl had told them: "He [the father] pulled down my pants . . . put his finger in there [pointing to her genitals] and then he pulled up my pants and put his 'wee-wee' in my mouth."[91] This tape-recorded interview formed the basis of a police report against the father.[92]

Yet, in spite of this evidence, the case turned sharply against the mother once the court appointed a mental health expert to assess the validity of the sexual abuse claims. After conducting six interviews with the mother and her children he wrote in his report: "I also find the mother utilizing numerous exclusionary maneuvers and she is presenting the father as inconsequential and unimportant [to the children]."[93] His testimony, in which he invoked Gardner's PAS theory, was harsh and clear:

MENTAL HEALTH EXPERT: My recommendation is that all the children should be placed immediately in the father's custody, and that the mother should have absolutely no contact with these children for thirty days.

FATHER'S COUNSEL: You are basing that on what concept that you are aware of?

MENTAL HEALTH EXPERT: Well, this is part of this Parental Alienation Syndrome and my observations and my opinion is that these children do not hate their father and that's one of the prime symptoms of Parental Alienation Syndrome is that the children hate their father. Children are not born with the gene to hate their father. So I see that all this alienation that's been going on by the mother has not worked. The father has been persistent in trying to get contact with these children, when it hasn't worked, now we have the atom bomb. This is right out of textbooks.

FATHER'S COUNSEL: So now you are saying since what other maneuvers mother might have gone through, the newest one is the allegation of sexual abuse [which] is just a new twist on the alienation syndrome?

MENTAL HEALTH EXPERT: This is an example of what Dr. Gardner calls escalating of more bizarre, more unusual allegations to try to get the father out of the children's lives and when these don't work, they get stranger and more bizarre.

Then they still don't work, then this is one sure way to get a father out of the children's lives absolutely.[94]

The expert was convinced that this was a clear-cut case of Gardner's Parental Alienation Syndrome; he told the court that it "matches right out of the textbooks what's classic in these Parental Alienation Syndromes. Just makes me even more confident that the other allegations haven't worked and here's the atom bomb."[95]

The expert was so confident in this diagnosis that he dismissed the concerns of the children's therapists: "Little weight should be placed on the impressionism [*sic*] and anecdotal intuitive statements made by the children's therapists."[96] In his testimony he was just as dismissive of the children's own statements:

> I don't place a lot of weight on what children have to say. I listen to them, but I don't place a lot of weight on what children have to say. Otherwise I would ask children which stocks and bonds I should buy, how should I run my life, I don't listen to what children say.[97]

Armed with a diagnosis of PAS, the court followed Gardner's recommendations practically to the letter. As we have seen, Gardner routinely recommended limiting the allegedly abused children's access to the parent who believed their report. In keeping with this approach, the court suspended the mother's visits with the children.

After almost six months of complete isolation, the court ordered supervised visitation between the mother and her children at a special clinic run by a program that operated through the court. The clinic closely monitored the mother's visits with her children. Naturally, the clinic's personnel were quickly introduced to the case's "running record"; its director later testified that the clinic was convinced the mother was guilty of PAS because of "information . . . received thus far."[98] There is no evidence that this "information" included any of the evidence supporting the mother's suspicions of abuse or the concerns of the children's therapists.

It was not enough for the mother to be constantly monitored during her short visits with her children. Soon, the program director of the monitoring clinic wrote to the judge to urge that the mother be forced to undergo therapy with her, the director, rather than with the therapist the mother was already seeing. To justify this demand, the director argued that "it would be necessary for the therapist to understand that [the mother's] treatment needed to be oriented towards her *alienating behavior* and not treat her as if she were a non-offending parent of molested children."[99] After all, she complained, the mother's current therapist was "reinforcing her image of herself as a parent of molested children." [100] The court agreed.

Now the mother lived in a closed world of mental health insanity. She was not supposed to consult a therapist she trusted. She was not allowed to speak to her children about the abuse they themselves reported. She was required to admit that she was mentally ill as a condition of being allowed to see or speak to her children at all. Every aspect of her life as a mother—as an on-going practical accomplishment—was now controlled by "experts" who in turn were guided by the theory of the mother as the "parental alienator."

Under the experts' influence, the family court took some bizarre steps. For example, at the time the judge stripped the mother of custody of the three children, he ordered her to have "no telephone contact" for a period of thirty days. At the expiration of that period, the judge ordered that all "telephone contact shall be monitored by an independent supervising adult or shall be recorded for later review."[101] Within a month, the program director, who—along with the children's father—was intently listening in on every conversation between the mother and her children, asked the court to suspend all telephone contact once again. Her reason? The mother was telling the children she loved them.

In an affidavit written in response to this "expert" attack on the mother's conversations, the mother's therapist had this to say:

> [The mother] was not told that she could not verbally express love for her children over the phone, as any normal parent does, without the children first expressing their love to her. I must take issue with the statements from the program director that [the mother] always expressed her love to the children first—that is not so. There are several places in the phone recordings that the children express their desire to visit with her and their love for her first, the most poignant of which is the first call between [the mother] and [the older daughter] when [the older daughter] broke down sobbing for several minutes.
>
> The program director criticizes [the mother] for talking with the children about their daily activities, their schooling, their playmates, and world news. At no time in any of the tape recorded phone conversations did [the mother] ask the children how their father was treating them, or make any suggestions about how they should or should not react around their father. If [the mother] is precluded from talking with the children about their normal daily activities, what is left to talk about?

It appears from the entire tone of the letter from [the program director] that no matter what [the mother] said or did, [the program director] could find fault with, doubt the wisdom of, or second-guess the motivation of [the mother] and her ordinary, everyday conversations with her children.[102]

Notwithstanding this protest, the court took the program director's advice, and—because the mother had told the children she loved them—suspended all telephone contact between this mother and her children for four years.

THE MOTHER WHO TOLD HER DAUGHTER SHE MISSED HER

In 1991, a New York mother, who had previously stipulated to joint custody with her ex-husband of their five-year-old daughter, started to worry about what was happening to the girl when she visited her father at his new home in Georgia. According to the mother, the girl returned from visits with her father in a belligerent mood and began to "act out" sexually. Concerned about the child's behavior, the mother took her to a psychologist. The child reportedly complained to the psychologist that her father made her sleep in the same bed with him and his girlfriend and that he fondled her genitals during the night.

The psychologist suggested to the mother that the child be evaluated by a clinic specializing in child sexual abuse trauma and referred the mother to a pediatric nurse who headed a sexual abuse program at the clinic. The nurse interviewed the girl and found that she had been sexually abused and that her father was the likely perpetrator. As the nurse later wrote to the family court:

> In my professional experience, I've evaluated over two thousand children for child abuse. I was a member of the Committee on Sexual Abuse, Office of Projects Department, Supreme Court of the State of New York, Appellate Division, First Department. I co-authored the chapter "Medical Protocol for Evaluation of Sexual Abuse" in the book published by this committee. I am confident about my assessment of [the child] that she is a sexually abused child who states her abuser was her father.[103]

But when the mother asked the court to restrict the father's visitation based on the evidence of sexual abuse, she was compelled to undergo an evaluation by a court-appointed mental health expert. After interviewing the child and her parents, the "expert" did not hesitate to label the *mother* as the source of all the trouble. According to the "expert," the real danger involved the threat the mother posed to the child's relationship with her father.

In her report to the court, the expert not only made the father-daughter relationship her central concern, but did not hesitate to predict that switching the child abruptly to the father's custody would be good—even necessary—for the child:

> [The child] will not, in my opinion, be traumatized if the physical custody is changed so that she [the child] resides in Georgia with the father and [his girlfriend]. It is the only way that she can have any kind of *father-daughter relationship* develop and it has to be done right away before any more damage is done that will be irreparable. One more period of six months [without the father] and I think it will be too late.[104]

Besides the abuse reports, this little girl presented some special problems. Since an early age, she had suffered from moderately severe hypoglycemia that required a diet of small, frequent meals.[105] The mother had been instructed by the child's pediatrician to keep a close watch on the child for signs of agitation and restlessness that could signal a precipitous drop in her blood sugar level.

The mother had always carefully followed the pediatrician's instructions. But now that she had been labeled an "alienator," her conscientious behavior became one more weapon against her. The mother was now judged entirely as a problem—an illustration of how mental health experts continually "negotiate" and "interpret" the meaning of maternal "fitness"—so that even her attention to the child's diet was seen as self-aggrandizing and "controlling," as in these comments by the same expert:

> [The mother] came equipped with orange juice, saying that [the child] had hypoglycemia and had to eat something every hour. She insisted she had to know how long the child was to be with me. . . . After 40 minutes a knock came on the door and the mother said she had to come into my office and personally give [the child] orange juice. . . . [The child's doctor was] giving the mother the license to use intrusive and controlling maneuvers about food intake with the child. It enabled her to present herself in the role of watchful guardian of the child's health. . . . [106]

The expert diagnosed the mother with "Narcissistic Personality Disorder . . . that interferes with her functioning as a mother."[107] The expert gave the following basis for the diagnosis after administering a battery of personality functioning tests to the mother:[108]

The test findings, both the Rorschach and the MMPI, point to a narcissistic character with hysterical traits and paranoid aspects, who feels emotionally unique and different; who has a related sense of elitism and entitlement. Her "found cause" of sexual abuse has enabled her to occupy a very high moral ground and she has found a "righteous cause" that effectively protects her against any dubiousness about her position or claims.[109]

The family court obligingly transferred the girl into the father's custody. Even after those proceedings ended, the findings of the court-appointed expert haunted the mother for many years. When she tried to visit her daughter in Georgia, a judge in that state (after receiving case information from the New York court) gave the father permission to engage a psychologist in Georgia to supervise the mother's visits and to monitor all her calls to her daughter. In keeping with the bizarre theorizing that had landed the girl with an allegedly abusive father in the first place, this new psychologist cautioned the mother to "talk less about your love and the fact that you miss her tremendously and talk more about your own personal life and your own day to day activities."[110] The child was only six years old at the time; her mother, like most mothers of children that age, tended to focus conversation on the child rather than on herself. But normal parental behavior was suspect in the strange world of family court quackery.

As time went on, the father made the child less and less available for visits. The mother made as many as thirty trips from New York to see the child in Georgia only to find that the child was not at home. The mother asked the court to enforce her visitation rights, but that proved futile; she encountered endless court delays (including an unexpected change of judges) and mounting legal costs until she was too financially drained to continue the battle.

Adding one injury to another, the father—even though he continued to interfere with the mother's visits—was allowed by the family court to demand weekly child support from the mother.

For the child's eighth birthday, the father seemed to relent, agreeing to allow the mother to visit the girl on her birthday. When the mother finished the nine-hundred-mile drive and arrived for the anticipated meeting, carrying several birthday presents for the girl she had not seen for a year, she was met by a sheriff and arrested for allegedly failing to pay child support. (Apparently the same court that had ignored her attempts to enforce her visitation rights had acted immediately on her ex-husband's request.) In her daughter's view, she was handcuffed and taken to a women's detention center, where she was placed in a "suffocating" jail cell. She recalls being "doubled over" in pain from severe menstrual cramps and "trembling uncontrollably"; she begged the prison guards for prescription medication that was in her purse, but they would not give it to her. When she was finally released six hours later, her ex-husband refused to allow her to see her daughter.

While visits between the mother and daughter were being stymied, the mother made every attempt to contact her daughter via telephone. Eventually the child did not even take her mother's phone calls. But the mother persisted; she continued to call her daughter twice a day, even though she rarely succeeded in speaking to her. She has continued this routine for well over a decade, though her daughter—now almost eighteen—has become almost a stranger to her. She keeps a written log of her failed attempts to contact the girl, a graphic record of the wedge driven between mother and child by misguided mental health theories and family court madness. In black felt marker at the bottom is the running tally of the times—over eight thousand now—she has tried without success to speak to the daughter she once tried to protect.

The Effects of Mental Health Labels

Mothers on the receiving end of the labels we have been examining feel their effects even outside family court. Women who have always been seen as competent people and mothers are now treated as if they were dangerously insane. How are they to explain to friends and neighbors why they no longer live with their children? Why they cannot even meet them without a supervisor present? When mothers are devalued by the family courts, there is nowhere to hide from the labels that have been applied to them. The mentally ill—even when they are not really mentally ill—are not treated as other people are.

For instance, one New York protective mother was found in the 1980s to be "delusional" about her belief in her daughter's sexual abuse (though substantial evidence supported her belief). The mother publicized her case by appearing on the nationally televised *Geraldo Rivera Show*. But when the show's producer called the family court judge to get his side of the story, the judge's law clerk told him that the mother was a "paranoid schizophrenic." This was not true: even the evaluator who had called the mother "paranoid" about the sexual abuse had not gone so far as to call her a "paranoid schizophrenic."[111] But she was to encounter similar experiences time after time, as she appeared on television or testified before legislators.

Such mothers suffer feelings of self-blame, inferiority, worthlessness.[112] One Kansas protective mother said, after she had finished a harrowing two-year family court trial in which she was ridiculed by the court and all its auxiliaries as "the crazy woman," that she emerged feeling she was "lower than dirt."

Chapter 8

Mothers and Madness

The "Aftershocks" of the System

One New York protective mother referred to her shattering experience in the family courts as a "moral earthquake." Because descriptions like this have often been offered to us by protective mothers, this mother's words are worth some consideration.

What did she mean by calling family courts a "moral earthquake"? Essentially, she meant that the foundation of her entire belief system had been shaken when she saw how courts, child welfare agencies, and their auxiliaries could turn so fiercely against her when she had done, as she said, "absolutely nothing wrong." She told us she felt "utter confusion" and difficulty "navigating" this "new world" of the family courts. All that had been familiar was gone: not only her six-year-old daughter but everything else that had seemed reliable. She had been financially secure; now she sank deeper and deeper into debt trying to defend herself against charges that she had "brainwashed" her child. She had been a respected authority in a modern academic field; the family court judge simply refused to believe that she had lectured extensively and published significant articles (though she had). No one had ever questioned her personal competence, either; now, at public appearances in which she described her case, she had to defend against "officials" who would slander her as "insane" or "paranoid schizophrenic" (which she was not).

Worst of all, what she had believed about America—the land of democracy, freedom, justice—was severely challenged. She had confronted a Kafkaesque court system that seemed to operate outside the law.

Another New York mother echoed these feelings several years later when she, too, became trapped in the bizarre world of the family courts. She told *New York Post* columnist Amy Pagnozzi: "You have to live through this to believe it."[1]

It is therefore not terribly surprising that some protective mothers are profoundly affected by their family court experience. In some cases the effects are so great that mothers behave in ways that, were it not for their family court experience, would have been quite alien to them.

In this chapter we examine some of the "aftershocks" of the family court earthquake—the sociological and psychological consequences to mothers who rebel against the system. We look at what has happened to mothers who fled with their children and to those who stayed behind to resist.

Protective Mother Syndromes

We believe that certain patterns of emotional response can be identified in protective mothers who have been attacked through the family court system. These "syndromes," as we will call them, seem to us to result from several features found together in such litigation: mothers have witnessed their children suffering and have found themselves unable to protect them; they have felt betrayed by a system they believed would help their children and themselves; they have been victims of verbal and legal attacks from family court "experts," child welfare personnel, and family court judges; they have lost their children, and in many cases even access to their children, as a result of the system. We will describe these "syndromes" below.

"HUNTED" SYNDROME

The constant feeling of being hunted is common in mothers who have become family court victims. Significantly, the feeling surfaces in mothers who are *not* fugitives, just as it does among mothers who are.

Those who take their children and try to hide from the police have obvious reasons to feel hunted. Their lives become a long series of "safe houses" in which they remain confined during the day, sheets or blankets covering the windows—venturing out only at night, and even then usually in wigs or other disguises. They are always afraid that, without a moment's notice, FBI agents or local police will descend on them. Capture and imprisonment is not their worst fear in such circumstances; worse than that is the fear of what will happen to their children, who are seldom allowed to see their mothers again and are usually returned, even against their will, to the fathers they have accused of abusing them.[2] And, as a matter of fact, nearly 80 percent of mothers who go into hiding with their children are caught by the FBI within the first six months.[3]

This fear is intensified by the isolation of fugitive mothers. Living on the run, these mothers are cut off from all that is familiar to them. In addition, fugitive moms are unable to develop new support systems; they cannot freely meet other parents and are often hesitant even to take their children to a playground for fear of getting caught.

"Hunted" Syndrome can lead to fatal mistakes. In 1996, a mother from Maryland died because she ignored a lump she had found in her breast while on the run. As a fugitive (with her daughter), she feared getting medical help because of the possibility that her medical records could lead the FBI to her. Her tumor was malignant, and it eventually killed her.

Protective mothers who are not on the run can feel equally threatened. They are not hunted by the FBI but may very well feel persecuted by CPS, and their emotional reactions are very similar. Moreover, they often suffer the loss of emotional "support systems" no less than those who become fugitives. University of Illinois researchers Carol Rippey Massat and Marta Lundy (1998) found that "[f]ifty-four percent [of mothers] reported that after disclosure [of sexual abuse] some family members were dissatisfied, and 35% reported that family members were angry. Forty-one percent indicated that some friends became less friendly. . . ."[4] The combination of relentless pursuit by family court and its auxiliaries and the erosion of support and comradeship gives rise to "Hunted" Syndrome.

Consider the case of a Brooklyn, New York, mother who was a schoolteacher with a master's degree in education. After two anguished years in a custody battle against her ex-husband—who was supported by CPS despite evidence that he had sexually abused both children—she was forced to quit the job she loved because of the number of days she had to take off for court appearances and court-ordered mental health examinations for herself and her children.

CPS's lawyer grilled the mother for twenty-one days, accusing her of having "brainwashed" her two young daughters (ages four and seven) into believing they had been sexually abused. At the end of the interrogation, CPS formally charged her with child neglect, "for instilling in the children a fear of sexual abuse by the father."[5]

At that time, the mother told one of us she felt that "the system is chasing me down," and she could not understand why. Both of her girls had physical symptoms of sexual abuse. The younger child's anus was infected with a sexually transmitted disease (chlamydia); "the older daughter's vaginal canal was found to be rounded instead of oval, roughened instead of smooth, and there was a stretching of the hymen."[6] In addition, the children were already showing signs of severe trauma. According to a newspaper columnist who covered the trial, her younger daughter "pulled a plastic bag over her head and said she wanted to die."[7]

But while the mother was forced by court order to send these girls on unsupervised weekend visits with their father, she was facing the pressure of CPS persecution. She was in constant fear of the agency's surprise visits, which took place about twice a week, always at different times so that she could not prepare for them. During the unannounced inspections—which took anywhere from one to two hours—the caseworkers would search the entire apartment, including private dresser drawers in her bedroom, looking for some sign of "brainwashing" materials, such as a book on how to recognize signs of sexual abuse in one's child. The mother knew that even the slightest hint of "brainwashing" would be held against her and would affect the fate of her children.[8]

The mother's sense of being "hunted" affected her daily behavior. Every morning, after sending her children to school and doing the minimal necessary chores, this woman found herself almost "paralyzed." She would stand at the window in her apartment with her eyes fixed on the huge clock atop the building housing the CPS agency that controlled her life. All she could think about, for hours at a time, was the agency's "threat" (which she related to one of us) that if she were to make any further reports of her children being sexually abused during weekend visits with their father, the court would see to it that she lost custody of her children. Unable to concentrate on any other subject, she stopped reading newspapers and withdrew from family and friends.

In the end, the persecution was more than she could bear; between the continuing evidence of abuse (which the court utterly ignored) and CPS's persecution, she came to believe that defeat was inevitable and took her children into hiding. Naturally, this gave the family court judge the needed rationale to transfer custody of both children to the father. However, the mother and her daughters eluded capture—their whereabouts remain a mystery. Questioned about the case years later by a reporter, the family court judge continued to claim he had acted properly and blamed the mother's flight for her loss of custody. But would she ever have defied the law, or a court order, had it not been for CPS's relentless pursuit—before she ever ran?

A similar irony can be seen in the case of an Idaho protective mother who was accused of causing her children to believe they had been sexually abused by their father. No evidence in the record suggested any history of paranoia. No mental health expert in the case diagnosed the mother as paranoid, despite the entire system's manifest hostility toward her.

In the course of family court litigation, two of her minor children were removed from her with no legal justification, based on evidence that was not shared with her or her lawyer. Her child support was slashed on flimsy grounds, she was repeatedly maligned by the judge, and her ex-husband's attorney seemed deliberately to serve her with threatening court papers just before family holidays.

After several years of this treatment, when the father sought full custody of the minor children, the mother allegedly began to exhibit some peculiar behavior, including missing court appearances. A new family court judge, awarding custody to the father, said that he based his opinion of the mother's mental state on the behavior he himself had witnessed. But this apparently objective approach was in fact grossly unfair: it ignored the extent to which the mother's fear of court appearances and extremely anxious behavior resulted from what she had experienced in family court. A fear of being hunted does not suggest insanity in someone who really has been hunted.[9]

"LOST LIMB" SYNDROME

Author and researcher John Edward Gill has chronicled how mothers cope with the loss of their children to the other spouse. Although his 1981 book[10] focused exclusively on mothers whose children had been kidnapped by their ex-husbands, rather than mothers who lost all contact with their children as the result of a family court order, the psychological effects he observed are felt by protective mothers who have lost custody: "their lives stop—emotions frozen . . . houses go uncleaned. Phones go unanswered, doorbells ignored. Some act like sleepwalkers, eyes glazed, their thinking distracted. . . . "

In 1987, a Queens, New York, protective mother coined the term "Lost Limb" Syndrome to describe how she felt when she lost custody of her five-year-old daughter. She meant that her loss felt as if she had lost her arm or leg and could never feel whole again.[11] Five years later, another protective mother, late at night after the day she lost custody of her three-year-old daughter, wrote some verses that display similar feelings:

> My tears flow unending
> And all I have left is my grief
> The memories of my daughter are still with me
> Yet, thoughts of her don't bring relief
>
> Gaps in my memory
> Silent photos I watch
> Trying to see
> And hear laughter

> Hours can go by
> Spiraling deeper in thought. . . . [12]

Mothers suffering from Lost Limb Syndrome may actually feel they are *personally* damaged, no longer capable of mothering. A California mother, for example, after losing custody following a lengthy trial (in which she was accused of coaching her child to make up sex abuse charges against the father), decided not to remarry and told one of us that, even if she did remarry, she would try not to have any more children.

In fact, some protective mothers speak of themselves as if they were literally incapable of having children. One Florida mother, for example, told us she stopped going for annual ob-gyn examinations after she was deprived of custody. She said, "It's useless to go for an exam . . . after all, what do I have left in the reproductive department?" A Washington State mother, after losing custody of her son to an allegedly sexually abusive father, went further than that: she told one of us that she actually had herself sterilized while in her midthirties, even though she intended to remarry (and later did).

Protective mothers often use the word "emptiness" to describe a grief in which they mourn children who are still alive. They often speak of yearning to hold their children, to put them to bed at night, kiss them in the morning. Instead, their houses contain empty cribs and beds, tables with an extra chair.

Another special aspect of protective mothers' grief is that time becomes their enemy. Severed from their children's lives at an early age, deprived of contact with them as they grow up, these mothers fight a losing battle against the calendar, remembering their children as they were when they were taken away—unable to cross the widening abyss between the child they lost and the much older one who inhabits a time and place alien to them. One protective mother kept her six-year-old daughter's room unchanged for more than ten years after the girl was removed by an ex parte court order, the little girl's clothes and toys waiting for her—waiting, that is, for a return that never came. At first this was a gesture of hope. As the days from removal became months, the months years, that room, frozen in time, became a kind of open household wound.

"MASOCHISTIC MOTHER" SYNDROME

Some protective mothers, despairing of any other way of regaining their children, try to endure whatever the family courts and CPS want them to suffer, simultaneously begging the court and its auxiliaries for the return of their children. They seldom succeed. But this pattern of behavior may continue anyway once it has begun.

Taken to its extreme, this pattern can end with the mother's suicide. In 1993, a Rockland County, New York, protective mother killed herself—and her child—with the exhaust fumes of her car. She had been faced with both a hostile family court system and an ultra-Orthodox Jewish community that had strongly sided with her ex-husband (who had been credibly accused of sexually abusing the child).[13]

Her tragic act was, in her eyes, the only way to remove herself, and her child, from a system she saw as bent on destroying both of them. She had come to feel that resistance was hopeless. The judge and law guardian, ignoring evidence of sexual abuse that included the testimony of the child's nursery school teacher and a leading sex abuse validator (who was chosen by the judge himself), had repeatedly threatened her with loss of custody if she persisted in believing the allegations of abuse. Just days before her suicide/homicide, this mother had called a New York State legislative office sympathetic to the plight of protective mothers and said: "I'm so afraid my child will end up like all the rest of the children who have been forced to live with sexually abusive parents." And when the court formally rejected the abuse allegations against her ex-husband and the law guardian (according to the mother) sneeringly told her she would have "the fight of her life" just to retain custody, she had had too much.[14] Self-destruction seemed the only way out.

Hers is not the only such case. Just a few years earlier, the *New York Daily News* reported that two Brooklyn mothers killed themselves after long court battles in Brooklyn Family Court.[15]

Damaged Lives

In some cases, the injuries suffered in family courts impel protective mothers to self-damaging choices, made essentially out of fear and insecurity. For example, some mothers who remarried after their family court experiences have stayed in bad marriages rather than undergo a divorce in the court system they have learned to fear. In some cases, protective mothers have actually agreed to give up custody of children (born in a later marriage) just to avoid going back to family court.

For example, one Texas protective mother, faced with a custody battle in her new marriage, declared: "After spending three years in the family courts, it's a place I could never go back to." She then "consented" to giving custody to her new husband—a decision she admits was made out of fear.

A mother from Woodstock, New York, who lost custody of her son in the early 1990s after repeated CPS intervention, fled to Mexico with her new partner and gave birth to a daughter there. The mother feared that the record built up against her by CPS, though undeserved, would prejudice her with her new child unless she stayed out of the United States altogether. Tragically, this mother's attempts to escape the courts had dire consequences. Living in poor conditions in a rural Mexican town, the mother contracted hepatitis B and died on her way to the hospital. She was forty-one and had been in good health until then.

Still other women put up a wall of denial around the damage they suffered in family courts. One of us has spoken to women who, after losing custody, have moved to a different part of the country and have remarried—not even telling their new husbands that they ever had children.

One North Carolina woman—now a high-level employee of the federal government—told one of us she had lost a child ten years earlier, to a man who had instigated CPS to remove the child from her after she brought sexual abuse charges against him. After she lost custody—and all visitation rights, too—she moved away and went back to school to complete her education, never disclosing to her new husband or to any of her colleagues that she ever had a child.

Other mothers we have interviewed gradually pulled away from their friends who had children, finding it too painful to participate in their friends' conversations about children. Some protective mothers actually made a point of becoming professionals, surrounding themselves with career-oriented women who they thought would be less likely to have a family.

Damaged Psyches

Protective mothers suffer more than the loss of a child. They also suffer deep feelings of helplessness and of remorse for having been unable to protect their children. In 1991, a Colorado protective mother lost custody of her four-year-old daughter after she reported alleged sexual abuse by the father. [16] A year later, her only contact with her daughter was one hour a week of tightly supervised visitation. Though she had no history of depression, she took antidepressant drugs for two months. Then she testified before a congressional committee about the pain of being unable to save her child:

> I am the mother of a precious 5-year old girl. My child has been the reason for my existence. For the past 3 years my whole being has been geared toward saving her from abuse. Fighting the system both body and soul has turned me into what the system has made and labeled me, an "hysterical mother." . . . There is no one, not even with the loss of a child through death, who could suffer more than a mother unable to save her child. That is the worst suffering of all.[17]

She gave a court-appointed expert an even more vivid picture of her despair over her helplessness:

> As her mother I have listened to her cries for help to friends, family, doctors, psychologists, social workers, and police, and I have watched her be let down and not protected. She used to say, "you will protect me Mom" and *I feel that I, too, have let her down.* All of these people tell her they are here to help her, but no one has been able to help her. I keep telling her I am still trying but it is very difficult after two years. I think she may begin accepting this as a way of life and there is no hope.[18]

This Colorado mother told one of us that her grief over the loss of her daughter was at its worst right after she left her child after each one-hour supervised visit, because that was when she felt most keenly aware of her own helplessness. After each such visit, she had to face the realization that her daughter would be going home to her father—the man the girl had said abused her. Yet the mother was not even allowed to talk to her child about her feelings, let alone the child's fears and almost certain sense of having been betrayed by the mother who was supposed to protect her.

This mother did make what efforts she could to fight the system in which she was trapped. Though forbidden by court order to speak at press conferences or to the media about her case, or about the protective mother problem at large,[19] she defied the "gag" order and became a leading spokesperson for other mothers. She made several trips to Washington, D.C., lobbying for new laws to protect mothers and children, and organized many rallies and candlelight vigils, which gave hope to other mothers in similar predicaments. After several years, her efforts won her unsupervised visitation with her daughter—a small accomplishment but not negligible in the world of family courts.

Self-Destructive Vigilantism

In a few cases, the psychic damage wrought by family courts has driven protective mothers to hostile, illegal, or dangerous behavior.

In 2003, a New York City mother took the law into her own hands, deciding to confront in her own way the judge who had removed her daughter from her. The result: she received a jail sentence after being charged with making harassing calls to the judge's chambers, writing threatening letters, and even stalking the judge (a woman) to her home.[20]

This mother had no criminal record before being jailed for contempt of court. Before she was entangled in the family courts, she had a perfectly respectable social and professional history. She lived in an apartment building, where she was well liked by her neighbors of more than ten years.

All this changed after she endured a six-year battle in a futile effort to regain custody of her daughter from her ex-husband. Medical evidence showed "an adhesion of the hymen to the interior aspect of the labia minora," which doctors found consistent with sexual abuse; the seven-year-old girl's stated that her father had "touched her vagina on multiple occasions with his hand, tongue and penis."[21] In fact, the local CPS agency filed formal charges alleging that the father had sexually abused the girl. But—consistent with the pattern we examined in chapter 6—the mother was also charged with "neglect," CPS claiming she "should have known about the abuse, but failed to take any steps to protect the child from further abuse."[22]

As in other cases we have presented here, CPS's accusations turned out to be cynical; after several months, during which the child—on the strength of the bilateral charges against both mother and father—was in foster care, the agency dropped the charges against the father. However, even though this should have meant the automatic dismissal of the "failure to protect" charge against the mother (since the charge assumed the occurrence of abuse by the father), the child was not in fact returned to the mother. The child was eventually given into the father's custody.

After the court ordered the change of custody, the mother became a hyper-activist. Struggling in vain against a hostile court system, she began to see the judge as a personal enemy and herself as a warrior unconcerned with rules. She created her own cable television program and used it to attack the judge, while publicizing other family court cases as well. Her actions —which were ultimately found to violate court orders—were intended to intimidate her "enemy." As for the consequences, she told one of us: "They already did the worst they could to me by taking my child, so what else did I have to lose?"

One would be hard pressed to say this mother was "crazy." She was never diagnosed with any serious mental illness and had never committed any crime (apart from defying a judge's orders). She had been capable of forming a close bond with her daughter, which is rarely possible for truly paranoid mothers. In fact, very few protective mothers of whom we have been aware were actually "crazy" in any clinical sense. Protective mothers earn the label "protective" by having a very strong bond with their children in the first place. They deplete their life savings fighting for protection from the courts; they move in with family members for shelter; they endure years of arduous court battles. None of this is typical of the mentally ill. Therefore, when a victim of family courts behaves in a fashion that would ordinarily justify the label of mental illness, we must seek the cause in something other than a diagnosis of mental illness.

This is equally of true of those rare protective mothers who resort to violence. A Maryland mother whose children were allegedly sexually abused is now serving a prison sentence for conspiracy to commit her ex-husband's murder.[23] Yet, before her ordeal in the family courts, this mother had never committed so much as a traffic violation. Nor was she found to be insane by the court-appointed evaluator, who also found no evidence of a "conduct disorder" in any of the tests he had administered to the mother.

But family court changed her. First, her allegations that the children's father had sexually abused them were ignored, despite the reports of psychologists who found no evidence that she had coached the children to report what they did. (The children reported spontaneously that their father had kicked one boy in the crotch, tickled his private parts, withheld food from him, ridiculed his artwork, and threatened to kill him and his mother by setting fire to their house. In addition, one of the elder boy's teachers reported to the boy's therapist that the boy had flinched when the teacher placed his hand near the boy's head; this teacher commented that "he had seen that before in children who've been abused, and that really bothered him.")[24]

Next, the law guardian appointed to protect the boys, having failed to persuade a Maryland court to remove the children from the mother, secretly went to officials in the District of Columbia and got an ex parte removal order from a court there—apparently on the strength of misrepresentations of fact made to caseworkers. Then, when the children had been removed from her, the mother was restricted to minimal, supervised visitation.

The mother reported to one of us that her boys continued to describe being abused by their father, but D.C. caseworkers and police officers were openly contemptuous of her reports. One D.C. official claimed—without any basis in the record—that she feared the mother would kill both her children and herself if she had the opportunity. The law guardian continued to claim that the mother was dangerous, though this was not the finding of any mental health professional in the case.

Branded insane, watching a lawless process unfold around her, helpless to protect children she believed were being abused, accused of planning murders, the mother finally did in fact undertake a crime. In January 2002, she arranged with her closest friend (and supporter in her belief that the children's father had abused them) for the friend to break into the father's home and kill him with a 9-millimeter pistol. Her friend entered his house, according to prosecutors, with child pornography (intending to leave it as evidence of pedophilia) and shot him once in the leg. He managed to wrest the gun from her and called the police. Both women were soon arrested and eventually convicted: the mother's friend of attempted murder, the mother herself of conspiracy to commit murder.

It is typical of the popular attitude toward such stories that although these incidents received prominent treatment in weekly magazines[25] and many newspapers, not one article adequately described the mother's agonizing experience in the family courts, or the shocking removal of her children through underhanded legal maneuvers and misrepresentation of facts, or the fact that the lawyer appointed to protect children who claimed their father was abusing them had insisted that the father should have custody, or the prejudices against her expressed by D.C. officials. They did not even comment on the crowning irony: that after the mother, imprisoned, told a judge she cared about nothing but her children, it was the boys' law guardian—the lawyer who had bent the truth to deprive the mother of custody in the first place—who persuaded the court to deny her request to have the children visit her, even though there was no evidence that she posed any danger to them. (The law guardian called her a "stressor.")[26]

And certainly when these things are considered, the mother's crime committed by a previously law-abiding woman—takes on a different aspect. No one is likely to condone the mother's actions. But they were, in part, an indictment of the family court system, a fact that so far has not been acknowledged in the popular press. It might be comforting to believe that protective mothers are all like this one and that courts are therefore justified in dealing harshly with them. In fact, the only thing really unusual about this case is the mother's violence. Apart from that, the madness of the case is common ground for protective mother cases all over the country—and, as with the other aftershocks treated in this chapter, this tragedy started with the system, not the mother.

Part III ||||||||||||||||||||||||||||||||||||||||||||||||||||||||||||||||||||||
CHANGES

Chapter 9

"Rebirthing" the Family Court System

Some activists have proposed a three-pronged approach to reforming the family court system: new laws, new policies for law guardians and child protective service workers, and a new mind-set to be instilled throughout the system. New laws can help to prevent the victimization of protective mothers in the courts; new policies can make law guardians and CPS agencies less likely to abuse their authority. But those familiar with the system believe that even substantial reform of laws and policies will not succeed unless they are accompanied by genuine changes in the attitudes of the participants. For instance, in 1997, at a special meeting at the White House Women's Office, attorney and domestic violence activist Joan Zorza[1] spoke with conviction about the need for a "radical" shift in the attitudes and perceptions of judges, law guardians, mental health experts, and others connected with the system.

What would such a "radical" change involve? Essentially it would require a rethinking of all the basic elements of the family courts and their auxiliaries—the rebirth of the entire system. That is, certain fundamental beliefs held by family court judges and their cadre of auxiliaries must be drastically revised. We examine some of these fundamental concepts below.

Parens Patriae

First of all, it is necessary for the family courts and their auxiliaries to rethink the implications of the doctrine known to lawyers as *parens patriae*. Under English common law, this doctrine, which literally means "the father of his country," conferred on the monarch the power to assume parental responsibility for any child (or someone else suffering a "disability") within his kingdom.[2]

This power (now assigned in democracies to the state, not to a king),[3] gives the state the authority to act in lieu of a parent in certain situations defined by law. It is this doctrine on which family courts rely when they make decisions concerning child custody "in the best interest of the child," or when they remove a child from an abusive home. As one legal treatise explains: "The state as 'parens patriae' is supreme guardian of all minors within its jurisdiction . . . [the] state's equity courts . . . may deprive either or both parents of custody and place minors in custody of a third person or institution regarding best interest of minors."[4]

The doctrine has the obvious benefit of providing protection for children whose interests are not being adequately protected by a parent or guardian. But it has spawned the notion among family court judges and related personnel that *they*—not parents—are ultimately responsible for the child care arrangement of any family that has once been subject to family court jurisdiction or to the intervention of a state agency. As a New Jersey court declared as far back as 1942: "The natural right of a father [parent] to the custody of his child is not an absolute property right, but rather a trust reposed in the father [parent] by the state as parens patriae."[5] Thus, over sixty years ago, the idea had already taken root that the state, in some sense, is the true parent, while mothers and fathers hold only a "trust" that the state has agreed to grant them.

That idea has become dogma in today's family courts. A New York family court in 1981 stated bluntly that because of *parens patriae* the state is a "superparent."[6] Two years later, a Maryland court amplified the idea still further, in language that Americans unfamiliar with matrimonial litigation might be surprised to find in the mouth of an official inside the United States:

> The authority by which the equity courts may safeguard the welfare of children emanated from the State's posture as *parens patriae. . . . In this paternalistic role,* the State imposes the obligation upon the parents to maintain, care for and protect their children. The State may regulate this custodial relationship whenever necessary . . . *and virtually without limitation when children's welfare is at stake.*[7]

Note that the court used the word "welfare" instead of "safety." This broad understanding of the doctrine can have far-reaching consequences. It is one thing to protect children who demonstrably need protection. It is quite another for courts, social service agencies, law guardians, and court-appointed mental health professionals to usurp the authority of a mother against whom no valid charges can be made and to impose their views, preferences, theories, and politics on her and her children—views that emphasize "a child's need to love both parents" (read "a father's rights over children of a divorced spouse") or the emotional "dangers" of a highly protective mother. When courts and social service agencies regard this as their proper function, their protective functions edge toward totalitarian powers, and social workers' armchair psychology becomes law.

To put the danger into clearer perspective, let us take a moment to examine how a family court judge resolved a visitation dispute that involved, not protective mother backlash, but an issue that (like today's cases involving protective mothers) combined popular misunderstanding with prejudice posing as psychology. *Matter of J. S. & C.*[8] concerned a dispute over the rights of a divorced homosexual father to visit his three children in 1974—at a time when homosexuality was no more acceptable to the general public than sex abuse allegations against fathers are today.[9] The children's mother sought to restrict the father's visitation severely; in particular, she was opposed to overnight visits between the father and any of the children. She also insisted that the father's lover, who lived with him, should not be present when the children visited. There was no evidence of abusive behavior on the father's part; in fact, it was not even claimed that he was in any way unfit as a parent. The children had no objections to seeing him. It is difficult to see, therefore, how the father could have posed a threat to the children's well-being. However, a New Jersey family court, after hearing testimony from the mother's expert, Richard A. Gardner—later to be notorious for his disastrously biased writings on child sexual abuse allegations—agreed with the mother and imposed serious restrictions on the father's visitation, including a ban on overnights and a rule that the father's lover could not be at home when the children visited.

The steps by which the court reached this conclusion are of great significance for anyone concerned about protective mother backlash. First, invoking *parens patriae,* the court rejected the father's claim that the state could interfere with his parental rights only if he "had impaired the safety or physical or mental health of the children."[10] (How often have protective mothers tried to assert the same claim, with no more success!) Rather, the court (using the expansive reading of *parens patriae* we have explored above) stated that "the parent's right to raise his child as he sees fit is *secondary to the State's power* to ensure the health *and welfare* of the child" (emphasis added). Thus, in effect, the court insisted on its power to substitute its own notion of the children's needs for that of a parent. Next, the court accepted Dr. Gardner's contention that the father's deep commitment to gay rights activism—"an obsessive preoccupation," Gardner had called it, though no one else found it "obsessive"—could "engender homo-sexual fantasies causing confusion and anxiety which would in turn affect the children's sexual development." How Gardner reached this conclusion is difficult to tell, and it was contradicted by two other expert witnesses. But the judge—without citing any evidence beyond Gardner's vague conclusions—claimed that the father's homosexuality "holds the possibil-ity of inflicting severe mental anguish and detriment on three innocent children." He even compared the father to a "bank robber" because he al-legedly advocated violations of New Jersey's sodomy statute. (Actually, the father had advocated *changing* the statute, not violating it, but who was counting?)

This decision illustrates all the elements of the *parens patriae* doctrine that have proven so dangerous to protective mothers. First, it shows how family courts interpret their right to "protect" children more broadly than state statutes (and Supreme Court precedents) appear to contemplate. Rather than stepping in only when a child is in danger—the original pur-pose of the laws that allow the state to override parental rights—family courts intervene to enforce what they believe is "good" for children. (And too many family court judges believe it is not "good" for fathers to be ac-cused of abuse.) Second, this case shows how a family court judge is will-ing to invoke his powers under *parens patriae* on very scanty evidence, once his prejudices are aroused. (And the popular myth of the vengeful, hyster-ical ex-wife heaping accusations on her former spouse is one of today's most stubborn prejudices.) Third, it shows how quickly a family court will accept junk science to lend support to a conclusion it has already reached.

This, then, is what has happened to a doctrine originally intended only to protect the helpless. To make matters worse, the doctrine of *parens patriae* has spilled out of courtrooms and into the ranks of family court auxiliaries—particularly the social workers and mental health profession-als who are called on to make judgments about the welfare of families involved in litigation. One protective mother after another has found a bureaucrat making the decisions for *her* children in matters that she has always believed (correctly) are secured to her by right. Caseworkers for child protective services can and do remove children from their homes without obtaining competent evidence that the children are in danger. Law guardians can and do seek drastic remedies when they feel unable to con-trol how a protective mother deals with her children. Even social workers who deal with such families under the auspices of a court order take it on themselves to decide what subjects a mother should discuss with her child during visits, or that she should not whisper—or even how often she should tell the child she loves her. (Examples of such conduct have been discussed in part II.)

Thus, in today's family court system, the doctrine of *parens patriae* has taken on proportions that threaten a more basic legal principle: the limitations on state power carved out by the Bill of Rights. For the right of parents to live with, and make decisions for, their children has constitutional status, and the deprivation of such rights without proper legal procedure violates the right to "due process of law" contained in the Fourteenth Amendment.[11]

So it is not reckless radicalism to demand the "rebirthing" of the fundamental mind-set of the family court system. This system must recognize both the legal and the prudential limitations inherent in any state-sponsored intrusions into private life. It must seriously rethink its claim to being a "superparent" with powers beyond those of mothers. An attitude that is contrary to constitutional law—even though it grows out of the well-known doctrine of *parens patriae* —must be reborn as something wiser.

Realities of Sex Abuse Reports

Judges and family court auxiliaries must also rethink the myth that women frequently, perhaps usually, make false reports of sex abuse to seek revenge against their spouse. This belief is deeply entrenched in the matrimonial bar and on the bench, although it flies in the face of published studies, as we have seen. It is therefore essential that everyone connected with family court litigation be educated about sexual abuse of children and the facts about sex abuse reports.[12]

There is disturbing evidence that lawyers and judges professionally responsible for handling charges of child sex abuse are strikingly ignorant of the facts concerning sex abuse reports. A prominent New York matrimonial attorney told one of us that most allegations of child sex abuse during divorces were fabricated by mothers "to get an advantage"—even though a study commissioned by the American Bar Association itself concluded that such fabrications are "rare." He even claimed that a professional evaluator's opinion that abuse had occurred was valueless because such validators were "feminists who had issues with men." Similarly, an appellate judge told investigative reporter Karen Winner, "You know what happens in every matrimonial case now? They go to the lawyer and the lawyer says, 'You know we're going to holler sexual abuse.' Everything stops. . . . That's become the password now . . . Holler sexual abuse and every goddamn thing slows down. It's getting to be a disaster now because that's the password now."[13] As we have learned, reality is very different: a mother who suspects sexual abuse is actually more likely to be told by her attorney *not* to mention the suspicion to anyone, and statistics show that women stand to lose more than they stand to gain by making such allegations.[14] It is painful to report that the family court system is unaware of the basic facts pertaining to one of its most sensitive functions. But that is the truth. Education is needed to correct it.

Recognizing the Importance of Family Court

Judges and lawyers must recognize the paradox that family courts wield awesome power over families yet are generally looked down on within the legal profession. Many lawyers see family courts as a "stepchild" of the court system, lacking the prestige of criminal courts or commercial litigation. It is no secret that many judges are ashamed to sit in family courts, seeing the position of family judge merely as a stepping-stone to another court, at best. And yet these courts are handling more and more cases involving decisions that can literally, and radically, change lives.[15] We cannot demand so much from our family courts without according them commensurate respect. And respect for the family courts must begin with family court personnel. They must realize the power they hold and conduct themselves with the restraint, dignity, and respect for legal process that such power demands.

Misuse of Mental Health Labels

Family courts must seriously rethink their freedom with labels such as "emotional disorder," "thought disorder," and the like when it comes to the treatment of protective mothers who clearly do not suffer from mental illness—that is, not anywhere but in the family court system. Serious mental illness affects only about 1 percent of the population, and those who are affected are not likely to marry. It is thus hardly reasonable to suppose that a substantial portion of the mothers who enter the family court system suffer from mental illness so severe that it prevents them from being fit parents. Yet this is exactly what the family courts are decreeing with respect to protective mothers—time after time, in case after case, once a court has concluded that the mother cannot *prove* that the abuse she reported actually occurred (prove it to the court's satisfaction, that is), the court goes on to label the mother "ill" according to one of the many special theories that have sprouted in the family court system. This makes no more sense than claiming that everyone who experiences heart palpitations has heart disease. The temptation to convert an inquiry into facts about alleged abuse into armchair psychologizing about the mother who made the abuse report must be resisted. Judges must not shirk their decision-making responsibilities by falling back on the "expertise" of a mental health professional, who often as not is really giving the judge a rationale for his own preconceived opinion.

Due Process

Lawyers in family courts must learn to demand—and expect—the same standards in legal procedure, ethics, and civil rights to which lawyers have grown accustomed in other courts. As we have seen, violations of due process rights are by no means uncommon in family courts. What *is* uncommon is for matrimonial attorneys to complain about such violations; and it is even more uncommon for the courts to respond to such complaints when they are made.

Changes of the magnitude and scope suggested in this chapter will necessarily involve the entire family court system. As the previous sections of this book have demonstrated, every level of that system is in need of serious reform. In the two chapters that follow, we propose a number of reforms designed to improve the functioning of the family courts and their auxiliary agents and to minimize the injustices that the system has inflicted on protective parents. Chapter 10 presents a range of ideas for judicial reform. Chapter 11 addresses reforms aimed at court "auxiliaries": law guardians, social service agencies, and court-appointed mental health experts. It must be stressed, again, that reforming parts and pieces of the system will not change much unless the participants shake off the attitudes, assumptions, and unquestioned habits that have made family courts places no mother wants to be.

Chapter 10

Reforming the Courts

A s we have seen, the family court system is composed of many parts. This chapter will discuss ideas for reform concerning the courts—the judges and lawyers who practice in family courts, and the kinds of procedures they employ. The next chapter will propose reforms for other parts of the family court system.

There are several general areas of malfunction that inhere in the family courts. One concerns the secrecy of proceedings—the unavailability of critical parts of the process to the litigants (particularly protective mothers), and the various rules barring public access and review of the proceedings. Another area desperately in need of reform is the set of rules and laws by which a mother can lose custody of her child without even knowing that a court action is proceeding against her, such as when a court awards a change of custody to a father who claims his ex-wife is a "flight risk" and therefore need not be notified of his petition. A further area of concern is the use of punitive measures against mothers who report suspicions of child sexual abuse, converting child custody into a sort of judicial football. The abuse of contempt powers by judges is a closely related problem. Finally, there is the role of family court judges themselves—so far the least scrutinized and most poorly supervised judges in the United States.

Some of the reforms we advocate involve changes in the laws and rules governing family court procedure. Although these are promulgated by each individual state, we believe that reforms in these laws and rules do not necessarily have to be achieved one state at a time. Rather, reform can be effected at one point—namely, at the level of federal legislation. This is because under the federal Child Abuse Prevention and Treatment Act (CAPTA),[1] the federal government provides funding to the child protective services of each state, provided that the state meets certain standards, including the adoption of certain procedures specified in the act. Therefore, amendments to CAPTA can be enacted that require the states to adopt the reforms urged here on pain of losing their federal support. This will effectively ensure compliance with all such federally established guidelines. In fact, we have previously urged precisely this approach to family court reform.[2]

Secrecy of Proceedings

We propose several reforms aimed at removing the cloak of secrecy from family court proceedings. Secrecy, in theory, exists to protect victims. In practice, it generally protects the guilty—particularly family court personnel guilty of malfeasance. It has long been recognized that secrecy contributes to abuses of proper legal norms. This is why criminal defendants are generally guaranteed public trials.

The first and most obvious target of these reforms is the "confidentiality" rule under which family courts seal the proceedings and records of most cases involving an allegation of child sexual abuse. It is difficult to believe that these rules have ever really helped their intended beneficiaries. The contrary is more often true, because freedom from public scrutiny allows family court judges and child protective service agencies to make decisions that would result in public outrage if they were better known. As one well-placed state government source told one of us, "If you're working for the city and you dump a load of cement in the street, everybody can find out about it. But if the same government messes up a child's life, it's secret, and that's why people get away with it." This succinctly explains why the confidentiality rules should be scrapped in child abuse cases.

These rules do not protect children. There is no evidence that abused children need to be screened from the public any more than adult rape victims do, yet rape trials cannot be sealed. On the other hand, there is extensive evidence that secrecy harms children. The protective mother of a child who was repeatedly bullied in secret interviews by the family court judge (who refused to credit her reports of abuse) testified to a state legislative committee that she did not believe the judge could have behaved so outrageously had the transcripts of his closed-doors interviews with the child been available to the public.[9] But they were sealed—supposedly for the child's "protection."

Confidentiality rules are unnecessary. By informal agreement, news organizations almost universally withhold the names of rape victims in their reports, as well as the names of certain other people whose need for privacy is obvious. This informal system, coupled with open trials, could function just as well in child abuse cases. It simply has never been tried.

Finally, confidentiality rules are hypocritical. One notorious New York family court judge actually distributed to numerous reporters unsolicited copies of a decision he wrote in a case alleging child abuse. When one of us investigated the case, more than one official of the CPS agency involved refused to divulge any specific information about the case, claiming it was "confidential"; but they did not hesitate to claim that the child's mother, who had supported the allegation of abuse by the father, was "mentally ill" (a claim not supported by the record in the case.) On another occasion, a reporter inquiring into a case in which a mother had lost temporary custody of her child after accusing his father of sexual abuse was told by the child's law guardian that a court-appointed psychologist had recommended the child's removal from the mother. After the reporter tried to contact the psychologist for confirmation, the law guardian admitted that this was not so. (The law guardian also misrepresented facts about the CPS petition in the case.) As these instances suggest, "confidentiality" has not meant confidentiality for protective mothers, nor protection for their children; it has only emboldened family court personnel to slander protective mothers, since they may reasonably assume in most cases that their statements cannot be checked.

It is logical that records of all family court proceedings should be available to the press and the general public, just as the records of other court proceedings are. The press may choose not to print the names of child victims, just as it routinely withholds names of adult rape victims. Why must cases involving minors involve a radical reversal of the general principle that secrecy invites misconduct? Can it really be said that children benefit from secrecy while rape victims and criminal defendants do not?

Sometimes a litigant before a family court tries to share the proceedings with the press. On many such occasions, family courts insulate themselves from public review by issuing "gag" orders, specifically barring mothers from describing any court proceedings to a third party. The (usually cynical) rationale for this is the "best interest of the child," who may allegedly be embarrassed by publicity; the real reason is more likely the desire for secrecy, and the real beneficiaries are bad judges. New Jersey activist attorney H. Joan Pennington testified before the House Judiciary Committee in 1992 that "gag orders are commonplace in these [protective parent] cases, supposedly to protect the children. In fact, such orders and files that are sealed are used to keep the public from being informed about the inequities rampant in the system."[4] In many cases judges have extended the force of such orders by warning mothers not even to talk about their cases to other mothers or to advocates. Mothers have been frightened to speak in front of support groups for fear that news of this might reach the judge. Such orders probably violate the First Amendment; they certainly do not protect children and should be abolished.

That family court secrecy is not really meant to benefit children is evident from the fact that the secrecy extends even to protective mothers who are directly involved in family court litigation. As we have seen, family court judges often hold private sessions with an allegedly abused child, barring the child's mother, and her attorney, from the private session. While in theory this is done to protect the child from the intimidation of the courtroom setting, we have shown that judges insulated from the eyes and ears of a protective mother's lawyer can be more intimidating, threatening, and downright abusive to a child reporting abuse than any trauma he or she is likely to encounter in a courtroom. Again, secrecy makes this possible— secrecy not only from the general public but from a child's parent. Amazingly, in some states (New York, for instance) family court judges can even seal the transcript of an in-chambers interrogation from the child's mother, even if the judge relies on this in reaching his conclusions concerning whether the child was abused or was being "harmed" by a mother who believed the child's report. This means that a mother may lose custody of her child—even visitation rights—on the strength of "evidence" she and her lawyer are never allowed to see. It is impossible to imagine a justification for this direct attack on constitutional principles of due process.

We propose, in general, the abolition of such private conferences in all child abuse and neglect proceedings; even in custody proceedings they should not be permitted unless all parties consent. If there are any extraordinary conditions that could really justify questioning a child outside the presence of the parents' lawyers, such circumstances must be closely defined by statute, and when a court finds them to be present, this must be stated clearly by the court on the record, with reasons. And *never,* under any circumstances, should the transcript (and tape recording, if it exists) of such an interview be sealed from a parent.

Another aspect of family court secrecy is the fondness of so many family court judges for off-the-record conferences. These conferences are not recorded by transcribers, and no official record of them is ever generated. But they can have momentous effects on a family court case. What is more, these conferences are often off-limits to the parties themselves, so that mothers learn what happened only afterward and only secondhand. We have commonly found that these conferences include critical events in a family court case: judges state conclusions before hearing the evidence; lawyers exchange "evidence" informally with the judge; law guardians and parents' counsels reach "understandings." In effect, many a family court case is decided in off-the-record conferences; yet a mother can never prove, afterward, what actually happened.

To take a single example: in a New York case, after a child reported being abused by her father, the case came before a family court judge. He met privately, off the record, with the lawyers, and insisted—for some reason never stated on the record—that the mother agree to have her child "remanded" to the Commissioner of Social Services. Though no one explained to the mother what this meant, it in fact enabled the judge to remove the six-year-old girl from her mother's custody a few weeks later without even holding the legally required hearing that must take place when such issues as changing custody are made. (The child was eventually moved into the father's custody, and evidence that he might have sexually abused the girl was systematically suppressed.) The mother's lawyer later told his client, remorsefully, that he had agreed to this bizarre procedure only because he was threatened: he was told that if he did not agree, the child would be taken from her mother's home that very day and placed into foster care. But there was never any record of this, since it all took place in an "unofficial" conference.

Such proceedings are improper and should be stopped. Anything that has a bearing on the conduct or outcome of a case should be on the record. And all parties have a right to be present at all on-the-record proceedings.

Finally, in any case in which a judge uses private proceedings to intimidate or threaten a child or parent, this should be grounds, in and of itself, for disqualifying the judge from further participation in the case. (The issue of judicial disqualification will be discussed later in this chapter.)

Surprise Removals/Changes of Custody

As we have seen, one of the most consistently outrageous features of family court dysfunction is the ease with which protective mothers can lose custody of a child without even knowing a court proceeding to take or change custody is under way. This evil can be cured through several direct reforms.

First, no state should permit a change of custody from one parent or guardian to the other on the basis of an ex parte hearing—that is, a hearing of which one parent or guardian does not receive notice. At the present time there are states, including California, that permit such changes without notification to the other parent.[5] In theory, these changes are only temporary, and they require evidence that the custodial parent is about to go into hiding with the child or flee the jurisdiction. But the laws are rampantly abused; mothers with no opportunity to defend themselves are routinely labeled "flight risks" if they have accused a father of abuse, and "temporary" changes of custody can quickly become permanent. Indeed, placing a child in the custody of a parent accused of abusing him/her generally has the effect of silencing the child's complaints of being abused and thus can lend apparent support to the alleged abuser's claim that he is being falsely and maliciously accused. In this way, many a protective mother has lost custody of her child for good.

It is true that some sort of mechanism must exist by which the relevant government agency can seek the emergency removal of a child from a home in which the child's life or safety is genuinely threatened. But two important limitations on this power must be stressed. First, such a removal must never be confused with a procedure for determining child custody as between parents. In other words, an emergency removal means a temporary placement of an endangered child in a safe and neutral setting—the state should not be allowed to move a child from one parent to the other until the parents have at least been notified of the court proceeding and have had an opportunity to appear. Second, the state must be required to prove the existence of a genuine emergency, such that notice to the custodial parent is simply impossible or would be dangerous to the child. The meaning of "emergency" should be spelled out in the state's laws and must not be presumed in vague formulas about "parental alienation" and so forth. State law should specify that a parent's mere belief that a child has been abused is *never*, in and of itself, grounds for a temporary or emergency removal.

A court order granting an emergency removal must reflect the seriousness of its consequences. When a family court grants the state's request for an emergency removal (whether or not at an ex parte hearing), the court must state in a written order, with specificity, the nature of the emergency and the evidence on which the finding of emergency was based. When such an order is ex parte, and a parent who was not given notice of the effort to remove the child is afterward able to demonstrate that notice in fact could have been given (without posing an undue risk to the child), the removal ordered pursuant to the ex parte hearing should be automatically invalidated, and a new hearing must be held on notice to both parties.

There is another loophole in the laws that allow "emergency" removal orders that must be plugged in order to protect the rights of custodial parents, particularly protective mothers. All states theoretically require that when a parent has lost a child without a hearing, that parent is entitled to a prompt hearing in order to seek the return of the child until a final determination can be reached. However, in case after case, protective mothers are effectively denied this right, bullied by judges and lawyers who tell them that insisting on this procedure will only delay the proceedings—and then, after learning the hard way that the system has no intention of giving them a prompt trial in any event, are told that they "waived" the right to seek the child's return by not seeking it immediately.

This catch-22 must be banned. State laws should specify that a parent or guardian's right to seek the return of a "temporarily" removed child—as well as the parent's right to a court hearing when a child is removed without one—*cannot* be waived. Rather, a request for the return of a temporarily removed child may be made at any time, so long as the parent can show that the child does not face imminent danger if returned to his or her home. In addition, the state should be required, at regular intervals until a final determination can be made by the court, to present evidence that continued removal of the child from the parent's home is necessary for the child's safety—otherwise the child should be returned automatically.[6] Moreover, "return" hearings, once demanded, must be heard and decided with all possible speed; in addition, a parent should be entitled to an emergency appeal of any removal order on the ground that it was not procedurally proper or that no proper emergency was established. (And if the appeals court upholds the removal, it must state, in writing, the reasons no procedural impropriety was found and an adequate basis for a finding that an emergency existed.)

In addition to these reforms, some of the abuses described in this book make it clear that a statutory clarification is needed of at least one other civil rights issue. It is clear that, in the system as it exists, children can be removed from their mothers on the basis of fundamentally flawed CPS petitions—petitions that fail to state any competent evidence or that violate basic norms concerning the statutory basis or the required service and attestation of such petitions. Yet, even when such petitions are revealed as legally invalid, family court judges have allowed their consequences to stand—thus permitting state agencies to force mothers to submit to illegal evaluations, to pressure them into waiving their legal rights, and to continue to hold children outside their homes without meeting the required legal standards.

This should be explicitly rejected by statute, since otherwise it appears that family courts will continue to rely on facially invalid CPS petitions whenever it suits them to do so. The law should provide that if a petition on which a removal is based is determined later to be legally invalid (for example, because the accused's civil rights were violated or because the required statutes were not followed), the removal resulting from the petition must be reversed automatically, with the child automatically being returned to its home. If CPS officials want to make new accusations against a parent after an illegal removal, they must start over, with a new petition, to be evaluated de novo by a court. This will protect the constitutional rights of all parents accused of abuse or neglect against the use of invalid petitions to gain control over their lives—and those of their children.

Punitive Rulings

We have seen, throughout this book, how family courts use rulings on custody and visitation as punitive measures to "discipline" mothers—and their attorneys and expert witnesses—who offer accusations or evidence of sex abuse by fathers. This practice is obviously wrong, and it is so common that it should be explicitly banned by statute.

To begin with, states should adopt specific language in the statutes governing custody, abuse, neglect, and visitation to the effect that a good-faith report or allegation by a parent or guardian that a child has been abused cannot be used as grounds for charging that parent or guardian with child abuse or neglect, nor as grounds for determining custody and/or visitation. This would give practical effect to the laws that already exist in many states that promise "immunity" to anyone who makes a report of suspected abuse, unless the report can be shown to be made maliciously. These laws protect nonparents from being sued for damages by someone they have accused of abuse, if that report is not ultimately confirmed by a court. However, *mothers* who report suspicions of abuse are not immune from the kinds of legal action that threaten them most: they can lose their children either to foster care or by means of a change of custody, even when their report was made in good faith. The reform we propose would change that. As stated above, this could be required by CAPTA as a prerequisite to a state's receipt of federal funds.

Something along these lines has already been enacted into law in California. In October 1999, California adopted an amendment to its Family Code[7] that provides:

> No parent shall be placed on supervised visitation, or be denied custody of or visitation with his or her child, and no custody or visitation rights shall be limited, solely because the parent (1) lawfully reported suspected sexual abuse of the child, (2) otherwise acted lawfully, based on a reasonable belief, to determine if his or her child was the victim of sexual abuse, or (3) sought treatment for the child from a licensed mental health professional for suspected sexual abuse. (b) The court may order supervised visitation or limit a parent's custody or visitation if the court finds substantial evidence that the parent, with the intent to interfere with the other parent's lawful contact with the child, made a report of child sexual abuse, during a child custody proceeding or at any other time, that he or she knew was false at the time it was made. Any limitation of custody or visitation, including an order for supervised visitation, pursuant to this subdivision, or any statute regarding the making of a false child abuse report, shall be imposed only after the court has determined that the limitation is necessary to protect the health, safety, and welfare of the child, and the court has considered the state's policy of assuring that children have frequent and continuing contact with both parents as declared in subdivision (b) of Section 3020.

Whether this reform has had the intended effect is debatable. Some observers in California maintain that family courts have so far ignored it. Moreover, the new law does not specify that its effect should be retroactive, and the family courts have refused to give it such effect, which means they have not reconsidered any of the cases in which mothers have *already* lost custody for making good-faith reports of abuse. In one case discussed in part II, for instance, a mother lost not only custody but all contact with her children because she reported suspected abuse by the father, even though the court never concluded that the mother knew the reports to be false or intended them solely as a means of interfering with the father's rights.

In that case, and in two others like it, the aggrieved mothers sought to regain custody after the passage of the new law. In each case, the judge refused to apply the law retroactively. Therefore, the children in these cases (and other similar cases) remained in the custody of their alleged abusers, and the children's contact with their mothers was still subject to restrictions.

In light of this, protective parent advocates have proposed a further amendment to the law, as follows:

> § 3027.5(c): Upon proper filing of a Notice of Motion or Order to Show Cause, the court shall conduct a review of any custody order made prior to January 1, 1999, in which the moving party alleges that the current custody order imposes supervised visitation, or limits or denies custody to a parent based, in whole or in part, on an allegation or finding that the parent had alienated a child from the affections of the other parent, engaged in conduct not in the child's best interests, or caused a child emotional abuse, and the underlying conduct consisted of (1) lawfully reporting suspected sexual abuse of the child, (2) otherwise acting lawfully, based on a reasonable belief, to determine if his or her child was the victim of sexual abuse, including questioning a child about suspected sexual abuse or (3) seeking treatment for the child from a licensed mental health professional for suspected sexual abuse. If, upon review, the court determines that the prior court order was based, in whole or part, on these allegations or findings and such underlying conduct, the court shall conduct a custody hearing, *de novo,* to determine the custody plan which would be in the best interests of the child(ren), in accord with subdivisions (a) and (b), above and other relevant statutes and case law related to the best interests of the child(ren).

It is typical of the warped state of America's family court system that this measure—clearly intended to remedy cases whose tragic results were based on procedures *already* renounced by the state legislature—encountered stiff opposition from establishment-oriented voices. While the new proposed amendment was supported by the Legislative Coalition to Prevent Child Abuse, the California Alliance Against Domestic Violence, the California Protective Parents Association, the California National Organization for Women, Child Abuse Solutions, Inc., the County Welfare Directors Association of California, the Domestic Violence Center of Santa Clarita Valley, and the State Commission on the Status of Women, it was opposed by the powerful California Judges' Association and the Family Law Executive Committee of the California State Bar.

The reasoning offered by the opponents was depressingly disingenuous: they claimed that the new bill amounted to undue interference with the courts' discretion (even in cases in which judges' decisions had contravened the legal standards set by the legislature in 1999)!

California's example supports our suggestion that a reform protecting parents from punishment for making a nonmalicious accusation of sex abuse against the other parent (or anyone else) should be made at the national level. Clearly the existing family court establishment resists such a measure, even though it is unwilling to state openly what this means: that family courts can and do punish mothers with the removal of their children when the mothers report legitimate suspicions of sex abuse. Given the attitude of the establishment, can anyone doubt the need for statutory reform forcing all states to cure this evil, on pain of losing all federal support?

Contempt Powers

Family courts are empowered, as are all courts, to hold a recalcitrant litigant in contempt of court. We do not deny the importance of such a power. But we do maintain that it has been grossly abused in family courts.

All too often, "contempt of court" is used as a disingenuous label that masks a court's illegitimate custody decision. Family courts use their contempt powers to award custody to the "nonoffending" parent, as though a change of custody were one of the punishments for contempt. In some cases, this is even done *before* a mother has violated an order—as in the case described in part II, chapter 4, in which an expert claimed that a mother was likely to kidnap her child because, when asked whether she would respect an order that forced her to give unsupervised visits to a father suspected of child abuse, she said, "If I have to be in contempt, I'll be in contempt." Even though there was no such order—let alone any violation of such an order—the mother promptly lost her child.

We propose some basic reforms that allow family courts to retain their contempt powers without abusing them.

First, the exact basis of any contempt ruling, criminal or civil, must be spelled out in writing whenever a judge finds a party in contempt of court. Second, the ruling must specify the nature of the order violated, how it was determined that the party was aware of the order, and the opportunity given the party to defend herself. Moreover, if the party is being held in civil contempt, she must be given a reasonable opportunity to "purge" herself. This means that if the court concludes that she is refusing to obey some order or directive, she must be given a reasonable opportunity to do so before a penalty is imposed. All too often in family courts, even mothers who say they did not intend to violate an order, and are willing to comply once informed, are punished with a loss of custody or visitation without being given an opportunity to correct the behavior frowned on by the court.

The abuse of contempt powers in family courts does not affect only litigants. Judges sometimes issue contempt citations against social workers or other mental health professionals—or threaten to do so—in order to prevent them from making reports of child abuse, or from treating abused children, or from presenting evidence of child abuse in court. We have seen, for instance, how a New York psychiatrist complained that a therapist who worked for a state-funded family therapy clinic, and who was treating a child for the effects of sexual abuse, was threatened by a family court judge that she would be held in contempt if she even attempted to contact the child again.[8] Such threats cripple the child protection system, for social workers and mental health professionals cannot protect children if they are intimidated from doing their jobs by judges who abuse contempt powers.

Accordingly, we propose the following: each state, in order to continue to receive funding under CAPTA, must require child protective service agencies to challenge a judge's contempt citation or threat of contempt aimed at social workers and other mental health professionals attempting to make a record of abuse.[9] After all, intimidation of mental health professionals by judges interferes with the capacity of CPS agencies to perform their legally mandated function. And, on the other hand, CPS agencies can place the power and prestige of the state behind practitioners who otherwise would stand alone before abusive judges. It should be stressed that this measure would *not* require CPS to defend contempt citations, or threatened contempt citations, in all cases—only when the threatened mental health professional was engaged in good faith in attempting to create or add to a record of abuse. Even if a court ultimately concludes that an allegation of child abuse is unfounded, it is wrong for mental health professionals to be punished with contempt citations for attempting to do their jobs.

Review of Sitting Judges

Judges enjoy virtually unlimited immunity from civil suits, no matter how outrageously they behave on the bench, even when their decisions violate the law. This is because our legal system requires the independence of judges, and a judge who can be sued by a losing litigant can never perform his or her job in an independent manner. For the same reason, it is very difficult to remove a judge from office.

This, however, only makes it imperative that family court judges—who, as we have seen, so often abuse their authority—be subject to some sort of review. We propose the periodic review of the performance of family court judges by a qualified and independent team of mental health professionals who will then report their findings publicly. Where family court judges are appointed, the review panel will offer advice and comments to the officials who make judicial appointments. In states that elect family court judges, the panel will publish its findings to inform the public.

The same periodic review should be applied to judicial hearing officers as well. Judicial hearing officers are individuals who are not judges, but who serve as "referees" when appointed to do so by a judge. In that role, the judicial hearing officer (JHO) presides over trials, hears motions, and makes decisions exactly as a judge would, except that his decisions are subject to review by the judge who assigned the case to him.

The importance of applying judicial review procedures to JHOs is illustrated by the example of Leon Deutsch, a Brooklyn, New York, family court judge until 1990. Judge Deutsch was notorious for his hostility to women; in cases involving sex abuse allegations, he allegedly ignored evidence of child abuse, misrepresented evidence so as to shift the blame to the protective mothers, browbeat and threatened children who reported being abused, and in one case threatened to hold a therapist in contempt simply for trying to treat a child for the effects of alleged abuse because he, Deutsch, believed the girl was "lying." In 1990, Deutsch voluntarily stepped down from the bench after a grievance against him was filed by New York State senator David A. Paterson, who had chaired hearings into family court abuses. (Senator Paterson complained that Deutsch had sent his law clerk, Steven Mostofsky, to his hearing room in order to intimidate the witnesses who were litigants before Judge Deutsch.) Just a few months after he "retired," however, Judge Deutsch was suddenly rehired by the state as a judicial hearing officer. Since he had officially left the bench, Deutsch never had to answer Senator Paterson's ethics grievance. But he continued to hear and decide exactly the sort of matrimonial cases he had so grievously mishandled in the past.[10] To prevent such occurrences, JHOs should receive the same sort of review we recommend for family court judges.

We also believe that, given the systemic malfunction of the family courts, there is a need for each state to establish a short-term special commission to review the case decisions of sitting family court judges in order to determine whether the rights of allegedly abused children and of protective mothers are being properly protected. We recommend that such commissions be in place for three years, during which time they should release annual reports. These commissions should consist of judges, psychologists (who are not court-appointed experts and therefore not dependent on judicial referrals), and laypersons.

Finally, it should be noted that many states have already established commissions to review gender bias in the courts. We recommend that such commissions should regularly devote part of their efforts to the protective parent backlash. To date, most gender bias studies examine general issues, such as how judges talk in court to female attorneys and similar issues of decorum. We believe these studies should specifically examine the penalization of mothers (and their lawyers, and sympathetic experts) for bringing sex abuse matters to the courts' attention.

Higher Court Review

Many states permit appeals only from "final" judgments. That is, only trial court orders that completely dispose of a case can be appealed to a higher court. In practice, for protective mothers, this means that when a child is "temporarily" removed from her custody—no matter how illegal the order may be—she cannot appeal the removal until the conclusion of a trial to determine *permanent* custody—which may take years. States that bar non-final appeals—"interlocutory" appeals, as lawyers call them—do provide for certain exceptions to the rule, and we propose that temporary child removals or custody changes, challenged on civil rights grounds, be included among the exceptions. Jeremiah B. McKenna, former chief counsel to the New York State Senate Committee on Crime and Correction and a frequent critic of the family court system, stated the simple truth when he said that "no order could be more final in an emotional sense than an order removing custody from a mother." In fact, forcing mothers to wait before appealing such orders is doubly unjust. First, the delay of a year or more that often results if interlocutory appeals are not allowed is an enormous length of time to a small child who has never lived away from his or her mother, and the harm done by such a separation cannot be undone even if the order is later reversed. Second, by the time an appellate court *is* asked to review a custody decision, family courts often question whether a sudden return to the mother, once the child has "adjusted" to a new environment, is in the child's "best interest." Thus, even if a mother can prove that her child should never have been removed, delay means that she may not be able to reverse the wrongful removal after proving her case! For these reasons, it is obvious that justice can be served only by allowing immediate appeals of child removal orders.

We further propose that the relevant statutes require the appellate courts to respond to every allegation of the invalidity of a removal order specifically and in writing, giving specific reasons for their holdings. (Some reasons for challenging these removals: the state's failure to give notice to the mother or her lawyer before obtaining the removal; improper exclusion of evidence; lack of a proper evidentiary hearing; false or missing statements in the removal order.)

Jurisdiction of Other Courts

It may come as a surprise to many readers to learn that while a man or woman who is wrongfully imprisoned can seek relief from the federal courts, a parent whose child has been wrongfully seized generally cannot petition the federal courts for the child's return. This is because the federal courts have created an exception to their jurisdiction known as the "domestic relations" exception, according to which federal courts will not review a "custody decision." Since federal courts generally look at all child placement issues as custody decisions, a mother can seldom vindicate her rights in the same federal court system most victims of state action turn to.

We propose that this be changed when it comes to cases that assert civil rights claims, even if these claims pertain to the removal of a child from his or her home. Custody decisions that involve the weighing of parental skills and so forth are, admittedly, not proper material for the limited jurisdiction of the federal courts. But civil rights complaints against seizures of children by improper agency action or illegal court order are not "custody cases." It is very much within the purview of the federal courts to prevent an agent or agency of a state government, or a private individual, from withholding a child from a parent without due process of law. Where such a claim is raised, federal courts must be required to exercise their jurisdiction so as to enforce basic constitutional rights. In fact, the close relationship between family courts and the state agencies who carry out the removals (which we have explored above in chapter 6) means that federal courts might well be the better forum to pursue a remedy in such cases—

once they were prevented from hiding behind the "domestic relations" exception.[11]

Judicial Training

We propose that every state require judges to attend judicial training seminars and lectures aimed at dispelling the popular myth that women use sex abuse allegations as a "weapon" to gain custody. In 1992, Louisiana Court of Appeals judge Sol Gothard pointed out that "too many judges have no understanding or knowledge of the dynamics of this [protective parent] problem [and] even worse, they have no compassion or empathy for the child victim."[12] A year later, New Jersey activist attorney H. Joan Pennington expressed her frustration over judicial ignorance:

> Judges, like everyone else, learn either by study, training, or trial and error. Self-motivated study carries the danger that the student might read only what appeals to them instead of learning the basic information in the field; judges may read fantastic, interesting theories which actually have no basis in fact. . . . Rather than learning through self-study, judges might learn through the most trusted method; training by experts in a formal, structured process, using professional teaching methods and curricula [but] judges are rarely required to attend any type of training and so it remains optional.[13]

We propose that such training be made mandatory for judges. It might be useful to ask the judges who take the courses to complete a questionnaire concerning their relevant knowledge, training, and beliefs.[14]

After the judges have completed the course, their responses might be taken again. It is likely that their attitudes toward many fundamental questions concerning child sex abuse allegations will be different from what they were before the course. That would be both a measure of progress and an index of the problems protective mothers have been facing for years at the hands of ill-informed judges.

These training programs will yield particular benefits if they include strong and memorable presentations. For example, it would be useful for judges to hear from parents who have personally suffered from the backlash of the family courts. They should also hear the views of mental health experts who have treated children suffering the injury of sexual abuse— and hear as well from those who have treated known child abusers. It can hardly be stressed too much, or too often, that men who abuse their children do not resemble the monster of popular myth. As one child abuse expert told us, "Men who sexually abuse children are Jekyll and Hyde. And only the abused child sees Mr. Hyde."

Disqualification of Judges

One essential component of any set of effective family court reforms is the protection of litigants from flagrantly abusive family court judges. Experience shows that a biased, hostile, or overtly misbehaving judge cannot simply be instructed to improve. Litigants can get the protection they need only if certain extreme sorts of judicial conduct are not only forbidden but are spelled out in the relevant laws as grounds for disqualifying the judge from further participation in the case in which such conduct occurs.

Such disqualifying conduct should include, at least: (1) refusal to hear evidence of abuse; (2) threatening or punishing a mother with loss of custody, visitation, or child support for making a claim of sexual abuse; and (3) attempting to coerce a mother into forfeiting basic rights, such as the right to have a decision reviewed by a higher court, in exchange for some sort of favorable ruling.[15]

Like other reforms we urge, this one can be effectively enacted nationwide by incorporating it into the Child Abuse Prevention and Treatment Act (CAPTA), 42 U.S.C. §§ 5101 *et seq.,* under which states qualify for federal monetary assistance in preventing and treating child abuse in exchange for meeting eligibility guidelines. CAPTA already forces the states to conform to federal law as a precondition for the receipt of federal funds. Thus, it is necessary only to add to the eligibility requirements specific guidelines such as those we have set out here.[16]

Chapter 11

Reforming the Court Auxiliaries

R eforming the family courts themselves is only part of the task ahead, if we are to rescue the system from ignorance, bias, and malfunction. As we have seen, family courts are integrally related to a number of auxiliary actors who play decisive roles in the way the system functions. Unless they are reformed along with the courts, reform will probably be fruitless.

Accordingly, we propose reforms for the three most important of the family court auxiliaries: law guardians, custody "evaluators," and social services agencies.

Law Guardians

Law guardians appointed to represent the "best interest" of minor children who have reported abuse (and supposedly to safeguard their rights in the family court process) bear a grave responsibility to their young clients—and to society. Who, outside the family court system, would imagine that this responsibility comes with almost a total absence of regulation or oversight? Yet, as we have seen, law guardians are virtually exempt from all control and regulation. Even if they knowingly suppress evidence that their clients have been abused, even if they recommend the clients' placement in conditions they know are dangerous, even if they claim to represent their clients' interests without so much as speaking to them—and we have seen examples of such conduct in part II—they enjoy almost complete protection from discipline and immunity from liability.[1]

This protection springs, in part, from the curious notion that the role of law guardian is closer to that of the judge than that of a legal advocate. If a lawyer does not properly represent his *adult* client, he is subject to discipline—and if he is negligent of his duties, he can be sued for damages. But this is not true of a law guardian who represents an *underage* client. The law almost everywhere favors law guardians with immunity from suit even when the law guardians are negligent, even grossly negligent, in their representation, because this privilege runs parallel to the immunity enjoyed by *judges*.[2]

It is hard to see who benefits from such immunity, other than incompetent or corrupt law guardians. Good ones are no more likely to be sued for their actions than other lawyers are. And why should lawyers appointed to represent clients whose tender age makes them particularly vulnerable to misconduct be protected from the consequences of such misconduct? We recommend that law guardians be subject to liability for negligent representation just as other legal advocates are, though they will remain protected from unfair complaints because their good-faith compliance with the accepted ethical standards should operate as a complete defense to a civil or disciplinary action.

ETHICAL GUIDELINES FOR LAW GUARDIANS

This brings us to the next problem: there are no such ethical guidelines in place. Law guardians appointed to represent children operate under no comprehensive set of ethical directives, such as those set out for judges in the Code of Judicial Conduct. Lawyers (most law guardians and GALs in family court matters are lawyers) and mental health professionals (and those GALs who are not lawyers are usually mental health professionals) do have general ethical standards that govern members of their professions. But these guidelines—which, as we will see, are rarely enforceable in any event under today's circumstances—do not address the special responsibilities of representing a minor child in abuse-related litigation.

We believe that a national set of such standards should be promulgated. They should include, at a minimum, such ethical guidelines for law guardians as the following:

1. A law guardian must communicate with her client. She must meet the child or children she represents, must consult them, where possible, before taking any action or position, and must inform them in an age-appropriate manner of what she is doing.[3]
2. When a law guardian feels that she must make a recommendation that is contrary to the wishes of the child, she must inform the court candidly of the child's wishes, state that her own recommendation contravenes the child's wishes, and offer clear reasons why she is making it despite the wishes of the child. This *must* be

part of the court record of any such recommendation, and the law guardian must be subject to questioning on this issue by either parent (or their lawyers).

3. A law guardian must conduct a fair, thorough, unbiased investigation into the relevant facts, including all allegations concerning abuse. The law guardian must properly document this investigation and inform the court and all parties, at the appropriate time(s), what evidence has been considered, which experts and witnesses have been consulted, and so forth.

4. The law guardian must share with the court, and the parties, any evidence relevant to the child's best interest, even if it does not tend to support the position she is taking. (For instance, if she has decided to recommend against a finding that abuse occurred, she is still obligated to share with the court all evidence suggesting that it did.)

5. The law guardian must bear in mind, at all times, that she represents the child and that she does not represent either of the parents. She is not an advocate for either of them, even if her recommendations will favor one over the other. Thus, she must not litigate, nor unnecessarily give the appearance of litigating, as one parent's unofficial advocate. For instance, it is unethical for a law guardian to arrange to pay the expenses of a witness chosen by one parent to testify against the other, or of an expert whose sole purpose is to support one parent or to criticize the other. (We do not mean to bar law guardians from obtaining their own expert witnesses, whose role is to evaluate all parties, even if their ultimate conclusions support one parent over the other. We have shown in part II, chapter 5, however, that law guardians have paid "experts" whose role was partisan from the outset and who should have been paid by the father whose case they were obviously intended to bolster.) Similarly, a law guardian should not pay court costs, filing fees, transcript costs, copying charges, or other such litigation costs incurred by one of the adversarial parents. Law guardians should also take care not to appear to take sides in other ways, such as sharing private notes at a counsel table with one parent during a trial.

6. A law guardian must not communicate secretly with expert witnesses or with either parent. Both parties should be informed of the communication between the law guardian and either parent,

or between the law guardian and an expert connected with the case. This is because law guardians, as we have seen, play an unusual role in family court litigation in which their special advisory relationship to the court makes them unlike adversarial litigants.[4] Thus, when a law guardian communicates with one side, the other has a right to know about it before the law guardian offers advice to the court based on such communication; and when a law guardian communicates with an expert witness, certainly both parties should be notified.

ENFORCEMENT OF ETHICAL GUIDELINES

The knowledge that they can be sued for negligent performance of their duties would help deter law guardians from flagrant misuse of their powers. But what about the ethical guidelines we advocate above? How can these be enforced?

Ethical guidelines that govern lawyers in general are enforced by disciplinary committees in every state. But, as we have seen, law guardians who represent minor children in family courts—even if they are lawyers, as most of them are—are exempt in practice from such review. Disciplinary committees decline to intervene, claiming that law guardians are answerable only to the judge who appointed them.

This is obviously wrong. Disciplinary rules should make plain that a lawyer remains subject to the authority of disciplinary committees even when he or she represents a minor child. At the very least, law guardians who are lawyers should be subject to the same ethical conduct standards and the same professional review as their colleagues.

But more is needed. Since the problems faced by law guardians are in some respects specialized, there should also be a special forum for reviewing law guardian misconduct, a subcommittee or division that specializes in ethical considerations relevant to lawyers who are appointed to represent minors in abuse-related litigation.

These committees must deal with at least one unusual procedural feature. Generally it is a lawyer's client or former client who lodges a complaint against him. In the case of a law guardian, the client is a minor and cannot be expected to file grievances. We believe these committees should accept complaints against law guardians from any party involved in the litigation—which, of course, includes the mother. Waiting for a child client to reach the age of majority is obviously impractical.

It is of great importance that these complaints be handled in a timely fashion. We have often found that disciplinary committees—even when they can be persuaded to respond to complaints against law guardians in the first place—refuse to consider the merits of a complaint, on the grounds that the case is still before the court. This excuse should be specifically rejected by a subcommittee specializing in law guardian complaints. After all, once a case is really over, disciplinary agencies are just as reluctant to intervene, using the excuse that the complaint is now too old for anything to be done about it. And even if the committee takes some action, correcting the inadequate or biased procedures of a law guardian will do little good if the real harm to the child—an improper removal or change of custody—has already been finalized.

SPECIFIC TERMS OF APPOINTMENT

Law guardians are also answerable to the judges who appoint them, and this gives family court judges an opportunity to curb law guardian abuses. It is an opportunity rarely exercised. However, there is one way in which family courts can limit such abuses or even prevent them before they occur. And this should be required of family courts as part of the rules that govern the appointment of law guardians.

The needed reform is simple: family courts, when appointing a law guardian to represent a minor child, must spell out the precise purpose of the appointment. For example, if the law guardian is appointed to represent the child because allegations of sexual abuse have been raised, the terms of his appointment should be limited to the responsibilities flowing from that purpose. The law guardian must behave only in keeping with the terms of his appointment; he has no powers outside those terms, and if he acts outside them, his actions are subject to challenge by a motion to the court.

The consequences of such a rule would be most keenly felt in cases in which a law guardian is appointed because of allegations of abuse, where those allegations are ultimately rejected by the courts. When this happens, the law guardian's appointment should automatically terminate. Thus, a law guardian who disbelieves the abuse allegations due to which he is appointed would at least be unable to continue to litigate in the case after the dismissal of the charges—as so many law guardians have done—as a free advocate for the accused father. In many cases, law guardians have even caused public money to be spent in advocacy for a father who seeks custody after being accused of abuse—even though the only reason the law allowed their appointment was to give the child a representative in court with respect to the abuse allegations.

For example, suppose a father accused of sexually abusing his child is found not to have committed the abuse—and the mother appeals. The law guardian appointed for the child to deal with the abuse allegations should *not* be permitted to file a brief with the appellate court on the father's behalf. If his position is that no abuse occurred, he should have no legal standing to defend a family court's finding to that effect. His role in the case is at an end.[5]

On the other hand, if the law guardian believes that abuse *did* occur and the family court rules otherwise, it is logical that he may file an appellate brief seeking the reversal of the lower court's ruling. In such a case his role continues; he is still an advocate for an allegedly abused child. However, once appeals are at an end and the courts have rejected the allegation of abuse, the law guardian has no more legal standing to take any action whatever.

The adoption of this rule would prevent law guardians from outlasting the rationale of their appointments. And it would bar law guardians from becoming free advocates for one parent over the other. For if a law guardian can file an appellate brief supporting a finding that no abuse by the father occurred (and opposing the appeal of the mother who believes it did), he is simply taking over the role the father himself should be playing in the litigation. This results in letting a private litigant have his custody case made for him by the state. A law guardian should not play such a role.

LAW GUARDIAN TRAINING

Just as family court judges should be required to attend courses that deal with child abuse allegations and the penalization of protective parents, law guardians ought to receive special training for the grave responsibilities their role thrusts upon them. The easiest way to accomplish this is to add such training to the requirements of continuing legal education (CLE), which many lawyers must satisfy in any case. It should be an elective, of course, to be taken only by those lawyers who take appointments as law guardians. But for them, such training would be an essential element of the reforms needed to curb family court abuses.

Custody Evaluators

Custody evaluators (generally psychologists) are, in one sense, a little farther along the road to progress than law guardians are: the American Psychological Association has already established standards and guidelines for custody evaluations. These guidelines curtail evaluators' authority to make custody and visitation recommendations to a court. But in another sense custody evaluators are no closer than law guardians are to meeting what we regard as "minimal standards of justice," because nothing in the guidelines addresses the peculiar problems faced by protective parents. As we have seen, custody evaluators can and do rely on unscientific theories to attack mothers who suspect their children's fathers of sexual abuse. They can and do ignore their proper function and play the mixed role of judge and prophet, urging family courts to punish mothers who suspect abuse for "violating" court orders (concerning visitation, shared custody, etc.) before any violations have occurred. And they allow their reports and evaluations—formulated without any of the protections that are part of a trial—to serve as the basis for catastrophic child removal and change-of-custody orders.

To make matters worse, family courts tend to accept uncritically the conclusions offered by custody evaluators. As Timothy Tippins, a distinguished matrimonial lawyer in New York, stated in a 2003 article in the *New York Law Journal:*

> Mental health opinions can spell the end of the line for the disfavored parent because of the indicia of authoritativeness they have come to carry, an aura that emanates from the assumption that the opinion rests on scientifically reliable and valid principles and procedures. Sadly, that assumption is often unwarranted. [6]

And Dr. Gary Melton and several of his colleagues, in a leading text on forensic custody evaluations, lamented:

> [T]here is probably no forensic question on which overreaching by mental health professionals has been so common and so egregious. Besides lacking scientific validity, such opinions have often been based on clinical data that are, on their face, irrelevant to the legal questions in dispute. [7]

For these reasons, we propose that the guidelines be expanded to include standards concerning the introduction of such non-science science as "Parental Alienation Syndrome" and the proper role of the evaluator in a case in which abuse is alleged. Specifically, an evaluator should not be permitted to recommend a change of custody as a punishment that a court would otherwise be forbidden to impose (such as in a case in which a mother has not violated a court order but the evaluator considers her suspicions of abuse as tantamount to such a violation). Likewise, an evaluator must be ethically limited to relying on theories and methodologies that pass muster under the applicable legal standards (as PAS does not).

Another important step toward a juster evaluation process is the standardization of the evaluations themselves. This has been proposed by attorney Lynne Hecht Schafran, Director of the National Judicial Education Program (a project of the NOW Legal Defense and Education Fund).[8] Activists Karen Anderson and Constance Valentine, who in 1998 founded the California Protective Parent Association, have drafted a protocol for custody evaluators in collaboration with attorney Meera Fox (who founded Child Abuse Solutions, Inc., a California-based consulting firm for matrimonial lawyers and expert witnesses who deal with child abuse charges that arise during custody litigation). This protocol lays out all the steps of a comprehensive evaluation. Fox has used this to train custody evaluators, and its wider use would probably lead to better, fairer, and better documented custody evaluations.

Of particular interest is the portion of this protocol that deals with possible sexual abuse of a child. It lists many behavioral indicators that differentiate children who report sexual abuse, based on the important work of William Friedrich, Ph.D., of the Mayo Clinic, published in the January 1993 edition of *Violence Update*.[9] According to this protocol, an evaluator must note the frequency of behaviors such as rubbing against or hugging complete strangers, making sexual sounds or trying to French kiss, verbalizing sexual words or acts, or engaging in flirtatious conversation—among many others—before reporting a conclusion as to the likelihood that sexual abuse occurred. If all evaluators followed such a guide, they would find it much more difficult to conclude glibly that a child who displays such behaviors was "coached" to report abuse by his mother. It is one thing to "coach" a child to report abuse; it is a very different matter to "coach" a child to display a wide variety of such overtly sexual behaviors.

Obviously, it is difficult to legislate how custody evaluators should evaluate data once an examination has been completed. However, it should be obvious that, at the very least, evaluators must accurately represent a subject's test scores. It should also be obvious that when both parents in a custody evaluation have similar test results or behaviors, the evaluator's resulting conclusions should be similar. When an evaluator reaches very different conclusions about two parents based on similar data, his methods are fundamentally suspect. Finally, it should be obvious that a so-called expert should not reach conclusions based on intuition or personal biases.

Unfortunately, cases that violate these rules are not at all rare. In a 1995 North Dakota case, for instance, an appellate judge registered concern with a court-appointed psychologist who had interpreted similar test results for the two parents in radically different fashion.[10] Although the father showed "anger and hostility," the psychologist dismissed these feelings as understandable and predicted (on the basis of no visible evidence) that they would disappear once the custody dispute was resolved. The mother's emotions, however, were a different matter: the psychologist attributed them to "hysteria" and called her allegations of being stalked and harassed (despite her description of several specific episodes) as "paranoid and delusional."

In another recent case, this one in New Jersey, the custody evaluator appointed by the court claimed that the mother was "narcissistic" and that, as a result, she could be expected to interfere with the father's relationship with the couple's child if she were granted primary custody. When the objective test results he obtained were reviewed by another psychologist, however, it turned out that the evaluator had not correctly represented the mother's test scores to the court. The second psychologist, an expert on the scoring of psychological tests, was sharply critical of the evaluator's methods:

> [T]here are significant questions as to the validity of his interpretation of these tests . . . . [The mother's] MMPI-2 profile revealed very little indication of any psychological problems, inappropriate interpersonal behaviors, or negative character traits . . . . There was no evidence, from her MMPI profile, of any excessive hostility, histrionic personality characteristics, or repression/defensiveness (although these characteristics were all cited by [the evaluator] in his report) . . . . In short, there is simply no evidence, in her MMPI-2 profile, to support *any* of the interpretations offered by [the evaluator] . . . . His failure to resolve, nor even acknowledge, the discrepancy between the two psychological tests administered is troubling, particularly given the fact that the more widely accepted and well-validated of the two tests revealed essentially no problematic behaviors or personality characteristics.[11]

(Family courts being what they are, there was nothing the mother could do to seek any sort of disciplinary action against the evaluator, who is presumably free to misinterpret test scores in future custody evaluations.)

And Dr. Jeffrey Wittmann, who has personally performed over 1,500 custody evaluations, makes it just as clear that conclusions based on personal, unscientific factors are not unheard of in custody evaluations:

Statements derived solely from "intuition," clearly limited clinical contact, speculation . . . or those representing strong personal bias unsupported by research or clinical data should be evaluated as "unscientific." . . . Mental health professionals often make less extreme, yet "unscientific" statements. . . . Our field is famous for supporting conclusions during testimony simply on the basis of "accumulated clinical experience," a phrase which may mean nothing more than accumulated personal bias.[12]

Examples and statements like these make it clear that custody evaluators do not always follow even minimally proper procedures.[13] Courts must therefore look carefully at all such evaluations and must explain, in their decisions, exactly how their judicial conclusions have been reached.[14] Such a procedure tends to expose reliance on skewed or biased analysis on the part of the evaluator and thus tends to minimize the abuse of the system by a biased expert.

As one judge on New York's highest court observed in a 1997 case:

Experts, who predict future consequences based on their professional theories and examinations of subject children, should not be elevated to the singular importance of, in effect, overriding the array of pertinently balanced jurisdictional protections afforded to decrees affecting one of society's most sacrosanct relationships—parent and child. Courts must beware lest the unique juridical authority to decide these cases be sacrificed to the sheer crosswinds of paid or even so-called independent experts.[15]

A few procedural reforms seem likely to curb at least some of the worst abuses in this area of family court litigation.

For one thing, though it is already spelled out in the Code of Judicial Conduct that a judge should not hold ex parte communication with an expert witness, it should be spelled out in no uncertain terms that for the expert, too, such behavior is per se unethical. It should be noted here that one prominent custody evaluator, Dr. Arthur Green (described above in part II, chapter 7), actually told one of us that he routinely spoke with the judge in a family court case as soon as he was appointed, to get what he called a "thumbnail" of the case. In practice, such communication is fraught with potential for abuse and is often used to give the expert his conclusion before he begins his evaluation.

Second, Timothy Tippins has argued—rightly, we believe—that the common practice of custody evaluators submitting their reports to a family court judge *before* trial must stop. This is because when an expert presents evidence in a court of law, his credentials and his methods are subject to preliminary questioning before his testimony can be admitted—a procedure known as voir dire. Then his conclusions may be challenged, either by objection or through cross-examination. As a result, the expert's conclusions—which can be devastating to one party or the other—may never be admitted into evidence at all. But if the expert's report is admitted ahead of time, without anyone having an opportunity to question or challenge the expert concerning how he reached his conclusions, the judge will already learn the expert's "findings" and may not be able to ignore them, even if they ultimately do not pass muster in his court once trial begins. Since family court judges act as juries as well in nearly all cases, this common procedure is completely unacceptable, bypassing important legal safeguards. It should be prohibited.

At the same time, it is critical that the expert's report, together with all the bases of the opinion and the circumstances surrounding the evaluation, be disclosed to the *parties* well before trial. This should be as detailed as possible. As the well-known custody evaluator David A. Martindale, Ph.D., has written:

> The role of an expert . . . is to assist the trier of fact. Doing so requires that evaluators report all pertinent information, including information supportive of a recommendation different from that offered in the advisory report. Custody evaluators are reasonably expected to be thorough in reporting the information that they have gathered.[16]

Moreover, expert witnesses should not be allowed to charge excessive fees for evaluations. In most cases, the evaluator's fee is paid by the litigants, and where the fee is excessive, the weaker financial party (usually the mother) suffers most. To make matters worse, hostile evaluators sometimes complain to the family court judge even before trial when a mother has been slow in paying her portion of the fee—asking the judge to order, under threat of contempt, that she make her payment. This tactic neatly turns a judge against an impecunious mother before her case has even reached trial, and it also serves as an extortionate device by which a mother afraid of incurring the court's wrath will pay any fee at all, no matter how high. For this reason, any measure that tends to standardize or limit such fees would be welcome. And experts should be required to commence separate proceedings to recover their fees.

It is possible that the use of "junk science" theories can be banned from family courts by specific legislation, but so far this seems unlikely. Controversial theories such as Parental Alienation Syndrome were the targets of proposed legislation in 2003 in two states, Texas and Virginia, but neither remedial bill became law. Thus, we believe that the implementation of standards like those laid out above is more likely to effect the necessary reforms. And if such reforms are made part of the systemic standards required by CAPTA, they—like the judicial reforms advocated above—can be effected at the national level.

Social Services

Every reader of this book will know, from reading chapter 6, that many abuses are committed by child protective services agencies in cases involving child sexual abuse allegations. As with the family courts themselves, the malfunction of CPS agencies is rooted in fundamental misconceptions that can be corrected only through the "rebirthing" of the system we discuss above in chapter 9. What we propose here are more pragmatic reforms aimed at containing at least the most obvious types of agency misconduct. Like the other reforms we propose, these can be made effectively at the federal level by incorporating them into CAPTA, as described above.

TRAINING

Obviously, CPS workers must (and do) receive training before they can serve as caseworkers for the state in such sensitive matters. Training is required of all such workers in each state. What is not currently required—as it should be—is training that deals specifically with family court abuses.

We propose that every social worker employed by a state CPS agency be required to take a course, to be accredited by the National Association of Social Workers, that will warn caseworkers of the impropriety of such conduct as:

1. Accusing a parent of abuse or neglect simply to force her to comply with agency directives.
2. Accusing a parent of abuse or neglect when there is no evidence that a child is in harm's way, simply because a caseworker would like to intervene in the family's affairs.
3. Accusing a mother of child abuse or neglect based on theories without scientific validity.

4. Accusing a mother of abuse or neglect when the definitions of abuse or neglect set out in the state's statutes are not met.

In addition, caseworkers should be trained in the basic elements of legal procedure involved in abuse/neglect cases. For instance, they should know the legal standards for seeking removals, emergency intervention, and the termination of parental rights. Our analysis in part II has shown that many CPS workers are either grossly ignorant of the legal standards or ignore them. This should be changed.

PROCEDURES

Again, it should be obvious that certain procedural reforms should be built into the applicable regulations governing the conduct of CPS agencies. These reforms are simple and—to family court outsiders—will doubtless seem unnecessary to state. But too many devastating disruptions of family life have occurred because CPS agencies have wantonly ignored even these procedural norms.

First, no CPS agency has the right to withhold agency records from a child's mother simply because CPS is pursuing a case against her. Unless a mother's parental rights have been terminated by a court order, only a specific court order may serve to allow a CPS agency to withhold any information or records in a case from the mother or her lawyer. And such orders may only be based on overriding need.

In most states, abuse or neglect petitions are signed by an employee of the social services agency responsible for issuing them. However, in many cases these petitions are signed by individuals who have no knowledge whatever of the facts of the case. Since these petitions can have devastating consequences, we propose that each such petition be signed, or at least countersigned or otherwise verified, by a caseworker who, by signing, claims to be personally familiar with the facts of the case and believes that the allegations stated in the petition are true and that abuse or neglect is properly alleged under the circumstances. This should be true a fortiori of motions or petitions seeking the removal of a child or some other action from a family court. In such cases, affidavits are nearly always required in support of the agency's request. But we believe that the relevant statutes should require that all such affidavits state explicitly that the signatory is personally familiar with the facts of the case and swears to the truth of the allegations contained in the papers. Too often, as we have seen, CPS agencies file such motions supported by generally worded affidavits from supervisors who do not claim (and certainly do not have) any firsthand knowledge of the facts. Such affidavits should be treated as legal nullities— but in practice they are not. And by the time a protective mother is able to challenge such a motion in court, CPS is usually prepared with a new set of allegations, so that the improper removal remains uncorrected for months—if, indeed, it is ever corrected. A specific statutory requirement of what should be a commonsense rule would deter courts from ordering removals when such evasive procedures are used by CPS.

We further recommend, as a deterrent to the use of invalid petitions by CPS, that the signing of clearly improper or baseless neglect or abuse petitions (or other CPS court papers) should be grounds for internal discipline by the agency.

Finally, state statutes should guarantee that CPS employees who disclose the truth about agency failure in cases involving abuse allegations may not be the objects of retaliation by the agency.

REGULATION AND CONTROL

We noted above that law guardians have, for too long, enjoyed virtually absolute immunity from lawsuits arising from their misconduct in abuse-related cases. The same is true of CPS agencies, which, as arms of government, are immune from suit as long as they work in "good faith." There are reasons for this. Government agencies would be hamstrung in their functions if they faced lawsuits from disgruntled citizens over every official act. That is why it makes sense to protect government when its employees act in good faith. But this immunity should not extend to knowingly improper or unlawful acts. Thus, there must be no immunity for such acts as perjury; making any knowingly false statements that lead a family court to take improper action; knowing or grossly negligent endangerment of children; or the conscious suppression of evidence. For such acts as these, the state government should be liable. Protective mothers who have suffered damages as a result of CPS misconduct should be able to recover compensation from the state government. This is not only just in itself; it will help to deter further misconduct by CPS caseworkers. All the warnings in the world are likely to be ineffective if the agencies know they have nothing to fear when they violate the guidelines.

We also believe that each state's commissioner of social services (or the equivalent), who presides over the state's CPS officials, should periodically review his or her agency's handling of child abuse/neglect petitions to determine whether such petitions are being properly issued and whether the agency is unduly penalizing mothers who make good-faith accusations of child sex abuse. The commissioner should also seek to determine whether the agency is improperly meddling in private custody cases even when it has no grounds for believing that child abuse or neglect has occurred.

Conclusion

We have set out in part III a rather lengthy list of reforms. Most of them, however, are really self-evident, or would be if basic principles of justice, common sense, and decency were not so often trampled on in the family courts. The rest follow simply and logically from the abuses we have analyzed throughout this book.

In the last analysis, we will have a healthy family court system only when the citizenry demands one. At present, most people believe—wrongly—that no one in the United States of America can lose something as precious as a child without something resembling basic due process of law. Most people believe that if they are good parents, they will not have to watch as their children are pulled from them by police officers. Most assume that if they have managed to live a normal, productive life for thirty years or more, they will not suddenly be declared "insane" in family court on the strength of a quack theory. Most assume that they cannot lose a child—perhaps never to see the child again—because of rumors, hearsay statements, or a prediction they might violate a court order at some future date. Most believe they cannot be penalized for trying to protect a child.

When American mothers realize just how vulnerable they and their children really are in the family court system of today, they will begin to demand a better one. Then, and only then, will sexually abused children and the women who try to protect them enjoy the security they have always deserved, within a family court system free of the forces of judicial madness it has been our unpleasant duty to record.

Notes

Unless otherwise indicated, all references to transcripts are to trial transcripts in unpublished cases and are referenced by date and page number(s). Names of parties and docket numbers of cases are omitted to protect the privacy of the parents and children involved in the proceedings.

Introduction

1. We use the term "family court" to refer to any trial-level court handling domestic relations matters, such as divorce, custody, visitation, or child support. In some states these courts are called by the name Family Court. In many jurisdictions, specific matters of child abuse and neglect are heard exclusively by the Juvenile Courts or Children's Courts. In some states these matters are heard by trial courts of general jurisdiction.

2. The term "protective parent" is used if the accused abuser is a father, stepfather, grandfather, or someone else within the immediate family circle. It is not applied to parents charging abuse by others, such as pastors or teachers.

3. Pennington, *The Judicial Training Act.*

4. Personal communication with Rita Henley Jensen, July 15, 2004. Women's eNews can be found at www.womensenews.org.

5. Letter from Bonnie Campbell to Amy Neustein, December 15, 1998.

6. Personal communication with Mariam Bell, February 4, 1994.

7. Lawson and Chaffin, "False Negatives in Sexual Abuse Disclosure Interviews."

8. Faller and DeVoe, "Allegations of Sexual Abuse in Divorce."

9. Arens and Lasswell, *In Defense of Public Order*, p. 180.

10. Our use of "methodical" does not necessarily imply *neatly* organized case management. Instead, what we describe as "methodical" is meant to be understood in strictly ethnomethodological terms: the systematic ways in which participants produce and interpret social interaction. Thus, even disorganization and sloppiness are seen as "methodically" ordered social practices in ethnomethodological studies of social interaction.

11. Decision of the Court of Appeals of Georgia, Fourth Division, December 23, 1999, p. 2.

Chapter 1. *An Overview of Family Court Madness—and Mothers' Mutiny*

1. Lombardi, "Custodians of Abuse."

2. Waller's film was shown at the New York International Independent Film and Video Festival, New York City, September 7, 2001.

3. The extreme penalty of loss of visitation, often imposed on protective parents, is especially remarkable because courts in general are extremely reluctant to deprive parents—that is, fathers—of visitation even with children who do not want to see them, unless the visits actually jeopardize the children's health or well-being. See *Mark-Weiner v. Mark, New York Law Journal,* August 24, 2001, p. 18, col. 4. Yet protective parents may be denied visits with children who love them.

4. Jacobbi and Wright, "Mothers Who Go to Jail for Their Children."

5. Galtney, "Mothers on the Run."

6. Quindlen, "The Good Mother," p. 15.

7. Fifield and Lesher, "A Child's at Stake."

8. The case was treated in a series of news articles by Bob Port of the *New York Daily News* from May to July 2004; see also Neustein and Lesher, "Courts See Moms as Guilty Till Proven Innocent."

9. Keating, "Children in Incestuous Relationships," pp. 113, 114.

10. Faller, "Child Maltreatment and Endangerment in the Context of Divorce."

11. Faller offers a conservative figure. Other researchers have found an even lower rate of false reports of abuse in divorce and custody proceedings. For example, D. P. Jones and J. M. McGraw (1987) reported that only 8 percent of total reports of sexual abuse were "fictitious." A year later, D. P. Jones and A. Seig (1988) reported in an American Bar Association publication the results of another study showing a "false" allegation rate of 20 percent—none of which, however, was determined to be a deliberate fabrication. In their 1992 article, J. M. McGraw and H. A. Smith found that the rate of false reports of abuse was 16.5 percent, a figure that would have been even lower had they removed from their sample the false report that had been made by an adolescent child against a parent.

12. Penfold, "Questionable Beliefs about Child Sexual Abuse Allegations during Custody Disputes."

13. Massat and Lundy, "Reporting Costs to Nonoffending Parents in Cases of Intrafamilial Child Sexual Abuse," p. 384.

14. Heim et al., *California National Organization for Women Family Court Report,* p. iv.

15. *Id.*

16. The report was produced by the Battered Mothers' Testimony Project at the Wellesley Centers for Women, November 2002. The report was authored by

Carrie Cuthbert, Kim Slote, Monica Ghosh Driggers, Cynthia Mesh, Lundy Bancroft and Jay Silverman.

17. Silverman et al., "Child Custody Determinations in Cases Involving Intimate Partner Violence."

18. The report was authored by Dianne Post and Kisa Corcoran.

19. See Rothman and Watson (1990). This report of the Judicial Council Advisory Committee on Gender Bias in the Courts was issued under the auspices of the Administrative Office of the Courts of California. The committee was chaired by Los Angeles Superior Court Judge David M. Rothman and Senator Diane E. Watson of Los Angeles.

20. Winner, *Findings on Judge Michael Dufficy, Commissioner Sylvia Shapiro, and Court-Appointees in Marin County's Superior Court in California,* p. 4.

21. Winner, *Placing Children at Risk: Questionable Psychologists and Therapists in the Sacramento Family Court and Surrounding Counties,* p. 7.

22. Kramer, "Justice Denied," p. 17.

23. Testimony given at a joint New York State legislative hearing sponsored by four committees: Assembly Committee on Judiciary; Assembly Committee on Children and Families; Senate Committee on Child Care; and Assembly Subcommittee on Family Law (March 9, 1989).

24. Nicholson and Bulkley, *Sexual Abuse Allegations in Custody and Visitation Cases.*

25. *American Jurisprudence Proof of Facts,* 3rd ed., vol. 33, section 303, p. 327.

26. *Id.,* pp. 315–316.

27. Men's Equality Now newsletter, September/October 1982. Apart from Armstrong, feminist writer Trish Wilson has looked into the activities of father's rights groups in her article "Will Paternal Paranoia Triumph?"

28. Columnist Mike McAlary ("Court with the Disney Touch") wrote that the judge was "regarded as extremely weak on sexual abuse cases" (p. 5).

29. Testimony given at a joint New York State legislative hearing sponsored by four committees: Assembly Committee on Judiciary; Assembly Committee on Children and Families; Senate Committee on Child Care; and Assembly Subcommittee on Family Law (March 9, 1989), p. 394.

30. Letter from Humberto Middleton, December 20, 1991.

31. Winner, *Divorced from Justice,* p. 133.

32. Kerrison, "Pleas for a Dying Child Go Unheeded," p. 14.

33. Kerrison, "Anguished Mothers Beg for Help," p. 2.

34. Kerrison, "Exposing Dads Who Rape their Children," p. 2.

35. Hanson, "The Sex Abuse Controversy," p. 258.

36. Nance, "Validation Evidence Poses Issue in Child Abuse Cases," pp. 1–2.

37. *Turner v. Turner,* 689 N.Y.S.2d 269 (3rd Dept., 1999). To understand the full impact of that ruling, one should bear in mind that the majority of sex abuse allegations are never substantiated sufficiently to result in a judicial finding of abuse. The nature of the act makes legal proof unusually difficult. This ruling, in

other words, could well mean that a mother who alleges sex abuse—even if her suspicions are understandable—stands a more than even chance of losing custody.

38. The action by the appellate court was all the more striking because such courts are generally very reluctant to reverse child custody decisions, since these decisions often turn on subjective assessments of the parents, who appear before the trial judge but not the appellate court.

39. 203 F. Supp. 2d 153 (E.D.N.Y., 2002).

40. The conference is now an annual event.

41. See Woodlin, "Newsome Gaining Public Support"; Skipper, "Mom Remains in Hattisburg Jail"; and Fentress, "Mothers Defy Court, Keep Children."

42. Keating, "Children in Incestuous Relationships," pp. 111–112.

43. Galtney, "Mothers on the Run."

44. Podesta and Van Biema, "Running for Their Lives"; Baer, "G.A. [Georgia] Woman Guides Abused Children toward Havens."

45. Pennington, *The Judicial Training Act,* p. 5.

46. Carpenter, "Children of the Underground."

47. Herbert, "Norton vs. Norton," p. 1.

Chapter 2. The New Legal Landscape

1. *New York Law Journal,* March 18, 2002.

2. Derdyn, "A Consideration of Legal Issues in Child Custody Contests."

3. Curran, "The Vulnerability of Court-Appointed Impartial Experts in Child-Custody Cases," pp. 1169.

4. Gardner wrote an article about PAS in 1985, and his first book-length discussion of the "syndrome" appeared in 1987: *The Parental Alienation Syndrome and the Differentiation between Fabricated and Genuine Child Sexual Abuse.* In 1992, Gardner published a guide for practitioners in recognizing and treating PAS, *The Parental Alienation Syndrome: A Guide for Mental Health and Legal Professionals.*

5. Hanson, "The Sex Abuse Controversy," p. 258.

6. Pennington, *The Judicial Training Act,* p. 10.

7. Brooklyn Citizen Court Monitors, *An Inside Look at the Brooklyn Family Court,* p. 7.

8. Goodhue, *Child Protection and the Family Court: A Study of Processes, Procedures and Outcomes under Article Ten of the New York Family Court Act.*

Chapter 3. Research Methods

1. M. Travers and J. Manzo (eds.).

2. Garfinkel, "The Origins of the Term 'Ethnomethodology,'" p. 18.

3. When we speak about "publicly" observable or accountable actions, we are referring to the other interactants in the social setting who, as members of that setting and as part of their routine practical social activities, engage in "publicly" demonstrating an understanding of the social conventions underlying that activity to one another, such as when an actor provides a "return greeting" upon being greeted by another actor. Failure to do so implies that the recipient of the greeting is angry, too busy, or possibly deaf/dumb or too mentally impaired to publicly demonstrate to the other actor his understanding of the social import of the greeting.

4. Garfinkel's 1967 study of the staff at the Los Angeles Suicide Prevention Center shows how members accomplish their inquiries into deaths by taking the "unique" context-dependent features of each case—cases that are by their very nature problematic and equivocal, since the only one who can tell an accurate story is now dead—and deciding "for all practical purposes" what happened by giving reasons that point to, document, instantiate a socially organized pattern of practical activity and mundane occurrences; and in so doing, reflexively re-create the underlying pattern of commonsense reasoning as it is derived from the particulars of each case.

5. For instance, when mothers needed to ask for advice from the health visitor, they employed certain conversational practices by which they could "display their own putative competence and capacity to cope with the problem for which they seek help and avoid the appearance of ignorance or incompetence which might arise from a simple request for information" (p. 388).

6. The law permits the filing of inconsistent allegations in such petitions. However, in cases like these, the inconsistency goes to the fundamental question of whether the petition ought to be filed in the first place. If the child in question was not abused, there is no legal basis for commencing a family court action. Thus, it is highly unlikely that CPS agencies would taint their petitions with such a basic ambiguity if the petitions were simply intended as factual records of the agencies' concerns in a given case.

7. According to Meehan, the running record "can be conceptually distinguished from an officer's 'mental dossier,' the term used by Cicourel (1968) to refer to the personal recollection of events or persons . . . [because] it is an occasion for revealing *selected* aspects of one's mental dossier on an individual, place, or event" (p. 199, emphasis added).

8. Ex parte communications are a breach of judicial ethics. Code of Judicial Conduct, Canon 3A(4). Nevertheless, as the examples in part II of this book will show, they are amazingly common in family courts.

9. In one case, for instance, a protective mother's child support was slashed to compensate the father for her supposedly "excessive" litigation—a favorite complaint against protective mothers. This ruling was upheld on appeal despite the mother's detailed proof that most of the litigation complained of had been prompted by the father, not the mother, and that the father's claimed expenses

were wildly inflated. The appellate judge simply declared that he would not "re-open" the issue—which had never properly been examined in the first place. The judge's comments at oral argument showed that he had *heard* about the mother from other court personnel. The oral "running record" provided the basis for his ruling, even though it was contradicted by documentary proof.

Chapter 4. Robed Rage

1. The practice of attorneys "contemplating" the judge as a guide to how to present their case occurs in other legal matters as well. As discussed in the previous chapter, Lynch (1997) points out that in criminal proceedings "attorneys invoke the judge as an organizational principle that locally governs the presentation of the case at hand . . . they incorporate the judge into the practical organization of the projected cases, and by so doing they realize the judge in their procedures for presenting cases at hand" (p. 103).

2. Appellate brief, January 31, 1989, p. 78. See Kerrison, "Incredible Return of Misogynist a Disgrace," p. 4.

3. Women are often blamed by judges for any hostility their children show toward their fathers. For instance, in one published case, the record shows that a divorced father (stationed overseas in military service) had a drinking problem, was "frequently violent when intoxicated," had assaulted his wife, and reportedly became hostile when he came to visit the children, on one occasion "breaking through a storm door to enter the house and breaking into the locked bathroom where the three children were hiding out of fear." However, even after the children testified that they did not want to be forced to visit their father (who had not attempted to visit them for several years before filing a motion seeking to enforce visitation), a family court judge fined the mother and ordered her to see to it that the children called their father daily, answered all his letters, and visited him for several weeks out of the year overseas. The judge claimed, "Mrs. Dennison [the mother] was doing her share of badmouthing, so to speak, her former husband. . . . Mrs. Dennison has been in there pitching so to speak, against visitation with Mr. Ridley. I do believe that is infectious. . . . Clearly, it is defendant [the mother] who has, by overt and covert means, influenced the children." An appellate court reversed the judge, stating, "We find no basis in the record for his conclusions." *Ridley v. Dennison*, 689 A.2d 793 (App. Div., 1997). Such reversals appear to be more the exception than the rule.

4. Transcript, October 21, 1986, pp. 6–8; transcript, October 22, 1986, pp. 5–6, 18–23.

5. An official report from a senior assistant state attorney to Connecticut's state's attorney (written in October 1998, after the boys had been placed with their father and the mother had been thrown in jail) also concluded that "a reasonable parent in [the mother's] position in February, 1994, would have believed that J. W.

and B. W. had been sexually abused by [the father] and [his sister]" and recites considerable evidence in support of this conclusion. The report goes on to state that "if her boys have been sexually abused," as the mother reasonably believed, "then surely she, who has seen the system deliver the boys to the abuser while it has sent her to jail, has been one of the most gravely victimized parents ever to seek protection from the legal system." Unfortunately, as this book demonstrates, her case does not stand alone.

6. Transcript, July 7, 1993, pp. 5–11.

7. Transcript of testimony in chambers, June 9, 1993.

8. Transcript, June 15, 1993; order dated June 15, 1993, pp. 1–2.

9. Affidavit supporting CPS petition, August 10, 1983. The affidavit also states that the infant's seven-year-old sister had personally seen the father touching the infant's genitals "for an extended period of time."

10. Affidavit of mother, July 25, 1986, p. 8.

11. *Id.*

12. *Id.*, p. 12.

13. *Id.*

14. Mother's affidavit, July 25, 1986, p. 10.

15. Transcript, December 23, 1997, p. 23. In 1999, New Jersey's Appellate Division reversed another family court judge for removing a child from her mother because the mother would not "change her subjective view of [the father's] prospective visitation with [the parties' daughter]," which she feared. The court stated that judges in custody and visitation matters "cannot reasonably require the parties to change their opinions and forsake their subjective fears. The court has the power to control and punish conduct, not thought." *P.T. v. M.S.,* 738 A.2d 385, 399 (App. Div., 1999). As discussed in other sections of this book, such appellate review of family court actions is rare, and it remains to be seen whether the Appellate Division's warning will have any effect on family courts in New Jersey. See below for a description of a still more recent New Jersey case in which a mother's children were removed from her without the evidentiary hearing clearly required by New Jersey's appellate court.

16. Jeremiah B. McKenna, report to New York State Senate Committee on Crime and Correction, October 31, 1987, p. 1.

17. *Id*, p. 1.

18. Testimony of the mother before the New York State Assembly Judiciary Committee, May 18, 1989.

19. A few (published) examples of such cases, drawn from a single state (New York), include the following: *Gagliardo v. Gagliardo,* New York Law Journal, January 1, 1989, p. 28 (the mother was ruled "unfit" to be the custodial parent because she prevented the father's visits due to sex abuse allegations that were ultimately ruled unfounded); *F.N. v. F.A.,* New York Law Journal, July 3, 1989, p. 29 (the father was awarded sole custody after the mother took the child out of state, believing the

child to have been sexually abused by the father; an expert witness testified merely that there was no "direct evidence" of abuse, not that the mother had acted in bad faith); *Turner v. Turner*, 689 N.Y.S.2d 269 (3rd Dept., 1999) (the father was awarded sole custody because the mother had made a good-faith child abuse allegation against the father that was ruled unsubstantiated; the court claimed that regardless of the mother's motives, her allegation rendered her unfit for custody because the charge had caused the temporary suspension of the father's visitation with the child; the court said the mother's "behavior casts significant doubt upon her capacity to provide for the emotional and intellectual development of the child").

20. Letter from Attorney Steve Mandel to the special prosecutor's office, June 20, 1990.

21. Pagnozzi, "Mom Was Trying to Help Her Kids, So Why Is She the One on Trial?" p. 13.

22. Code of Judicial Conduct, Canon 3A(4).

23. Attorney affirmation, Appellate Division, July 24, 1986, p. 8.

24. Sworn affidavit, July 25, 1986, p. 14.

25. This statement was part of an unsuccessful motion for a stay of the order changing custody. What makes the judge's order particularly astounding is that New York law does not provide for a change of child custody without a full court hearing at which *both* parents (and anyone else with actual custody of a child) are given an opportunity to appear and be heard, whereas in this case the judge transferred the child to the father without a hearing, let alone any advance notice to the mother. New York Domestic Relations Law § 75–e; see *Priscilla S. v. Albert B.*, 102 Misc. 2d 650, 424 N.Y.S.2d 613 (1980). Family courts often seem to overlook such questions of due process.

26. Court transcript, June 15, 1993.

27. Memorandum decision, February 22, 1994, p. 2.

28. *Id.*, p. 6.

29. Decision of January 30, 1995, p. 5.

30. Psychologist's report, February 28, 2002.

31. Attorney's affirmation in support of the mother's motion for greater visitation rights with the children, July 2003. No factual or legal opposition to these papers was filed by CPS or any party to the case.

32. *New Jersey Division of Youth and Family Services v. J.Y.*, 352 N.J. Super. 245, 800 A.2d 132 (App. Div., 2002).

33. Report of the State of New York Commission on Judicial Conduct, Matter of Judge Louis Grossman, November 20, 1984, pp. 1–9. Subsequent quotations are taken from this report.

34. Determination, State of New York Commission on Judicial Conduct, November 20, 1984, p. 7.

35. *Id.*, pp. 7–8.

36. *Id.*, pp. 5–6.

37. Dr. Arthur Green is described at length in chapter 7.

38. There is no record that the family court judge even forwarded these transcripts to the appellate court, as required by New York law; New York Family Court Act § 664(b), Civil Practice Law & Rules § 4019; see *Fleishman v. Walters,* 40 A.D.2d 622. In theory, an appellate court should not accept a family court custody ruling if it is based more on private interviews than on evidence taken in court; *People ex rel. Kessler v. Cotter,* 285 A.D. 206. In practice, appellate courts rarely give family court decisions close scrutiny.

39. Transcript of hearing, July 13, 1989, pp. 2–6.

40. Interview on radio program *New York & Company,* WNYC (New York, New York), November 30, 1989.

41. *Lincoln v. Lincoln,* 24 N.Y.2d 270.

42. Letter of Dr. Robert Geffner, June 5, 1999.

43. *State ex rel. Rich v. Bair,* 83 Idaho 475, 365 P.2d 216 (1961).

44. *Kinsella v. Kinsella,* 696 A.2d 556 (1997) (New Jersey Supreme Court), quoting with approval the 1991 report of a task force of the American Psychiatric Association. The court's opinion reviewed similar statements from the courts of other states.

45. Memorandum decision, January 29, 1999. As further evidence of the anger that motivated the judge, the decision contains derogatory statements about the mother that are unsupported by the record.

46. Written statement of Robert Geffner, Ph.D., June 1999. Dr. Geffner wrote that he still thought disclosure might violate ethical guidelines and even federal law. Evidently that was less important to the judge than the desire to control—or punish—the protective mother.

47. Mother's complaint to the New York State Grievance Committee, March 5, 1999, p. 2.

48. *Id.*

49. Nassau County Medical Center report, June 14, 1993.

50. Two other mothers whose cases had been before Judge Deutsch reportedly committed suicide. (Mike McAlary, "Court with Disney Touch," p. 28; Viva, "Women and Children Last," p. 115.)

51. Testimony before New York State Senate, July 13, 1989, p. 1.

52. Jayakar testimony, May 18, 1989, p. 20.

53. *Id.,* pp. 21–22.

54. *Id.,* p. 22.

55. *Id.,* p. 23.

56. Transcript, November 29, 1990, p. 17.

57. Psychiatrist's report, November 13, 1990.

58. Transcript, November 29, 1990, p. 2.

59. *Id.,* p. 5.

60. *Id.,* p. 6.

61. *Id.,* p. 16.

62. *Id.,* p. 3.

63. *Id.,* p. 7.

64. Decision of May 1993. Despite the relatively cautious wording of this decision, its real meaning was perfectly obvious to other judges who inherited the case. An appellate judge would describe the earlier decision this way: "[The judge] questioned her motivations, her credibility and her mental stability. It is clear that he did not believe any part of plaintiff's allegations of abuse involving the daughter. His findings were based upon a fully developed record following an extensive evidentiary hearing." (Memorandum decision, March 28, 1995.) This confirms that the real "record" of a case like this is not the official legal one, for as a matter of fact the abuse allegations had never been resolved by the court; they were withdrawn when the father agreed to forgo all contact with the girl. Nor did the earlier judge ever actually conclude that the charges had been false. The "fully developed record" so calmly referred to by the appellate judge simply did not exist in any legal sense. The "record" had been written, so to speak, between the lines.

65. Decision of June 15, 1993, p. 2.

66. Decision of December 18, 1997.

67. Appellate brief, September 1998, and reply brief, October 5, 1998. Remarkably, none of these points were denied by the father's attorneys. Their brief continued the pattern of burying the mother under hostile epithets; they scarcely even attempted to justify the (by then) familiar labels. They called the mother "litigious" even though they did not deny that it was the father, not the mother, who had insisted on litigating the issues raised in the appeal. In another flourish (unadorned with facts), they complained that the father's income "was being consumed by attorney's fees caused by a vindictive ex-wife, who will not stop." Yet they left completely unchallenged the mother's showing that nearly three-fifths of the father's claimed legal expenses could not possibly be attributed to her actions.

68. Memorandum decision, January 29, 1999.

69. The same judge, in an earlier opinion, had actually claimed that the trial judge was the real victim—he castigated the "machinations" of the mother's attorneys as they struggled to bring her children home and said their "disrespect" for the trial judge who had taken the children away without a proper hearing was "appalling" (Memorandum decision, January 30, 1995).

70. Neustein, Burton, and Quirk, "Concerning the Plight of Children in Cases of Parental Abuse," p. 19.

71. Motion for recusal, March 22, 1996.

72. Personal communication of the mother's lawyer to Amy Neustein, July 3, 2003.

73. Testimony of Julia Heit, Hearing before the Subcommittee on Select Edu-

cation, Committee on Education and Labor, U.S. House of Representatives, 102nd Congress, Second Session, April 20, 1992, pp. 73–74.

74. These hearings were sponsored by four committees: Assembly Committee on Judiciary; Assembly Committee on Children and Families; Senate Committee on Child Care; and Assembly Subcommittee on Family Law. Hearing dates were March 9 and May 18, 1989.

75. Hemphill, "The Agony of Yacov Riegler," p. 6.

76. Memorandum of Jeremiah B. McKenna to the New York State Senate Committee on Crime and Correction, April 13, 1987.

77. Trial testimony of Dr. Sidney Fein, May 8, 1989, p. 8.

78. Nance, "Validation Evidence Poses Issue in Child Abuse Cases," p. 1.

79. University of California, Davis, Medical Center, Sacramento, July 7, 1996, pp. 3–4.

80. Mother's formal complaint to the presiding judge overseeing the trial court, January 28, 2002, p. 1.

81. Transcript, February 20, 1998, p. 31.

82. Judge's statements, reading from a letter written by the court-appointed visitation supervisor, transcript of February 20, 1998, p. 38.

83. Such orders are in fact quite common in protective mother cases. The mother—though not accused of any sort of violence—is precluded from important ceremonies, such as religious confirmations or school graduations, as part of her isolation from her child.

84. Transcript, April 25, 1997, p. 110.

85. Transcript, October 31, 1996, pp. 3, 9–10. The judge's mention of "witchcraft" here refers to statements he made earlier that day about the notorious Salem witch hunts: "History tells us that the witchcraft fright that went through Salem, Massachusetts, was hysterical and, as we know, unfounded on any factual basis" (p. 3).

86. Transcript, November 1, 1996, p. 59.

87. Transcript, February 20, 1998, pp. 11–12.

88. *Id.*, p. 16.

89. *Id.*, p. 34.

90. *Id.*, pp. 32–33.

91. *Id.*, p. 16.

92. *Id.*, p. 12.

93. One protective mother we spoke with was surprised that in her custody proceedings involving sex abuse allegations, unlike routine custody proceedings that do not involve abuse allegations, the court and its auxiliaries became so entirely focused on litigation issues (for instance, the mother's presumed making of a false report of abuse to the child protective service agency or the police) that they never even inquired into whether or not she was the primary caretaker of the child.

The mother, a busy professional, had her own mother care for her child and feared being asked questions about basic caretaking matters such as the child's eating and sleeping habits. To her surprise, these questions never came up; the proceeding seem to shy away from nurturing concerns altogether.

Chapter 5. Lawless Law Gaurdians

1. The family law literature often uses the terms "law guardian" and "guardian ad litem" interchangeably, though in fact there are some differences between the two. Simply put, a guardian ad litem is an attorney or a layperson appointed by the court to protect the interests of a minor child (or incompetent) involved in litigation. A law guardian is an attorney appointed to act as the lawyer for a minor child in a divorce or child abuse case—that is, to represent the child on the assumption that the child's interests may not be adequately represented by either of the parents. We use the term "guardian ad litem" only when referring to published articles or case records where that specific term has been used. Otherwise we refer to all court-appointed representatives for minor children in family court litigation as "law guardians."

2. Lidman and Hollingsworth, "The Guardian Ad Litem in Child Custody Cases," pp. 255, 256, n. 4.

3. The National Center on Women and Family Law (1982–1996), operating under a federal grant from the Legal Services Corporation, served as a legal research and training center for women and family law.

4. *Guarding Our Children: A Review of Massachusetts' Guardian Ad Litem Program within the Probate and Family Court* (March 2001).

5. Ducote, "Guardians Ad Litem in Private Custody Litigation."

6. 42 U.S.C.S. § 5106a.

7. Lidman and Hollingsworth, "The Guardian Ad Litem in Child Custody Cases," p. 306.

8. Sometimes, in fact, a family court judge will rein in a law guardian whose advocacy veers outside the definition of his or her role, but this is more the exception than the rule. In one Wisconsin case we studied, a law guardian failed to persuade the judge to give a father found to have engaged in "inappropriate [sexual] conduct" greater visitation rights than the evidence justified. In that case, the judge had speculated to the lawyers, on the record, that he might release the father from supervised visitation at some *future* date. The law guardian then directly confronted the judge, seeking a "specific time" for the removal of those restrictions. (Significantly, it was not the father's lawyer who made this aggressive request on the father's behalf but the lawyer for the children allegedly abused by him.)

The judge, however, did not give way to the law guardian's pressure. Rather, he qualified his earlier statement:

I did not set a specific time for that because I think that depends upon insofar as a counselor or therapist might be able to recommend it, I think that depends in large part upon the successful completion of therapy, whatever that term might mean, and that could be a matter of a short period of time or a more lengthy period of time. I really don't know. (Transcript of oral decision, November 20, 1992, p. 31)

The mother told Amy Neustein that she had feared losing custody of her sons, despite the serious allegations of abuse, because of the extraordinary "camaraderie" between the law guardian and the children's father, who appeared pro se throughout a two-week trial. The law guardian not only zealously cross-examined the mother's witnesses but called—as her own witness—a CPS caseworker to testify that the mother had "neglected" her children by making "false" charges of sexual abuse. That "camaraderie" did not pay off for the father in this particular case.

9. Ethnomethodologists Harold Garfinkel and Egon Bittner (1967) first introduced the concept of "contractual" uses of records—that is, records with "projected external careers" (to be used outside the immediate organizational setting, as opposed to their internal purposes). In their 1967 study of outpatient clinic records ("Good Organizational Reasons for 'Bad' Clinic Records"), Garfinkel and Bittner offered a new way of analyzing how, unlike records for internal use, official records are produced and used in organizational settings. As an example, they pointed to how "the contents of clinic folders are assembled with regard for the possibility that the relationship may have to be portrayed as having been in accord with expectations of sanctionable performances by clinicians and patients" (p. 199).

10. Court transcript, July 7, 1993, pp. 6, 13.

11. Letter dated July 15, 1993.

12. Letter to law guardian dated August 25, 1993.

13. Application for ex parte modification of physical custody filed by law guardian, February 14, 1994.

14. Transcript, November 20, 1996, pp. 10–12. It is, alas, typical of family court procedure that an earlier judge had not hesitated to remove custody from the *mother* in *her* absence—even though no evidence ever suggested the mother posed any threat of harm to the children. But the mother could not get a court to consider a temporary removal of custody from her ex-husband, even though there was an imposing mass of evidence of abuse, *plus a doctor's letter indicating an emergency,* until all attorneys—including the ex-husband's attorney—were "prepared."

15. Transcript, November 20, 1996, pp. 11–13.

16. Transcript, February 16, 2001; order, February 21, 2001.

17. Order (District of Columbia), February 21, 2001.

18. Transcript, November 8, 2000, pp. 29, 35.

19. Letter, June 22, 2000, pp. 2, 4–5.

20. Caseworker memorandum, February 8, 2001, p. 4.

21. Evaluation, p. 9.

22. Caseworker memorandum, p. 5.

23. Transcript, November 8, 2000, p. 43.

24. The caseworker's memo contains other false statements that may have originated with the GAL, though her memo does not directly say so. For instance, the memo states (p. 3) that the court-appointed psychologist in Maryland found that the mother "has no rational thoughts at this time," that she "is getting worst [*sic*]," that her "disorder is hard to treat," and that she had "fired 4–5 of her attorneys." *Not one* of these statements actually appears in the psychologist's testimony.

25. Strictly speaking, the "law guardian" in this case was an agency, the Legal Aid Society of New York, Kings County. The references to the "law guardian" here apply to the supervising attorney assigned to the case, who indeed personally handled nearly all of the litigation on behalf of the agency.

26. Transcript, March 17, 1987.

27. Appellant's brief, January 31, 1988, pp. 20–21; affidavit of Marjori Schecter, November 13, 1992; transcript of state legislative hearing, May 14, 1993, pp. 20–32.

28. Fifield and Lesher, "A Child's at Stake."

29. Letter of law guardian, June 8, 1993.

30. Closing argument of law guardian, June 9, 1993, pp. 168–169.

31. Transcript, July 27, 1993.

32. Attorney for [children's] position re: custody/visitation, August 11, 1993.

33. Letter of December 4, 1995 from Dr. Lenore Walker.

34. Affidavit of law guardian in support of motion for Order to Show Cause, signed December 16, 1993 (entered December 23), p. 2.

35. The Children's Hospital, Child Advocacy and Protection Team, October 1, 1991, pp. 2, 4–5.

36. Id., p. 4.

37. Humana Hospital Aurora, September 20, 1991, p. 1.

38. The Children's Hospital, Child Advocacy and Protection Team, October 1, 1991, p. 6.

39. Law guardian's closing argument, February 19, 1991, p. 3.

40. Verified motion for payment of expert witness consultation fee, November 6, 1989, p. 2.

41. Decision of the Kentucky Court of Appeals, dissenting opinion of Judge Michael O. McDonald, March 17, 1995, p. 33.

42. *Id.,* pp. 30–31.

43. As noted earlier in this book, "ex parte" contact between a judge and one of the attorneys in a case, without the others' knowledge and consent, is a breach of legal and judicial ethics (emphasis added).

44. Dissenting opinion, p. 33.

45. *Id.,* p. 34.

46. *Id.,* p. 33, n. 7.

47. Bennett, "Book Citing Hardin Case Stirs Debate," p. B1.

48. Judge McDonald later gave permission to have his dissenting opinion published in full in the popular press. See Winner, *Divorced from Justice*, appendix VI, pp. 270–280.

49. Bennett, "Controversial Case Can't Be Cited Later," p. B1.

50. Appellate decision, p. 37 (emphasis added).

51. Mother's complaint to the New York State Grievance Committee, March 5, 1999, p. 2.

52. Grace Moran, chief counsel for the State of New York Grievance Committee for the Tenth Judicial District, March 23, 1999.

53. Mother's complaint to the New York State Grievance Committee, March 5, 1999, p. 1.

54. *Krause v. Krause* (Docket No. C 02–5277 JSW, N.D. Cal.).

55. We have not located any cases in which children, having reached the age of majority, were permitted to sue their former law guardians for legal malpractice. However, some case law in New York suggests that such a suit might be possible if the law guardian is clearly incompetent or fails to act in good faith. See *Matter of Jamie TT,* 191 A.D.2d 132, 599 N.Y.S.2d 892 (3rd Dept., 1993); *Marquez v. Presbyterian Hospital et al.,* Index No. 7583 (Sup. Ct., Bronx Co.). Even this hint of possible legal liability for bad law guardians appears to be the exception rather than the rule.

56. Krause, "Letting Children Speak for Themselves," p. 4.

57. 537 A.2d 1227, 109 NJ 396.

58. Personal communications with the mother from November 1993 to December 1999.

59. Agus, "A Mother's Cry from the Grave," p. 8.

60. Petition of law guardian, October 5, 1992, p. 2. The law guardian's petition claimed that her inability to contact the mother that day posed an "imminent risk of harm" to the child. This bit of nonsense worked in family court; when faced with a *real* court—the Appellate Division—the law guardian did not even bother filing papers in opposition to the mother's arguments seeking to vacate the order (*New York Law Journal,* November 30, 1992, p. 31, col. 3). As we have seen, family courts are a breed apart, and law guardians know it. Unfortunately, law guardians are rarely subjected to higher court review.

61. This mother was not the only one to complain about this particular law guardian. We have examined three other cases involving her. In one case, the law guardian allegedly threatened the mother with prosecution for "neglect" if she did not stipulate to a custody award to the father after a controversial expert (Dr. Arthur Green) made that recommendation. The mother fled with her child. In the second case, the mother, who became a vocal activist, was "arrested, jailed, handcuffed behind her back and attached to the wall of the cell" for "several hours" for bringing her daughter to a hospital where the doctors found serious evidence of

sexual abuse (Agus, "Standing Fast to Get Her Kids Back," pp. 4, 34). In the third case, despite a report of sexual abuse by the father, the mother lost custody and all visitation rights. When she died of heart failure at forty-six, her parents were denied all access to their granddaughter.

62. Berger, "Three Deaths," p. 25.

63. Report of Virginia Strand, Ph.D., November 27, 1992, p. 3.

64. Sherman, "'No Choice,'" p. 8.

65. Buckmaster, *Let My People Go,* p. 13.

66. Agus, "A Mother's Cry from the Grave," p. 8.

Chapter 6. Anti–Social Services

1. Hearing transcript, Subcommittee on Select Education, Committee on Education and Labor, U.S. House of Representatives, 102nd Congress, Second Session, April 20, 1992, p. 85.

2. *Id.*

3. A typical regulation in New Jersey specifies that one of the purposes of CPS is to "[p]reserve and strengthen family life": New Jersey Administrative Code 10:133C-2.3(a)(2); N.J.S.A. 30:4C-1(a). This principle means that family ties must be encouraged and preserved to the greatest extent possible under the circumstances of a given case.

4. See transcript of decision, June 22, 2001, p. 14.

5. Personal communication with one of us.

6. Transcript, March 17, 1987.

7. The study was funded by a grant from the National Center on Child Abuse and Neglect (grant # 90–CA-1519).

8. Personal communication between Amy Neustein and Professors Marta Lundy and Carol Rippey Massat, January 21, 1994.

9. Personal communication between Amy Neustein and Dr. Lundy, July 17, 1996.

10. The published results of this study can be found in Massat and Lundy, "'Reporting Costs' to Nonoffending Parents in Cases of Intrafamilial Child Sexual Abuse," and Massat and Lundy, "Service and Support Needs of Non-offending Parents in Cases of Intrafamilial Sexual Abuse." In 1996, Drs. Massat and Lundy invited Amy Neustein to lecture at Jane Addams College of Social Work on the protective parent problem.

11. Letter, February 8, 1994, p. 2.

12. Forrest, "Children Die," p. 4.

13. Harman affidavit, October 19, 1992, pp. 1–2.

14. Letter dated January 24, 1996, pp. 1–2.

15. Memorandum of social worker, February 8, 2001.

16. *Id.;* psychological evaluation, November 21, 2000, p. 9; letter of psychologist summarizing his review of the transcript of children's interviews at Child Advocacy Center in June–July 2000 (undated), pp. 2–3.

17. Letter of therapist, June 22, 2000.

18. Temporary Custody Order (Maryland), February 21, 2001.

19. Transcript of deposition, June 6, 2001, pp. 147, 158–159.

20. Family Court Act § 1012(f).

21. C.S.R. § 19-3-102(1).

22. California Penal Code § 11165.2.

23. See *In re E.H.,* 718 A.2d 162 (D.C., 1998).

24. Family Court Act § 1027(b).

25. C.R.S. § 19-3-405(2).

26. Code of Virginia § 16.1-252(E).

27. In the case of a Brooklyn, New York, mother, the judge instructed CPS to charge the mother with neglect because she had changed therapists for her sexually abused children without first seeking the permission of the court. Even if her actions were in violation of a court order (for which contempt remedies could have been sought), her actions certainly did not qualify as "neglect" under the statute. See Pagnozzi, "Mom Was Trying to Help Her Kids."

28. Personal communication with Michael Lesher, May 1997.

29. New York State Department of Social Services, October 4, 1995, pp. 1–2.

30. Discharge summary, November 21, 1994, pp. 1–2.

31. Neglect petition, May 31, 1996, p. 3 (emphasis added).

32. *Id.*

33. The source of these claims was, in fact, the DA's counselor, who in turn heard them from a social worker who had met the mother at the battered women's shelter and (according to the mother) had pressured her to place her son with a foster care agency with which the social worker was professionally connected. When asked by a journalist if she had diagnosed the mother as mentally ill (with homicidal tendencies), the social worker admitted that she was not qualified to make any such diagnosis. But case notes clearly show that she did make it—and told the counselor so (CPS case summary notes, May 30, 1996; counselor's notes, May 30, 1996). So the petition against the mother was the outcome of an improper diagnosis, conveyed to a judge in the form of double hearsay. But as usual in family court, agency chatter was accepted as truth until long after the child was removed from his home.

34. We describe in chapter 3 how family courts rely on the "running record," which is built up by and shared with "insiders," at key points in the legal decision-making process. The "running record" may well be based on claims or beliefs that are not grounded in fact.

35. CPS case summary notes, November 15, 1995.

36. Affidavit for *Ex Parte* Custody Order, February 28, 1989, pp. 1–3.

37. Addendum to affidavit for *Ex Parte* Custody Order, March 1, 1989, p. 1. Ironically, CPS evidently had a budget for the costs of foster care placement but not for proper monitoring of visits. Unfortunately, CPS's choice in this case is similar to many others made regularly by CPS agencies across the country. Investigative reporter Richard Wexler found that CPS agencies readily place children in foster homes rather than provide preventive services aimed at keeping families together. In *Wounded Innocents,* Wexler argues that the reason for this is that "the orientation of practitioners and the financial incentives . . . encourage taking children away from their parents" (p. 250).

38. Addendum to affidavit for *Ex Parte* Custody Order, March 1, 1989, p. 2.

39. Published proceedings of the congressional hearing before the Subcommittee on Select Education (see note 1 above), April 20, 1992, p. 35.

40. Testimony of child, December 9, 1986. The child testified that her father "stuck his finger in my gina [*sic*] and my bottom and he cut me with a knife."

41. Written testimony, submitted to Subcommitee on Select Education, *Congressional Record,* April 15, 1992, pp. 18–21.

42. Neglect petition, August 25, 1987, p. 2.

43. *Id.*

44. Hearing before the Subcommittee on Select Education, Committee on Education and Labor, U.S. House of Representatives, *Congressional Record,* April 20, 1992, p. 23.

45. *Id.,* pp. 22–23.

46. *Id.,* p. 36.

47. Medical report, March 8, 1988, p. 2.

48. Testimony before the Subcommittee on Select Education of the Committee on Education and Labor, U.S. House of Representatives, 102 Congress, Second Session, April 20, 1992, p. 35.

49. Petition, February 11, 1993, p. 3.

50. Police report, June 27, 1993.

51. Neglect petition, June 28, 1993.

52. Agus, "Standing Fast to Get Her Kids Back."

53. *Id.,* p. 34.

54. Part of this mother's activism was directed at another case, involving the same judge and law guardian as her own. We discuss the tragic ending of that case—the despairing mother killed herself and the child—elsewhere in this book.

55. Petition, September 18, 1986.

56. Memo from special counsel to New York State Committee on Crime and Correction, April 13, 1987, pp. 7–10.

57. Transcript, October 22, 1986, pp. 24–26.

58. *Id.,* p. 26.

59. *Matter of Marie B.,* 62 N.Y.2d 352, 477 N.Y.S.2d 87 (1982).

60. Transcript, October 17, 1986, pp. 58–60.

61. Transcript, March 17, 1988, pp. 38–39.

62. Physician's affidavit, June 10, 1998, p. 2; trial transcript, May 8, 1989, p. 8.

63. Transcript, May 8, 1989, pp. 8–10.

64. The National Child Abuse and Neglect Data System, which collects data from all fifty states—and prepares an annual report for the Children's Bureau for the Administration on Children, Youth and Families of the U.S. Department of Health and Human Services—has studied this problem for thirteen years. The findings of prior years have been more or less consistent with those in the 2002 report, which is the most current.

65. McDonald, *Child Maltreatment 2002*, p. 51.

Chapter 7. Mental Heath Quackery

1. Tippins, "Custody Evaluations," p. 3.

2. Gould, *Conducting Scientifically Crafted Child Custody Evaluations*, p. 33.

3. Niggemyer, "Parental Alienation Is Open Heart Surgery," p. 573.

4. *People v. Fortin*, 184 Misc. 2d 10, 706 N.Y.S.2d 611 (Sup. Ct., Nassau Co., 2000), *aff'd*, 289 A.D.2d 590, 735 N.Y.S.2d 819 (App. Div., 2001). The defense in that case would have presented testimony from Dr. Gardner himself.

5. Unpublished opinion, 2003 WL 1785921 (Cal. App. 6 Dist.).

6. In a recent case, a Maryland appellate court vacated the family court's custody award to a father and ordered the family court to rehear the case. Significantly, the appellate judges supported the mother's claim that "the trial court erred when it relied on the Parental Alienation Syndrome as a basis for rejecting her [the mother's] claims that [the father] had abused the child." While the appellate court did not rule on the merits of PAS, it did caution the family court that if PAS "is raised in the rehearing, there should be evidence to support its validity." Unpublished decision of Court of Special Appeals of Maryland, *E.V. v. J.M.*, 151 Md. App. 31 (2003).

7. Traubmann, "Junk Science Has Its Way in Court."

8. Gardner had been the father's expert in the case; Green, who had never appeared before in Silbermann's court, was selected by the judge at random from a list of experts.

9. Transcript of decision, March 28, 1991.

10. Turkat, "Management of Visitation Interference," pp. 17–18.

11. Smith and Coukos, "Fairness and Accuracy in Evaluations of Domestic Violence and Child Abuse in Custody Determinations," pp. 42, 54.

12. Corwin et al., "Child Sexual Abuse and Custody Disputes," p. 98.

13. Summit, "The Child Sexual Abuse Accommodation Syndrome."

14. Post and Corcoran, *Battered Mothers' Testimony Project*, p. 26.

15. It should be noted, however, that in actual family court cases the "experts" do not hesitate to invest extraordinary time and labor scrutinizing the accusing

mother. She may undergo months of court-ordered forensic testing. Many protective mothers interviewed for this book have expressed amazement that while *they* were subjected to time-consuming testing, the parent accused of abuse rarely was. Perhaps changing family courts' priorities would shift, rather than increase, family courts' burdens in such cases.

16. As discussed in more detail below, Gardner never clearly explained how he knew when sex abuse charges were false in the first place.

17. Gardner, *True and False Accusations of Child Sex Abuse,* p. 209.

18. Green, "True and False Allegations of Sexual Abuse in Child Custody Disputes," p. 452.

19. Hanson, "The Sex Abuse Controversy," p. 258.

20. Deblinger, Stauffer, and Steer, "Comparative Efficacies of Supportive and Cognitive Behavioral Group Therapies."

21. Gardner and Green do not appear to have addressed the fact that the *fathers* in these divorces may also experience sexual deprivation, a fact that might, after all, lead to a heightened likelihood of sexual abuse.

22. Gardner, *True and False Accusations of Child Sex Abuse,* pp. 220–221.

23. Green, "True and False Allegations of Sexual Abuse in Child Custody Disputes," pp. 451–452.

24. See Corwin et al., "Child Sexual Abuse and Custody Disputes," p. 102.

25. Froning, Letter to the Editor, p. 665; Faller, *Child Sexual Abuse.*

26. Corwin et al., "Child Sexual Abuse and Custody Disputes," p. 102.

27. Green, "True and False Allegations of Sexual Abuse in Child Custody Disputes," p. 454.

28. Report, July 7, 1987. Dr. Anne Meltzer, who actually drafted New York State's guidelines for sex abuse evaluations, had stated her "strong reason to believe" the child had been abused; psychiatrist Dr. Carmen Alonso found no mental illness in the mother.

29. "Betty C" would later testify before the U.S. Congress, Subcommittee on Select Education of the Committee on Education and Labor, House of Representatives, 102nd Congress, 2nd Session, at a hearing looking into abuses of the family court system and the misuse of mental health testimony. Hearing transcript, April 20, 1992, pp. 90–97.

30. Personal communication between Arthur Greenspan, M.D., former associate director of Mount Sinai Medical Center Headache Clinic, and Amy Neustein, January 18, 1999.

31. New York State Assembly Judiciary Committee, March 9, 1989, and May 18, 1989; U.S. Congress, Subcommittee on Select Education of the Committee on Education and Labor, House of Representatives, 102nd Congress, 2nd Session, April 20, 1992.

32. Kaplan and Kaplan, "The Child's Accusation of Sexual Abuse during a Divorce and Custody Struggle."

33. Faller, Corwin, and Olafson, "Literature Review," p. 7.

34. Gardner wrote prolifically about "parental alienation syndrome" (PAS), a term he first coined in 1985 in a brief article, "Recent Trends in Divorce and Custody Litigation." His first full discussion of the syndrome, however, appeared in 1987 in *The Parental Alienation Syndrome and the Differentiation between Fabricated and Genuine Child Sexual Abuse.* Then, in 1992, Gardner published an actual guide for practitioners in recognizing and treating PAS, *The Parental Alienation Syndrome: A Guide for Mental Health and Legal Professionals.*

35. Gardner, *True and False Accusations of Child Sex Abuse,* p. 193.

36. See Gardner, "Rebuttal to Kathleen Faller's Article," p. 310.

37. Bruch, "Parental Alienation Syndrome and Parental Alienation."

38. *Id.,* p. 530, n 11.

39. *Id.,* p. 531 (emphasis added). Although it is generally accepted that psychosis rarely appears until late adolescence, Gardner claimed that "three and four year olds are the best subjects for programming a sex-abuse accusation" (*True and False Accusations of Child Sex Abuse,* p. 194) and maintained they are receptive to the induction of a folie à deux psychosis.

40. Personal communication between James Yudes, Esq., and Michael Lesher, June 1997.

41. Apolo, "Munchausen Syndrome by Proxy," p. 92.

42. Sinanan and Haughton, "Evolution of Variants of the Munchausen Syndrome," p. 465.

43. Rand, "Munchausen Syndrome by Proxy: A Complex Type of Emotional Abuse Responsible for Some False Allegations of Child Abuse in Divorce," p. 135. It should be noted that Rand's "contemporary" version of MSBP differed sharply from the syndrome as originally defined. Rand was willing to apply the MSBP label even when mothers had not induced any symptoms in their children, nor exposed them to invasive or dangerous procedures, whereas these were formerly both important elements of the syndrome.

44. Rand, "Munchausen Syndrome by Proxy: Integration of Classic and Contemporary Types," p. 83.

45. Faller, "Allegations of Sexual Abuse in Divorce," slide #10.

46. Physician's letter to the court, May 4, 1996.

47. Mental health expert's report to the court, March 22, 1996, p. 9.

48. Testimony of expert, April 24, 1996, p. 20.

49. Mental health expert's report to the court, March 22, 1996, pp. 9–10.

50. Transcript, April 24, 1996, p. 19. Not only did the mental health expert leave her expertise behind in making this prediction, she overlooked the practical factors militating against flight: the child required steady medical supervision from the caretakers she had had since birth, and there was no evidence that the mother had ever considered fleeing the jurisdiction or, indeed, ever defied a court order.

51. Mental Illness and the Workplace, a conference sponsored by the Association of Health Services Research and National Alliance For the Mentally Ill, December 8–9, 1999.

52. Gardner, "Should Courts Order PAS Children to Visit/Reside with the Alienated Parent?" p. 102.

53. *Id.*

54. Gould, *Conducting Scientifically Crafted Child Custody Evaluations,* p. 33.

55. For example, see *Sullivan County Dept. of Social Services v. Richard "C",* 260 A.D.2d 680, 687 N.Y.S.2d 470 (3rd Dept., 1999); *Gadomski v. Gadomski,* 256 A.D.2d 675, 681 N.Y.S.2d 374; *Rogowski v. Rogowksi,* 251 A.D.2d 827, 674 N.Y.S.2d 480.

56. Mental health report, February 12, 1987, p. 7.

57. *Id.*

58. If the judge and his clerk did this—and no one has ever denied Green's claim, which was repeated in press coverage of the case—they acted in violation of the canons of judicial ethics.

59. On instructions from the counsel to New York State Senate's Committee on Crime and Correction, the mother tape-recorded this interview with Dr. Green. The family court judge denied her motion to admit these tapes into evidence. Transcript, January 19, 1988, p. 24.

60. Report to the court, July 7, 1987, p. 2.

61. The use of vague psychological signs to predict "rebellion" has its historical precedent in the antebellum South. Henrietta Buckmaster pointed out in *Let My People Go* that when black fugitive slaves were caught and tried before the courts, charges of "mental instability" against them often overlapped with charges of criminal actions, which gave rise to the term "flighty nigger." That is, slaves were accused of being unsteady and/or dishonest for having tried to escape—"one week they swore they had no desire for freedom and the next week disappeared" (p. 17).

62. Judge's notes, January 17, 2001; custody evaluation, June 20, 2003.

63. Decision, July 14, 1988, p. 23.

64. *Id.,* p. 38.

65. *Id.,* p. 99.

66. *Id.,* p. 104.

67. *Id.,* p. 62.

68. Trial transcript, June 12, 2001, pp. 45–50.

69. *Id.,* June 22, 2001, p. 39.

70. Once a protective mother has been branded with one of the labels beloved of family court judges, almost anything she says or does may be used against her as further "proof" of her "illness." For example, one protective mother, responding to her allegedly abusive ex-husband's second demand to reduce his child support payments (though he admitted to an annual income of about $130,000), told the judge she had begged her ex-husband not to take her to court, saying she had been willing to settle for anything he would pay; even if he paid no child support at all,

she said, she would find a way to care for her children, because she loved them. In granting the father's request to slash his child support obligation, the judge went out of his way to criticize the mother's comment, which he said was intended to malign the father by implying that his attempt to reduce child support called into question "the level of love that he has for his sons." In fact, the judge claimed in his written decision that the mother (who had tried to stay out of court) was "obsessed" with litigation, while the father (who insisted on several court hearings aimed at reducing his child support) "loved" his children (decision, December 23, 1997).

71. Gardner, "Should Courts Order PAS Children to Visit/Reside with the Alienated Parent?"

72. Gardner, "Rebuttal to Kathleen Faller's Article," p. 310. In spite of intense public criticism, Gardner repeated the same assertions about PAS in an article published in 2001 (see preceding note), claiming the use of a consistent "definition of the parental alienation syndrome . . . since [his] first publication on the disorder in 1985."

73. Faller, "The Parental Alienation Syndrome," p. 106.

74. *Id.*

75. Transcript, July 15, 1985, pp. 4–5.

76. New York Penal Law §§ 130.65(3), 130.00(3).

77. Mother's attorney's affirmation to Appellate Division, July 24, 1986.

78. Peachtree Psychological Associates, child custody evaluation, February 17, 2000, p. 24.

79. *Id.*, p. 6.

80. Transcript, emergency hearing for change of custody, February 18, 2000, p. 19 (emphasis added).

81. *Id.*, p. 49.

82. Transcript of emergency hearing, February 18, 2000, p. 48–49.

83. Attorney Richard Ducote's letter to the members of the Cobb County Bar Association and the Metro Atlanta Board of Mental Health Professionals, April 29, 2002.

84. Peachtree Psychological Associates, child custody evaluation, p. 26.

85. Transcript, pp. 52, 53.

86. *Id.*, p. 53.

87. *Peachtree Psychological Association,* child custody evaluation, p. 26.

88. Therapist's affidavit, October 31, 1996, pp. 3–4.

89. Therapist's affidavit, October 6, 1996, p. 3.

90. Medical report, January 24, 1996, pp. 2–3.

91. MDIC report, March 12, 1996, p. 41.

92. Transcript, September 26, 1996, pp. 29–33.

93. Evaluator's report to the court, December 6, 1995, p. 11.

94. Transcript, March 6, 1996, p. 20.

95. *Id.*, p. 28.

96. Evaluator's report, p. 11.

97. Transcript, March 6, 1996, p. 34.

98. Transcript, November 1, 1996, p. 33.

99. Report of visitation program director, January 24, 1997, p. 7 (emphasis added).

100. *Id.,* pp. 8–10.

101. Findings and order after hearing, October 2, 1996, p. 4.

102. Therapist's affidavit, December 27, 1996, pp. 2–4.

103. Letter of pediatric nurse to the court, October 1, 1992.

104. Mental health report on the child, November 9, 1991, p. 10 (emphasis added).

105. Letter to the law guardian from the chief of pediatrics at New York Medical College, Department of Pediatrics, June 8, 1992, pp. 1–2.

106. Mental health report on the child, p. 5.

107. Mental health report on the mother, November 9, 1991, p. 7.

108. The tests included the Wechsler Adult Intelligence Scale (WAIS); Rorschach; the Minnesota Multiphasic Personality Inventory (MMPI); the Goodenough-Draw-a-Person test; and the Millon Clinical Multiaxial Inventory (MCMI).

109. Mental health report on the mother, p. 6.

110. Psychologist's letter to the mother, November 6, 1992, p. 2.

111. Dr. Arthur Green's report to the court, July 7, 1987.

112. Similar emotional responses were found in a study of Australian mothers who had received undeserved mental illness labels from family courts. In "Misdiagnosed Children, Misdiagnosed Parents," unpublished doctoral dissertation (2003), Helen Hayward-Brown reports the day-to-day psychological effects on a mother who was wrongly diagnosed with Munchausen Syndrome By Proxy after making a sex abuse charge against her ex-husband. Hayward-Brown describes a mother's tortuous progress through the courts: "Her story became a stream of consciousness throughout an entire day—anxiety, stress and emotion became clearly evident. Her narrative was punctuated by high levels of fear and anger . . . [and] her distress could particularly be seen in her attempts to try and comprehend what happened to her" (p. 180).

Chapter 8. Mothers and Madness: The "Aftershocks" of the System

1. Pagnozzi, "Mom Was Trying to Help Her Kids," p. 13.

2. When the FBI captures a fugitive mother, the child usually goes directly into the father's custody. This is so even if the mother had legal custody at the time she went on the run, because in most such cases the fathers seek a change of custody in their favor once the mothers disappear. Unable to defend themselves in court, the mothers lose custody. Even if this has not happened, their imprisonment for "kidnapping" is usually enough to persuade an already hostile family court to switch

custody to the father. See Pennington and Woods, *Legal Issues and Legal Options in Civil Child Sexual Abuse Cases,* pp. 17–19.

3. Personal communication with Kathy Rosenthal, director of Children's Rights of America, formerly a founding member of the National Center for Missing and Exploited Children, May 12, 1993.

4. Massat and Lundy, "Reporting Costs to Nonoffending Parents in Cases of Intrafamilial Child Sexual Abuse," p. 379.

5. Report of Jeremiah B. McKenna, chief counsel to New York State Senate Committee on Crime and Correction, October 31, 1987, p. 1.

6. *Id.,* p. 2. In 1986, Bob Herbert, then a regular columnist for the *New York Daily News* (now a *New York Times* columnist), did a three-part series on this case, beginning on October 28, 1986, titled "Who Serves the Children?"

7. Herbert, "Who Serves the Children?" p. 29.

8. Perhaps the most outrageous thing about these surprise visits was that CPS never gave any reason for insisting on them. Normally such tactics are used when parents are accused of inadequate care such as unsanitary conditions or lack of food—conditions that can be concealed if the parents know when to expect a CPS visit. In this case, in the absence of any such charge, the visits were clearly intended mainly to harass and frighten the mother—which they did.

9. See chapters 4 and 5 for more details of her case.

10. *Stolen Children: How and Why Parents Kidnap Their Kids—and What to Do about It,* p. 167.

11. Della Howard, "Lost Limb Syndrome."

12. Charlinda Joseph, "Family Court Stolen Innocence."

13. Apart from our research for this book, we have devoted considerable study to the Orthodox Jewish community's reaction to intrafamilial (and stranger) sexual abuse. Protective mothers such as this Rockland County mother often encounter, in addition to a hostile family court, ostracism from their own religious communities, whose leaders are either conspicuously silent about the abuse charge or strongly supportive of the alleged offender—leaving the child victim and the protective parent standing alone. Such a situation can provoke self-destructive behavior, as was the case with this protective mother. See Neustein and Lesher, "The Silence of the Jewish Media on Sexual Abuse in the Orthodox Jewish Community"; Neustein and Lesher, "Does the Jewish Community Sacrifice Victims of Sexual Abuse?"; and Lesher, "Speaking with Their Silence."

14. The mother spoke with one of us the same day these devastating events took place in court. The next day, she and her daughter were dead.

15. Mike McAlary, "Court with Disney Touch," p. 28; Viva, "Women and Children Last," p. 115.

16. See chapter 5 for more details on this case.

17. Hearing before the Subcommittee on Select Education of the Committee

on Education and Labor, U.S. House of Representatives, 102nd Congress, Second Session, April 20, 1992, pp. 141–142.

18. Mental health report, March 21, 1992, p. 2 (emphasis added).

19. Such orders are not uncommon in family courts. In theory, they are intended to "protect" a child from the invasion of her privacy. We suspect that protection of the family court system from public scrutiny is more often the actual motive. In any event, how these orders can be squared with the First Amendment is a question we hope to see matrimonial attorneys explore in the future.

20. Notice of Application for Recognizance or Bail, January 18, 2003.

21. CPS petition, March 7, 1997, p. 2.

22. *Id.*

23. See chapter 5 for more details concerning the case.

24. Therapist's letter, June 22, 2000, p. 3; teacher's report, June 8, 2000.

25. Fields-Meyer, "In the Dead of Night"; Jaffe and Rich, "Deadly Triangle."

26. Jaffe and Rich, "Deadly Triangle."

Chapter 9. "Rebirthing" the Family Court System

1. Editor of *Sexual Assault Report,* a bimonthly publication of the Civic Research Institute, a nonprofit educational resource center founded in 2001 for lawyers, public prosecutors, and mental health professionals handling matters of sexual abuse and rape in criminal and civil proceedings. Zorza was formerly staff counsel at the National Center for Women and Family Law.

2. *In re Turner,* 94 Kan. 115, 145 P. 871.

3. *Helton v. Crawley,* 241 Iowa 296, 41 N.W.2d 60.

4. *Words and Phrases,* p. 100.

5. *Gardner v. Hall,* 132 N.J. Eq. 64, 26 A.2d 799 (Chancery Div., 1942), quoting *Lippincott v. Lippincott,* 97 N.J. Eq. 517, 128 A. 254.

6. *Matter of Female S.,* 111 Misc. 2d 313, 444 N.Y.S.2d 829 (Fam. Ct., 1981)

7. *Kennedy v. Kennedy,* 55 Md. App. 299, 462 A.2d 1208 (Md. App., 1983) (emphasis added).

8. 129 N.J. Super. 486, 324 A.2d 90 (Chancery Div., 1974).

9. Indeed, homosexuality was still officially listed as a mental disorder by the American Psychiatric Association until 1973, just one year before this case was decided.

10. That this argument was based directly on a decision of the U.S. Supreme Court—*Wisconsin v. Yoder,* 406 U.S. 205, 92 S. Ct. 1526, 32 L. Ed. 2d 15 (1972)—did not help.

11. *Stanley v. Illinois,* 405 U.S. 645, 92 S. Ct. 1208, 31 L. Ed. 2d 551 (1972); *Santosky v. Kramer,* 455 U.S. 745 (1981).

12. It is well known that misguided attitudes about rape—that victims "asked for it," that it was related to female promiscuity—have long interfered with rape prosecutions. Education has slowly begun to change this. It is not unreasonable to hope that mistaken beliefs about sex abuse reports can similarly be altered through education.

13. Winner, *Divorced from Justice,* p. 133.

14. See chapter 1.

15. McAlary, "Court with Disney Touch."

Chapter 10. Reforming the Courts

1. 42 U.S.C. §§ 5101 *et seq.*

2. Neustein and Lesher, "Legislative Solutions to the Protective Parent Backlash."

3. See part II, chapter 4.

4. Pennington, *The Judicial Training Act,* p. 10.

5. States such as California originally enacted provisions for ex parte changes of custody to shield battered women from having to face their abusers in court. Ironically, the same laws have often served the interests of abusive fathers, who can now seize custody without notice to their wives.

6. This has already been proposed by New York State assemblywoman Cecile Singer, who urged the New York State Legislature in 1991 to require CPS to affirmatively demonstrate every ninety days the need for continued placement of a child away from its home, pending final determination of an abuse or neglect complaint.

7. California Family Code § 3027.5.

8. See part II, chapter 4.

9. Adding this eligibility requirement to CAPTA addresses the backlash against mental health professionals by providing them with the assistance of a state child welfare agency in challenging an actual or threatened punitive contempt ruling or threat of contempt.

10. In 1998, another complaint against Deutsch—then a JHO—was addressed to New York's chief administrative judge for matrimonial matters. The administrative judge wrote to the complainants on September 9, 1998, advising them that "Judicial Hearing Officer Leon Deutsch was not redesignated to serve as a Judicial Hearing Officer for another term" and therefore declining to pursue the complaint further. In April 2003, however, we learned that Deutsch was still serving as a JHO. The administrative judge did not respond to inquiries. It would seem that bad family court judges are as hard to get rid of as bad pennies. And Deutsch has yet to answer any of the complaints against him.

11. Today's trend is that wherever federal courts *can* decline jurisdiction over a child-related case, they do so. Partly, no doubt, this reflects overcrowded dockets

throughout the federal trial courts. But it also reflects a prejudice that litigation involving children is simply not as important and prestigious as other sorts of cases.

12. Gothard, "Children in Courtrooms," p. 115.

13. Pennington, *The Hardest Case*, p. 20.

14. Such a questionnaire was formulated in 1993 by one of us at the request of attorney Sherry Quirk, senior partner at the firm of Verner Liipfert in Washington, D.C.

15. Such a case was reported to us. After a judge determined that a father had abused his child, the case was referred to a judicial hearing officer notoriously hostile to mothers. The hearing officer heeded the law guardian's recommendation that the abusive father's visitation be increased. The mother then asked the judge to remove the law guardian. He agreed to do so—but only if the mother waived her right to have the judge (who had already ruled that the father had committed abuse) review the hearing officer's findings. If our recommendations are adopted, such behavior will be automatic grounds for disqualifying a judge or a hearing officer.

16. Congress, in its enactment of CAPTA, evidently anticipated future amendments to its guidelines by establishing the National Center on Child Abuse and Neglect. NCCAN's stated purpose is to review how child abuse cases are handled by the courts and the child protective service agencies, to see whether their performance is in compliance with the goals of child protection set forth under CAPTA. The findings of a preliminary study funded by NCCAN (that were confirmed when the study was completed) showed "a consistent pattern of punitive responses [to the nonoffending parent] to the reporting of child maltreatment . . . a pattern of obstruction of investigations . . . in apparent contradiction of the legal requirements of CAPTA" (Carol Rippey Massat, coprincipal investigator of the NCCAN-funded study, in a letter to George Burgasser, acting chief of Child Exploitation and Obscenity Section, U.S. Department of Justice, February 8, 1994, p. 2).

Chapter 11. Reforming the Court Auxilaries

1. For example, in *Krause v. Krause* (Docket No. C 02–5277 JSW, N.D. Cal.), a California federal district court judge ruled in 2003 that a woman could not sue the court-appointed attorney who had urged her placement with her father when she was a minor, despite allegedly knowing of his abusive behavior and conspiring to manipulate the family court proceeding. The court stated, "Under governing California law . . . therapists, guardians and court-appointed attorneys, are accorded quasi-judicial immunity . . . attorneys for children in child abuse actions are granted immunity from damages claims." A similar holding is found in *Fox v. Wills*, Docket No. 01075, Court of Special Appeals of Maryland, 2002.

2. The reason for this privilege is that if judges could be sued for their official

acts, they would face the threat of litigation every time they decided a case, particularly when they ruled against a powerful litigant. Thus, judicial immunity from suit is one of the safeguards of an independent judiciary.

3. We have been astonished at the number of law guardians who have made critical recommendations on behalf of their young clients—including recommendations that caused small children to be removed from the only homes they had ever known, in the absence of any evidence that they faced any danger while living there—without having so much as spoken to or laid eyes on them.

4. Ordinary lawyers may communicate with others (though not with the court) without giving notice to all other parties. Judges, however, may not do so, since their role requires impartiality. Similarly, law guardians, who do not represent either parent against the other and who offer advice to the court in this relatively impartial role, should be required to follow rules concerning ex parte contact similar to those that judges follow.

5. It may be objected that the law guardian's role is not definitely over, since the appellate court could reverse the family court, causing it to conclude that child abuse occurred after all and therefore requiring (once again) the appointment of a law guardian. However, since the law guardian in this scenario has maintained that no abuse occurred, a reversal by the appellate court should result in the appointment of a *new* law guardian, one prepared to put the appellate court's ruling into practice. Even if the former law guardian is to be reappointed, it can be only with a radically new mandate.

6. Tippins, "Custody Evaluations," p. 3.

7. Melton et al., *Psychological Evaluations for the Courts,* p. 484.

8. Schafran, "Evaluating the Evaluators." Schafran proposes that all custody evaluations contain the same required elements, including a list of all parties interviewed, an explanation of their relationship to the litigants, a listing of all abuse allegations made by any party, abuse findings, and a listing of evidence that led to the findings.

9. Friedrich, "Sexual Behavior in Sexually Abused Children."

10. *Severson v. Hansen,* 529 N.W.2d 167 (N.D., 1995).

11. Report of psychologist to the court, April 2, 2003, pp. 2–3.

12. J. Wittmann, "Child Advocacy and the Scientific Model in Family Court," pp. 77–78.

13. Indeed, in 1999, two mental health professionals published an article calling for a complete "moratorium of mental health professionals' participation in child custody evaluations" until the profession developed better and more reliable procedures for reaching conclusions in such cases. Otherwise, they argued, "the mental health professional cannot ethically conduct these evaluations." O'Donohue and Bradley, "Conceptual and Empirical Issues in Child Custody Evaluations," p. 320.

14. For an analysis of how judges can best work with expert medical testimony in other kinds of cases, see Neustein, "Getting Straight Answers from Experts."

15. *Matter of Sayeh R. v. Monroe County Dept. of Social Services,* 91 N.Y.2d 306, 693 N.E.2d 724 (1997) (Bellacosa, dissenting on a jurisdictional issue).

16. Martindale, "Cross-examining Mental Health Experts in Child Custody Litigation," p. 488.

References

Agus, C. (1993a). "A Mother's Cry from the Grave." *New York Newsday,* June 24, p. 8.

Agus, C. (1993b). "Standing Fast to Get Her Kids Back." *New York Newsday,* July 11, pp. 4, 34.

American Jurisprudence Proof of Facts, 3rd Ed. (1995). Vol. 33, section 303.

American Psychological Association Presidential Task Force on Violence and the Family (1996). "Violence and the Family". *American Psychological Association,* 40.

Apolo, J. (1999). "Munchausen Syndrome by Proxy: The Syndrome of Fabricated Illness in the Pediatric Patient." *International Pediatrics* 14 (2): 90–93.

Arens, R., and Lasswell, H. D. (1961). *In Defense of Public Order.* New York: Columbia University Press.

Armstrong, L. (1983). *The Home Front: Notes from the Family War Zone.* New York: McGraw-Hill.

Armstrong, L. (1994). *Rocking the Cradle of Sexual Politics: What Happened When Women Said Incest.* Reading, Mass.: Addison-Wesley Publishing Company.

Atkinson, J. M. (1979). "Sequencing and Shared Attentiveness to Court Proceedings." In G. Psathas (ed.), *Everyday Language: Studies in Ethnomethodology,* pp. 257–286. New York: Irvington Publishers.

Atkinson, J. M., and Drew, P. (1979). *Order in Court: The Organization of Verbal Interaction in Judicial Settings.* London: Macmillan.

Baer, S. (1989). "G.A. [Georgia] Woman Guides Abused Children toward Havens." *Baltimore Sun,* February 26, pp. 1A, 14A.

Bennett, B. (1996a). "Book Citing Hardin Case Stirs Debate." *Lexington Herald-Leader,* December 15, p. B1.

Bennett, B. (1996b). "Controversial Case Can't Be Cited Later." *Lexington Herald-Leader,* December 15, p. B1.

Berger, J. (1993). "Three Deaths: A Mother, a Daughter, the Truth." *New York Times,* June 26, pp. 21, 25.

Berliner, L. (1988). "Deciding Whether a Child Has Been Sexually Abused." In E. B. Nicholson and J. Buckley (eds.), *Sexual Abuse Allegations in Custody and Visitation Cases,* pp. 48–69. Washington, D.C.: American Bar Association.

Brooklyn Citizen Court Monitors (1986). *An Inside Look at the Brooklyn Family Court.* New York: The Fund for Modern Courts.

Bruch, C. S. (2001). "Parental Alienation Syndrome and Parental Alienation: Getting It Wrong in Child Custody Cases." *Family Law Quarterly* 35 (3): 527–552.

Buckmaster, H. [1941] (1992). *Let My People Go: The Story of the Underground Railroad and the Growth of the Abolition Movement.* New York: Harper and Brothers; Columbia: University of South Carolina Press.

Carpenter, M. (1997) "Children of the Underground." *Pittsburgh Post-Gazette,* December 14–21.

Chesler, P. (1986). *Mothers on Trial: The Battle for Children and Custody.* Seattle: The Seal Press.

Cicourel, A. (1968). *The Social Organization of Juvenile Justice.* New York: John Wiley.

Corwin, D. L., Berliner, L., Goodman, G., Goodwin, J., and White, S. (1987). "Child Sexual Abuse and Custody Disputes: No Easy Answers." *Journal of Interpersonal Violence* 2 (1): 91–105.

Curran, W. J. (1985). "The Vulnerability of Court-Appointed Impartial Experts in Child-Custody Cases." *New England Journal of Medicine* 312 (18), May 2, pp. 1168–1170.

Cuthbert, C., Slote, K., Driggers, M. G., Mesh, C. M., Bancroft, L., and Sliverman, J. (2002). *Battered Mothers Speak Out: A Human Rights Report on Domestic Violence and Child Custody in the Massachusetts Family Courts.* Wellesley, Mass.: Battered Mothers' Testimony Project at the Wellesley Centers for Women.

Deblinger, E., Stauffer, L. B, and Steer, R. A. (2001). "Comparative Efficacies of Supportive and Cognitive Behavioral Group Therapies for Young Children Who Have Been Sexually Abused and Their Nonoffending Mothers." *Child Maltreatment,* 6 (4): 332–343.

Denike, M., Huang, A. and Kachuk, P. (1998). *Myths and Realities of Custody and Access.* Vancouver, Canada: The FREDA Centre for Research on Violence against Women and Children.

Derdyn, A. P. (1976). "A Consideration of Legal Issues in Child Custody Contests." *Archives of General Psychiatry* 33: 165–171.

Drew, P. (1992). "Contested Evidence in Courtroom Cross-Examination: The Case of a Trial for Rape." In P. Drew and J. Heritage (eds.), *Talk at Work: Interaction in Institutional Settings,* pp. 470–520. Cambridge: Cambridge University Press.

Ducote, R. (2002). "Guardians Ad Litem in Private Custody Litigation: The Case for Abolition." *Loyola Journal of Public Interest Law,* 3: 106–151.

Durkheim, E. (1938). *The Rules of Sociological Method.* Glencoe, U.K.: The Free Press.

Dziech, B. W., and Schudson, C. B. (1989). *On Trial: America's Courts and Their Treatment of Sexually Abused Children.* Boston: Beacon Press.

Everson, M. D., and Boat, B. W. (1989). "False Allegations of Sexual Abuse by

Children and Adolescents." *Journal of the American Academy of Child and Adolescent Psychiatry* 28 (2): 230–235.

Faller, K. C. (1988). *Child Sexual Abuse: An Interdisciplinary Manual for Diagnosis, Case Management and Treatment.* New York: Columbia University Press.

Faller, K. C. (1998). "The Parental Alienation Syndrome: What Is It and What Data Support It?" *Child Maltreatment* 3 (2): 100–115.

Faller, K. C. (2000). "Child Maltreatment and Endangerment in the Context of Divorce." *University of Arkansas Little Rock Law Review* 22: 429–452.

Faller, K. C. (2002). "Allegations of Sexual Abuse in Divorce." PowerPoint presentation given at *Seventh Annual Northern New England Conference on Child Maltreatment.* Portland, Maine, September 13.

Faller, K. C., Corwin, D. L., and Olafson, E. (1993). "Literature Review: Research on False Allegations of Sexual Abuse in Divorce." *American Professional Society on the Abuse of Children (APSAC) Adviser* 6 (3): 1, 7–10.

Faller, K. C., and DeVoe, E. (1995). "Allegations of Sexual Abuse in Divorce." *Journal of Child Sexual Abuse* 4 (4): 1–25.

Fentress, G. (1987). "Mothers Defy Court, Keep Children." *Sun Herald* (Gulfport, Miss.) August 15, p. C-1.

Fields-Meyer, T. (2002). "In the Dead of Night: A State Department Worker Is Charged with Trying to Kill Her Best Friend's Ex-Husband." *People* 57 (8), March 4, pp. 123–126.

Fifield, A., and Lesher, M. (1996). "A Child's at Stake: A Custody Fight Becomes a Political Nightmare." *Village Voice,* October 1, pp.10, 12–13.

Finkelhor, D. (1986). *A Sourcebook on Child Sexual Abuse.* Thousand Oaks, Calif.: Sage Publications.

Forrest, S. (1996). "Children Die—but No Caseworkers Punished." *New York Post,* January 17, p. 4.

Friedrich, W. N. (1993). "Sexual Behavior in Sexually Abused Children." *Violence Update* 3:1–20.

Froning, M. L. (1988). Letter to the Editor. *Journal of the American Academy of Child and Adolescent Psychiatry* 27 (5): 665–666.

Galtney, L. (1988). "Mothers on the Run." *U.S. News and World Report* 104 (23), June 13, pp. 22–33.

Gardner, R. A. (1985). "Recent Trends in Divorce and Custody Litigation." *Academy Forum* 29 (2): 3–7.

Gardner, R. A. (1987). *The Parental Alienation Syndrome and the Differentiation between Fabricated and Genuine Child Sexual Abuse.* Cresskill, N.J.: Creative Therapeutics.

Gardner, R. A. (1992a). *The Parental Alienation Syndrome: A Guide for Mental Health and Legal Professionals.* Cresskill, N.J.: Creative Therapeutics.

Gardner, R. A. (1992b). *True and False Accusations of Child Sex Abuse.* Cresskill, N.J.: Creative Therapeutics.

Gardner, R. A. (1998). "Rebuttal to Kathleen Faller's Article." *Child Maltreatment* 3 (4): 309–312.

Gardner, R. A. (2001). "Should Courts Order PAS Children to Visit/Reside with the Alienated Parent? A Follow-up Study." *The American Journal of Forensic Psychology* 19 (3): 61–106.

Garfinkel, H. (1967). *Studies in Ethnomethodology.* Englewood Cliffs, N.J.: Prentice-Hall.

Garfinkel, H. (1974). "The Origins of the Term 'Ethnomethodology.'" In R. Turner (ed.), *Ethnomethodology,* pp. 15–18. Harmondsworth, England: Penguin Education.

Garfinkel, H., and Bittner, E. (1967). "Good Organizational Reasons for 'Bad' Clinic Records." In H. Garfinkel (ed.), *Studies in Ethnomethodology,* pp. 186–207. Englewood Cliffs, N.J.: Prentice-Hall.

Garfinkel, H., and Sacks, H. (1970). "On Formal Structures of Practical Actions." In J. C. McKinney and E. A. Tiryakian (eds.), *Theoretical Sociology: Perspectives and Developments,* pp. 337–366. New York: Appleton-Century-Crofts.

Gill, J. E. (1981). *Stolen Children: How and Why Parents Kidnap Their Kids—and What to Do about It.* New York: Seaview Books.

Goodhue, M. B. (1989). *Child Protection and the Family Court: A Study of Processes, Procedures and Outcomes under Article Ten of the New York Family Court Act.* Albany: New York State Senate Committee on Child Care.

Gothard, S. (1992). "Children in Courtrooms: A Commentary." *Journal of Child Sexual Abuse* 1 (3): 115–117.

Gould, J. W. (1998). *Conducting Scientifically Crafted Child Custody Evaluations.* Thousand Oaks, Calif.: Sage Publications.

Green, A. H. (1986). "True and False Allegations of Sexual Abuse in Child Custody Disputes." *Journal of the American Academy of Child Psychiatry* 25 (4): 449–456.

Hanson, G. (1988). "The Sex Abuse Controversy": Letter to the Editor. *Journal of the American Academy of Child and Adolescent Psychiatry* 27 (2): 258.

Hayward-Brown, H. (2003). "Misdiagnosed Children, Misdiagnosed Parents: Chronic Illness and the Spectre of Munchausen Syndrome by Proxy." Ph. D. dissertation, Charles Sturt University, NSW Australia.

Heim, S., Grieco, H., Paola, S. D., and Allen, R. (2002). *California National Organization for Women Family Court Report 2002.* Sacramento, Calif.: California NOW.

Hemphill, C. (1990). "The Agony of Yacov Riegler: Bureaucracy Fails to Save Brooklyn Boy." *New York Newsday,* December 16, pp. 6, 22–23.

Herbert, B. (1986). "Who Serves the Children?" *New York Daily News,* October 28, p. 29.

Herbert, K. (2001). "Norton vs. Norton: When Opposites Sides Clash, Courts Have Tough Choice." *Morning Call* (Allentown, Pa.) October 14, p. 1.

Heritage, J., and Sefi, S. (1992). "Dilemmas of Advice: Aspects of the Delivery and

Reception of Advice in Interactions between Health Visitors and First-Time Mothers." In P. Drew and J. Heritage (eds.), *Talk at Work: Interaction in Institutional Settings*, pp. 359–417. Cambridge: Cambridge University Press.

Heritage, J. C., and Watson, D. R. (1979). "Formulations as Conversational Objects." In G. Psathas (ed.), *Everyday Language: Studies in Ethnomethodology*, pp. 123–162. New York: Irvington Publishers.

Holstein, J. (1983). "Jurors' Uses of Judges' Instructions." *Sociological Methods and Research.* 11: 501–518.

Holstein, J. (1988). "Studying 'Family Usage': Family Image and Discourse in Mental Hospitalization Decisions." *Journal of Contemporary Ethnography* 17: 261–284.

Holstein, J. A. and Gubrium, J. F. (1995). "Deprivatization and the Construction of Domestic Life." *Journal of Marriage and the Family* 57 (4): 894–908.

Jacobbi, M., and Wright, R. (1988). "Mothers Who Go to Jail for Their Children." *Good Housekeeping* 207 (4): 158, 234–238.

Jaffe, H., and Rich, C. (2002). "Deadly Triangle." *Washingtonian* 37 (9), June, pp. 52–57, 107–114.

Jones, D. P., and McGraw, J. M. (1987). "Reliable and Fictitious Accounts of Sexual Abuse to Children." *Journal of Interpersonal Violence* 2 (1): 27–45.

Jones, D. P., and Seig, A. (1988). "Child Sexual Abuse Allegations in Custody or Visitation Cases: A Report of 20 Cases." In E. B. Nicholson and J. Bulkley (eds.), *Sexual Abuse Allegations in Custody and Visitation Cases*, pp. 22–36. Washington, D.C.: American Bar Association.

Kaplan, S., and Kaplan, S. (1981). "The Child's Accusation of Sexual Abuse during a Divorce and Custody Struggle." *Hillside Journal of Clinical Psychiatry* 3 (1): 81–95.

Keating, S. S. (1988). "Children in Incestuous Relationships: The Forgotten Victims." *Loyola Law Review* 34: 111–123.

Kerrison, R. (1989a). "Anguished Mothers Beg for Help: 'Protect Our Kids from Sex Abuse.'" *New York Post*, March 10, p. 2.

Kerrison, R. (1989b). "Exposing Dads Who Rape Their Children: Albany Has Taken First Bold Step." *New York Post*, March 13, p. 2.

Kerrison, R. (1990). "Incredible Return of Misogynist a Disgrace: Judge Rewarded for Awful Offenses." *New York Post*, August 31, p. 4.

Kerrison, R. (1992). "Pleas for a Dying Child Go Unheeded." *New York Post*, November 7, pp. 7, 14.

Komter, M. L. (1995). "The Distribution of Knowledge in Courtroom Interaction." In P. ten Have and G. Psathas (eds.), *Situated Order: Studies in the Social Organization of Talk and Embodied Activities*, pp. 107–128. Washington, D.C.: University Press of America.

Komter, M. L. (1998). *Dilemmas in the Courtroom: A Study of Trials of Violent Crime in the Netherlands*. Mahwah, N.J.: Lawrence Erlbaum Associates, Publishers.

Kramer, Jill. (2002). "Justice Denied: Money Talks in Family Court, Hurting the Cases of Many Dependent Women." *Pacific Sun* (Mill Valley, Calif.) November 20, pp. 13–18.

Krause, A. (2000). "Letting Children Speak for Themselves: Youth in Court Need Attorneys Who Represent Their Interests Fairly, Strongly." *San Francisco Daily Journal,* July 17, p. 4.

Lawson, L., and Chaffin, M. (1992). "False Negatives in Sexual Abuse Disclosure Interviews." *Journal of Interpersonal Violence* 7 (4): 532–542.

Lesher, M. (1996). "Speaking with Their Silence: A Troubling Child Sex Abuse Case in Orthodox Community Raises the Question, Where Are Our Leaders?" *Jewish Week,* 209 (27), November 1, p. 28.

Lidman, R. C., and Hollingsworth, B. R. (1998). "The Guardian Ad Litem in Child Custody Cases: The Contours of Our Judicial System Stretched beyond Recognition." *George Mason Law Review* 6: 255–306.

Lombardi, K. (2003). "Custodians of Abuse." *Boston Phoenix,* January 10, p. 1, 12–20.

Lynch, M. (1997). "Preliminary Notes on Judges' Work: The Judge as a Constituent of Courtroom 'Hearings.'" In M. Travers and J. F. Manzo (eds.), *Law in Action: Ethnomethodological and Conversation Analytic Approaches to Law,* pp. 99–130. Aldershot, England: Ashgate/Dartmouth.

Martindale, D. A. (2001). "Cross-examining Mental Health Experts in Child Custody Litigation." *Journal of Psychiatry and Law* 29 (4): 483–511.

Massat, C. R., and Lundy, M. (1998). "'Reporting Costs' to Nonoffending Parents in Cases of Intrafamilial Child Sexual Abuse." *Child Welfare* 77 (4): 371–388.

Massat, C. R., and Lundy, M. (1999). "Service and Support Needs of Non-offending Parents in Cases of Intrafamilial Sexual Abuse." *Journal of Child Sexual Abuse* 8 (2): 41–56.

Matoesian, G. (1993). *Reproducing Rape: Domination through Talk in the Courtroom.* Chicago: University of Chicago Press.

Maynard, D. W. (1984). *Inside Plea-Bargaining: The Language of Negotiation.* New York: Plenum.

McAlary, M. (1989) "Court with Disney Touch." *New York Daily News,* June 2, pp. 5, 28.

McDonald, M. (1998). "The Myth of Epidemic False Allegations of Sexual Abuse in Divorce Cases." *Court Review* 35: 12–19.

McDonald, W. R. (2004). *Child Maltreatment 2002.* Prepared by the National Child Abuse and Neglect Data System (NCANDS) for the Children's Bureau for the Administration on Children, Youth and Families of the U.S. Department of Health and Human Services. Washington, D.C.: U.S. Government Printing Office.

McGraw, J. M., and Smith, H. A. (1992). "Child Sexual Abuse Allegations amidst

Divorce and Custody Proceedings: Refining the Validation Process." *Journal of Child Sexual Abuse* 1 (1): 49–62.

Meehan, A. J. (1997). "Record-Keeping Practices in the Policing of Juveniles." In M. Travers and J. F. Manzo (eds.), *Law in Action: Ethnomethodological and Conversation Analytic Approaches to Law,* pp. 183–208. Aldershot, England: Ashgate/Dartmouth.

Melton, G. B., Petrila, J., Poythress, N. G., and Slobogin, C. (1997). *Psychological Evaluations for the Courts, 2nd ed.* New York: Guilford Press.

Myers, J. E. B. (1997). *A Mother's Nightmare—Incest: A Practical Legal Guide for Parents and Professionals.* Thousand Oaks, Calif.: Sage Publications.

Nance, S. (1989). "Validation Evidence Poses Issue in Child Abuse Cases." *New York Law Journal,* October 5, p. 1.

Neustein, A. (1986). "Getting Straight Answers from Experts: A Comprehensive Guide to What They Appear to Be Saying." *Judges' Journal* 25 (3): 31–33, 56.

Neustein, A., Burton, J. R., and Quirk, S. A. (1993). "Concerning the Plight of Children in Cases of Parental Abuse." Memorandum to U.S. Attorney General Janet Reno. Washington, D.C.: American Coalition for Abuse Awareness.

Neustein, A., and Goetting, A. (1999). "Judicial Responses to the Protective Parent's Complaint of Child Sexual Abuse." *Journal of Child Sexual Abuse* 8 (4): 103–122.

Neustein, A., and Lesher, M. (1999). "Legislative Solutions to the Protective Parent Backlash." *Family Violence and Sexual Assault Bulletin* 25 (2–3): 19–26.

Neustein, A., and Lesher, M. (2002a). "Does the Jewish Community Sacrifice Victims of Sexual Abuse?" *Jewish Exponent* 211 (22), May 30, p. 37.

Neustein, A., and Lesher, M. (2002b). "The Silence of the Jewish Media on Sexual Abuse in the Orthodox Jewish Community." In D. S. Claussen (ed.), *Sex, Religion, Media,* pp. 79–87. Lanham, Md: Rowman and Littlefield Publishers.

Neustein, A., and Lesher, M. (2004). "Courts See Moms as Guilty Till Proven Innocent." *New York Daily News,* June 21, p. 39.

Niggemyer, K. (1998). "Parental Alienation Is Open Heart Surgery: It Needs More than a Band-Aid to Fix It." *California Western Law Review* 34: 567–587.

Nicholson, E. B., and Bulkley, J. (eds.) (1988). *Sexual Abuse Allegations in Custody and Visitation Cases.* Washington, D.C.: American Bar Association.

O'Donohue, W., and Bradley, A. R. (1999). "Conceptual and Empirical Issues in Child Custody Evaluations." *Clinical Psychology: Science and Practice* 6 (3): 310–322.

Olafson, E., Corwin, D. L., and Summit, R. C. (1993). "Modern History of Child Sexual Abuse Awareness: Cycles of Discovery and Suppression." *Child Abuse and Neglect* 17: 7–24.

Pagnozzi, A. (1990). "Mom Was Trying to Help Her Kids, So Why Is She the One on Trial?" *New York Post,* February 23, p. 13.

Palmer, S. E., and Brown, R. A. (1999). "Responding to Disclosures of Familial Abuse: What Survivors Tell Us." *Child Welfare Journal of Policy, Practice and Program* 78 (2): 259–282.

Penfold, P. S. (1997). "Questionable Beliefs about Child Sexual Abuse Allegations during Custody Disputes." *Canadian Journal of Family Law* 14 (1).

Pennington, H. J. (1992). *The Judicial Training Act.* Testimony before the U.S. House of Representatives, Judiciary Committee, August 6.

Pennington, H. J. (1993). *The Hardest Case: Custody and Incest.* Trenton, N.J.: National Center for Protective Parents.

Pennington, H. J., and Woods, L. (1990). *Legal Issues and Legal Options in Civil Child Sexual Abuse Cases: Representing the Protective Parent.* New York: National Center on Women and Family Law.

Podesta, J. S., and Van Biema, D. (1989). "Running for Their Lives, Defying the Law to Save Their Children from Alleged Sexual Horrors, Fugitive Parents Turn to Their Last Hope: The New Underground Railroad." *People* 31 (3), January 23, pp. 70–88.

Pollner, M. (1979). "Explicative Transactions: Making and Managing Meaning in Traffic Court." In G. Psathas (ed.), *Everyday Language: Studies in Ethnomethodology,* pp. 227–255. New York: Irvington Publishers.

Post, D., and Corcoran, K. (2003). *Battered Mothers' Testimony Project: A Human Rights Approach to Child Custody and Domestic Violence.* Pheonix: Arizona Coalition against Domestic Violence.

Quindlen, A. (1994). "The Good Mother: Sexual Abuse and Custody Battles." *New York Times,* December 10, p. 15.

Quinn, K. M. (1988). "The Credibility of Children's Allegations of Sexual Abuse." *Behavioral Sciences and the Law* 6 (2): 181–199.

Rand, D. C. (1990). "Munchausen Syndrome by Proxy: Integration of Classic and Contemporary Types." *Issues in Child Abuse Accusations* 2 (2): 83–89.

Rand, D. C. (1993). "Munchausen Syndrome by Proxy: A Complex Type of Emotional Abuse Responsible for Some False Allegations of Child Abuse in Divorce." *Issues in Child Abuse Accusations* 5 (3): 135–155.

Reynolds, B. (1993). "Children's Cries for Help Deserve More Attention." *USA Today,* May 21, p. 11A.

Reynolds, B. (1995). "Judges Sentence Kids to Life of Pain." *USA Today,* November 3, p. 11A.

Rosen, L. N., and Etlin, M. (1996). *The Hostage Child: Sex Abuse Allegations in Custody Disputes.* Bloomington: Indiana University Press.

Rothman, D. A., and Watson, D. E. (1990). *Achieving Equal Justice for Women and Men in the Courts.* San Francisco, Calif., Judicial Council of California Administrative Office of the Courts.

Russell, D. E. H. (1983). "The Incidence and Prevalence of Intrafamilial and Extrafamilial Sexual Abuse of Female Children." *Child Abuse and Neglect* 7: 133–146.

Russell, D. E. H. (1986). *The Secret Trauma: Incest in the Lives of Women and Girls.* New York: Basic Books.

Schafran, L. H. (1987). "Documenting Gender Bias in the Courts: The Task Force Approach." *Judicature* 70 (5): 280–290.

Schafran, L. H. (2003). "Evaluating the Evaluators: Problems with 'Outside Neutrals.'" *Judges' Journal* 42 (1): 10–15, 38.

Sherman, R. (1993). "'No Choice,' She Kills Self and Daughter." *National Law Journal,* July 26, p. 8.

Silverman, J. G., Mesh, C. M., Cuthbert, C. V., Slote, K., and Bancroft, L. (2004). "Child Custody Determinations in Cases Involving Intimate Partner Violence: A Human Rights Analysis." *American Journal of Public Health* 94 (6): 951–957.

Sinanan, K., and Haughton, H. (1986). "Evolution of Variants of the Munchausen Syndrome." *British Journal of Psychiatry* 148: 465–467.

Skipper, D. (1987). "Mom Remains in Hattisburg Jail." *Hattisburg American,* August 22, p. 2A.

Smith, R., and Coukos, P. (1997). "Fairness and Accuracy in Evaluations of Domestic Violence and Child Abuse in Custody Determinations." *Judges' Journal* 36 (4): 38–42, 54–56.

Stern, N., and Oehme, K. (2002). "The Troubling Admission of Supervised Visitation Records in Custody Proceedings." *Temple Law Review* 75: 271–311.

Summit, R. C. (1983). "The Child Sexual Abuse Accommodation Syndrome." *Child Abuse and Neglect* 7 (2): 177–193.

Thoennes, N., Pearson, J., and Tjaden, P. G. (1988). *Allegations of Sexual Abuse in Custody and Visitation Cases: An Empirical Study of 169 Cases from 12 States.* Denver: The Association of Family and Conciliation Courts.

Thoennes, N., and Tjaden, P. G. (1990). "The Extent, Nature, and Validity of Sexual Abuse Allegations in Custody and Visitation Disputes." *Child Abuse and Neglect* 14 (2): 151–163.

Tippins, T. M. (2003). "Custody Evaluations—Part 1: Expertise by Default?" *New York Law Journal,* July 15, p. 3.

Traubmann, T. (2003). "Junk Science Has Its Way in Court." *Ha'aretz,* August 15.

Travers, M., and Manzo, J. F. (eds.) (1997). *Law in Action: Ethnomethodological and Conversation Analytic Approaches to Law.* Aldershot, England: Ashgate/Dartmouth.

Turkat, I. D. (1997). "Management of Visitation Interference." *Judges' Journal* 36 (2): 17–21, 47.

Turner, V. (1974). *The Ritual Process.* Harmondsworth, England: Pelican Books.

Viva (1989). "Women and Children Last: How the Family Court Serves to Punish the Very People It Was Created to Protect." *New York Woman,* November, pp. 110–115.

Waller, G. (2001). *Small Justice: Little Justice in America's Family Courts.* New York International Independent Film and Video Festival, New York City, September 7.

Watson, D. R. (1990). "Some Features of the Elicitation of Confessions in Murder Interrogations." In G. Psathas (ed.), *Interaction Competence,* pp. 263–295. Washington, D.C.: University Press of America.

Watson, R. (1997). "The Presentation of Victim and Motive in Discourse: The Case of Police Interrogations and Interviews." In M. Travers and J. F. Manzo (eds.), *Law in Action: Ethnomethodological and Conversation Analytic Approaches to Law,* pp. 77–97. Aldershot, England: Ashgate/Dartmouth.

Weick, K. E. (1969). *The Social Psychology of Organizing.* Reading, Mass.: Addison-Wesley.

Wexler, R. (1990). *Wounded Innocents: The Real Victims of the War against Child Abuse.* Buffalo: Prometheus Books.

Wilson, T. (1997). "Will Paternal Paranoia Triumph? The Organization of Angry Dads." *On the Issues* 6 (1): 20–21.

Winner, K. (1996). *Divorced from Justice: The Abuse of Women and Children by Divorce Lawyers and Judges.* New York: ReganBooks.

Winner, K. (2000a). *Findings on Judge Michael Dufficy, Commissioner Sylvia Shapiro, and Court-Appointees in Marin County's Superior Court in California.* New York: The Justice Seekers, Inc., February 28.

Winner, K. (2000b). *Placing Children at Risk: Questionable Psychologists and Therapists in the Sacramento Family Court and Surrounding Counties.* New York: The Justice Seekers, Inc., May 15.

Wittmann, J. J. (1985). "Child Advocacy and the Scientific Model in Family Court: A Theory for Pretrial Self-assessment." *Journal of Psychiatry and Law* 13 (1,2): 61–82.

Woodlin, R. (1987). "Newsome Gaining Public Support." *Sun Herald,* (Gulfport, Miss.), August 28, p. A-1.

Words and Phrases (1964). St. Paul, Minn.: West Publishing Company.

Index